NATIONAL UNIVERSITY
LIBRARY   SAN DIEGO

Going Public

GOING PUBLIC

The Theory and Evidence on
How Companies Raise Equity Finance

Second Edition

TIM JENKINSON

ALEXANDER LJUNGQVIST

OXFORD
UNIVERSITY PRESS

OXFORD

UNIVERSITY PRESS

Great Clarendon Street, Oxford OX2 6DP

Oxford University Press is a department of the University of Oxford.
It furthers the University's objective of excellence in research, scholarship,
and education by publishing worldwide in

Oxford New York

Athens Auckland Bangkok Bogotá Buenos Aires Cape Town
Chennai Dar es Salaam Delhi Florence Hong Kong Istanbul Karachi
Kolkata Kuala Lumpur Madrid Melbourne Mexico City Mumbai Nairobi
Paris São Paulo Shanghai Singapore Taipei Tokyo Toronto Warsaw

with associated companies in Berlin Ibadan

Oxford is a registered trade mark of Oxford University Press
in the UK and in certain other countries

Published in the United States
by Oxford University Press Inc., New York

© Tim Jenkinson and Alexander Ljungqvist 2001

The moral rights of the authors have been asserted

Database right Oxford University Press (maker)

First edition published 1996
Second edition published 2001

British Library Cataloguing in Publication Data

Data available

Library of Congress Cataloging in Publication Data

Jenkinson, Tim, 1961–
   Going public : the theory and evidence on how companies raise equity finance /
Tim Jenkinson, Alexander Ljungqvist,—2nd ed.
      p. cm.
   Includes bibliographical references and index.
   1. Going public (Securities)   I. Ljungqvist Alexander. II. Title.
   HG4028.S7 J46 2001   658.15′224–dc21   2001033955
ISBN 0–19–829599–5

10 9 8 7 6 5 4 3 2 1

Typeset by Florence Production Ltd., Stoodleigh, Devon
Printed in Great Britain
on acid-free paper by
Biddles Ltd., *www.biddles.co.uk*

Foreword

I have been doing academic research on initial public offerings (IPOs) for over twenty years, and publishers frequently ask me if I would be willing to write a book on the topic. Since the first edition of Jenkinson and Ljungqvist's *Going Public* appeared, my answer has been simple: the book that I would write has already been written. This second edition expands and updates their earlier work, incorporating analysis and evidence on the dramatic changes that have occurred in the IPO market in recent years. The book presents both theory and evidence in a comprehensive manner. It summarizes the results of the authors' own work, as well as that of literally hundreds of published articles by others.

First, a minor point: Alexander Ljungqvist's name is pronounced 'yoong-kwist'. He's truly an international type of guy. Born and raised in Germany to German–Swedish parents, he has studied in Germany, Sweden, and the UK, and now teaches in the USA at New York University's Stern School of Business. Tim Jenkinson is British, and teaches at Oxford. Both authors have a mastery of the worldwide IPO market.

This book, as befits a work published by Oxford University Press, is not aimed at investors asking 'How can I make a quick killing in IPOs?' Rather, it describes and analyses many of the patterns that exist in the IPO market. It not only tells you what happens, but also addresses why it happens. When the authors compare the evidence in scores of countries, they find that there are some patterns that exist everywhere, and some systematic differences across countries. For example, the IPO market is highly cyclical in every country, and every country has positive first-day returns. In other words, on average, IPOs are underpriced relative to what the market is willing to pay as soon as they start trading. But the underpricing is much more severe in some countries than others. This is partly because the way that IPOs are sold varies across countries, and the book analyses why the contracts used make a difference.

The main method for selling IPOs in the USA, the firm commitment contract, is gaining market share in other countries. Firm commitment is really a misnomer, since the underwriter doesn't make a firm commitment to raise the funds for a firm until the last moment. Another name is 'book-building', for the underwriter keeps track of orders for shares in a notebook (or, more realistically, in a spreadsheet) to gauge the level of demand before setting the final offer price. One of the controversial features of book-building is that underwriters allocate shares to investors on the basis of favouritism. At first glance, this feature raises questions about fairness. But, as the authors explain, allowing favouritism in the allocation of shares may be desirable, for it makes it more difficult for an investor to cherry-pick the hot issues.

The book describes some of the main features of IPO markets: short-run underpricing, hot issue markets, and poor long-run performance. It presents explanations for the patterns. It discusses privatizations, corporate governance issues, and a host of other related issues. For someone trying to understand the IPO market, it is a treasure trove of information, providing a comprehensive description and analysis of existing theories. But it should be kept in mind that there are not always definitive answers, and the IPO market can change rapidly. In September 1996, Alexander Ljungqvist and I both attended the first German IPO conference, organized by Professor Richard Stehle of Humboldt University in Berlin. The conference brought together every German investment banker involved with IPOs, as well as academics. Not a single person predicted that Germany was on the verge of a boom in IPOs by young technology companies. Likewise, nobody predicted that Frankfurt's Neuer Markt would shortly become the centre of financing for Europe's emerging technology companies.

As recently as October 1998, no one was predicting the magnitude of the internet bubble's effect on first-day returns. Yet 1999 and the first half of 2000 saw an average first-day return of 70 per cent in the USA, a level unprecedented for the world's largest and most developed capital market. In the twenty-five years before 1998, only 39 US IPOs had first-day returns of 100 per cent or more. But 1999 alone saw 117 IPOs double in price in the USA. My prediction is that the internet bubble of 1999 will be to IPO researchers what the Great Depression of the 1930s is to macroeconomists: the outlier event that defies conventional explanation, and generates articles for years and years. As a starting point for understanding these phenomena, I can't think of a better place to start than by reading *Going Public: The Theory and Evidence on How Companies Raise Equity Finance,* by Tim Jenkinson and Alexander Ljungqvist.

8 November 2000

Jay R. Ritter

Cordell Professor of Finance,
University of Florida

Preface to the Second Edition

The first edition of *Going Public* was published in 1996. The original idea behind the book was to survey and synthesize the enormous amount of academic research that had been produced on initial public offerings. We wanted to write the book in a non-technical manner that would be accessible to practitioners involved in the IPO process, policy-makers interested in encouraging equity markets or in privatization issues, academics doing research in the area, non-specialist colleagues wishing to update their knowledge of the IPO literature for teaching or research reasons, and students of corporate finance. We also wanted to write it from an international perspective, drawing on evidence from different countries. The significant institutional and legal differences that exist across countries are directly relevant to both the theoretical literature on IPOs and the policy debates about the regulation of the IPO process.

The success of the first edition has led us to stick faithfully to this model in this second edition. We made a number of predictions and judgements in the original edition, not all of which have materialized over the last five years. However, we ended the book by stating that 'our firmest prediction is that initial public offerings will continue to be the subject of intense academic debate'. This prediction has certainly been realized: research on IPOs has taken a number of significant steps forward over the last five years. On the theoretical front, one of the most interesting lines of research has been on the role of intermediaries in overcoming the endemic information problems that may prevent IPOs from being accurately priced. And on the empirical side, more recent research has (as we predicted) undermined considerably the 'stylized fact' that IPOs underperform significantly in the longer term. These important advances in research make this a good time to produce a second edition.

The last five years have also witnessed some remarkable develop-ments. 'Hot issue' periods for IPOs have long been noted, but the extraordinary returns seen on IPOs during 1999 and the first half of 2000—as noted by Jay Ritter in his foreword—are quite unprece-dented. This most recent 'hot issue' period, which coincided with the internet bubble, may now be over, but the periodic development of such market conditions excites considerable interest in the IPO process, not only from academics but also from policy-makers. Excep-tional price movements, both upwards and downwards, often result in the spotlight being turned on the market intermediaries, and this has certainly happened in a number of countries recently. Is the investment banking industry competitive? Do analysts accurately assess the value of companies going public? How is the allocation of shares in an IPO, especially a 'hot issue', determined? Are retail investors getting a fair deal? Should the whole IPO pricing and allo-cation process be disintermediated using an internet auction? All these questions are currently being asked. In some countries there are formal investigations being conducted by regulatory bodies. The research presented in this volume is directly relevant to many of these questions. But there remain many unresolved issues, and advances on some key questions are currently constrained by a lack of data on such key issues as the pricing and allocation process.

There have been other important developments over the last few years. There has been a huge increase in the number of IPOs in many countries, often associated with the establishment of new stock mar-ket segments aimed at younger, high-growth, companies. There has also been a marked change in the techniques used to take companies public in many countries. In particular, the use of book-building techniques—long practised in the USA—has spread to many other countries.

All these developments have only served to increase interest in IPOs among both practitioners and academic researchers. We hope, therefore, that this revised edition of *Going Public* is timely.

T.J.J.

A.P.L.

Oxford and New York
December 2000

Contents

Part III **Policy Implications**

Part I

THE IPO MARKET

CHAPTER 1

Introduction

Whether or not to 'go public' is an important decision in the life cycle of a company. Going public involves having the shares in a company quoted on a stock exchange, and companies usually go public via an initial public offering (IPO) of their shares to investors. Stock exchanges serve two main functions: to facilitate the raising of new equity capital, and to enable trading in shares and other securities to take place. The capital-raising function is usually referred to as the primary market and the subsequent trading as the secondary market. It is important to an economy that both markets operate efficiently. If going public is relatively easy and inexpensive, this will increase the availability and lower the cost of equity finance. Similarly, a liquid and transparent secondary market will encourage investors to participate in the stock market and should again increase the availability of equity capital and lower investors' required returns.

The shares sold at the IPO can be either newly created or existing shares. In the case of new shares, the proceeds from selling these to investors accrue to the company. When existing shares are sold the proceeds obviously accrue to the original investors. In practice, some IPOs consist entirely of new equity, with the original investors retaining their shares, some IPOs involve selling only existing equity, with no new money being raised for the company, but with the original owners selling some of their shares, and many consist of a combination of the two. Even if new equity capital is not required, and the original investors simply want to sell part, or all, of their stake in a company, the ability to do this efficiently will encourage entrepreneurship and, ultimately, economic growth.

This book focuses on the efficiency of the IPO process. This focus on IPOs does not completely exclude subsequent equity issues, as some theories that we shall consider in Part II of the book relate choices at the IPO—for example on what proportion of the equity to sell, or on underpricing—to longer-term financing strategies. However, although considerable international variation exists, in many countries the majority of companies raise external equity finance only once—at the time of the IPO. Thereafter, they tend to rely upon retained earnings and debt (from banks or through issuing bonds) to finance their operations, and the importance of the stock exchange as a source of additional finance becomes less important. As a result, the efficiency of the IPO process, and the performance of companies that have gone public, has been the subject of considerable academic research. One of the aims of this book is to synthesize the enormous quantity of theoretical and applied research on IPOs, and to evaluate the contribution that academic research has made to our understanding of the costs and benefits of going public.

The important functions of an IPO in providing finance to companies and in providing an 'exit route' for the original entrepreneurs and investors—such as venture capitalists—would be reason enough to justify considerable research interest. However, the scale of the academic research has been driven, in large part, by the existence of two apparent anomalies.

First, there is now overwhelming international evidence of *initial underpricing*. That is, the shares in companies that go public are offered to investors at prices considerably below the prices at which they subsequently trade on the stock market. Later in this chapter we describe the various IPO procedures and timing in more detail, but the important implication of initial underpricing is that it can be thought of as raising the cost—to the original owners—of raising equity finance. Going public involves two types of cost. There are the *direct costs* of an issue, for example underwriting fees, selling commissions, legal expenses, accountancy, and audit fees in addition to the less quantifiable costs in terms of management time. Many of these costs are relatively fixed, and so there are considerable economies of scale. But in addition to these direct costs, there are also the *indirect costs* associated with underpricing of the shares. When shares are sold at a price below that at which they subsequently trade, the initial owners essentially 'leave money on the table' for the investors who purchase the shares at the IPO.

In the case of sales of secondary equity, the wealth loss associated with underpricing is obvious: the original shareholders could have sold their shares at a higher price had they retained them and sold them in the after-market. In the case of primary equity sales, the wealth loss occurs via the dilution of the original shareholders' stakes in the company. Initial underpricing of the IPO will mean that the new investors will have acquired their stake in the company for less than it was worth, to the detriment of the original shareholders. Put another way, in the absence of underpricing, the company could have raised the same sum of money by selling fewer shares, and thereby would have avoided diluting the holdings of the original investors.

How important this underpricing is will depend critically upon what proportion of the equity is being sold at the IPO. For example, suppose the company sells shares equivalent to 20 per cent of its total equity capital at the IPO. If these shares are, in the event, priced at a 10 per cent discount to the market price, then the amount 'left on the table' is only 2 per cent of the market value of the company. In contrast, if the entire equity capital were sold at the IPO, then the original owners would have suffered the full 10 per cent loss. The importance, in financial terms, of underpricing is therefore directly related to the proportion of the company that is sold at the IPO. However, the decision on how much of the company to sell is itself a complex one, involving issues of liquidity, stock exchange regulations, corporate control, and risk.

Of course, there are plausible reasons to expect some limited underpricing of IPOs on average. First, transaction costs are not negligible on any equity market, with bid–ask spreads often being a few percentage points, depending on the liquidity of the stock. If an investor is to be enticed to change her portfolio, she may require a limited incentive in the form of an initial discount. Second, there is a risk that the market price may fall below the issue price. If IPOs were priced, on average, with zero discount, risk-averse investors would, in the absence of specific information that would allow them to discriminate between winners and losers, prefer to buy shares in the after-market. Hence the initial discount on IPOs might be interpreted as a return for bearing risk. However, as will be seen in the next chapter, observed initial underpricing is typically too large to be explained away in this way.

The second anomaly that has generated much research is the evidence that the shares of companies that go public appear to suffer *long-run underperformance*. That is, relative to other quoted companies, investors appear to lose out by continuing to hold the shares of companies that have recently gone public. As a result, the immediate gain that investors typically make as a result of the underpricing of IPOs tends to be accompanied by poor relative performance thereafter. Such underperformance seems to last a surprising length of time, with some studies suggesting significant poor returns up to five years after the initial flotation. In fact, as we shall discuss in Chapter 6, the evidence on long-run underperformance is much less definitive than that for initial underpricing.

Economists are intrigued and perplexed by such anomalies. They are intrigued first because the presence of such statistical anomalies may have implications for the underlying structure of financial markets. One important lesson that a company learns when it goes public is that it cannot do it alone. Various financial intermediaries are involved in the IPO, including the investment bank that acts as a sponsor for the company, the underwriters of the share issue, and the brokers who find buyers for the shares. It is on the advice of these intermediaries that companies set the price of their shares. However, conflicts of interest can arise. For example, if the sponsor also acts as the lead underwriter, then there may be some incentive to price the shares cheaply as underwriting risk is thereby reduced. Of course, if markets are competitive, one might expect that companies going public would be able to 'shop around' to find the financial intermediary that would offer the best price. However, in financial markets, where information is imperfect and reputations are all-important, the competitive paradigm of new entrants—in this case financial intermediaries—appearing quickly to compete with incumbents and correct such anomalies appears very strained.

An alternative way in which underpricing might, in principle, disappear is through potential purchasers bidding up the price of the shares, as would be the case in an auction. However, in some circumstances investors may not be able to participate in an issue, and so such competitive forces may be absent. Even when investors can participate in an IPO, it is not uncommon to observe considerable over-subscription for the shares, which necessitates the rationing of shares to investors. The fact that companies, in association with their advisers, do not generally set the issue price at their best estimate of the subsequent market trading price has stimulated much academic research. Some of this research has suggested that underpricing is an equilibrium outcome that can be explained by the informational, institutional, or competitive structure of the market. We investigate many of these issues in some detail in this book and draw implications for the design of efficient institutional structures.

The second important reason why economists have been intrigued by these apparent anomalies is that they both violate the fundamental tenet of 'no arbitrage'. In other words, the existence of systematic trading rules that make money should be transitory at best. In the case of long-run underperformance the trading rule is simple: investors should sell the shares almost immediately they start trading (known as *stagging* in the UK or *flipping* in the USA). In this way, investors fortunate enough to be allocated shares at the IPO would benefit from the initial underpricing but would not suffer the long-run underperformance. This is a simple trading rule that would be highly profitable if the empirical observations were correct. Moreover, if people followed this rule, the phenomenon of long-run underperformance would tend to disappear. Economists are perplexed when such trading opportunities persist, as they tend to indicate the irrationality of investors, or the uninformed nature of investors, or, perhaps, the size of transaction costs. We reassess the existing empirical evidence on these anomalies in Chapter 2.

Of course, if the empirical 'anomalies' are found to be particularly endemic and long-lived, then a natural response is to reassess the reasons why they were viewed as anomalous in the first place. Much of the theoretical work on IPOs produced in recent years has considered whether it is possible to rationalize persistent initial underpricing as an equilibrium outcome of a consistent economic model. Various arguments have been advanced which suggest that companies might, under certain assumptions, *choose* to underprice their shares, ranging from the view that underpricing can act as a signal of the quality of the firm's management or future profitability to the belief that underpricing is a form of insurance against possible legal action. Theoretical models that predict long-run underperformance are considerably less abundant, but various explanations have recently been advanced.

In the second part of the book we survey and critique the various theoretical explanations of IPO performance, drawing upon international evidence to test their validity. Reference to data from many countries is particularly useful in this respect as the respective institutional, regulatory, and legal differences often allow one to perform better tests of theoretical propositions. Although there are few countries in the world that have escaped an empirical study of IPO performance, until recently much of the theoretical literature has been based on the US model of IPOs. But many of the predictions of this theoretical literature rely upon particular institutional and regulatory characteristics of the US stock market. The assumptions underlying some of the most widely advanced theories are often grossly violated in countries outside the USA. As a result, while many of the theories are certainly not inconsistent with US evidence, few of them can claim to explain the consistent international evidence on IPO underpricing and long-run underperformance. Part of the rationale of this book is to correct the US bias in the literature on IPOs and, in particular, to pay close attention to the various institutional arrangements and ways of going public that exist in different countries.

A final reason why IPOs have recently been the focus of much research is the worldwide trend towards privatization. Companies can be privatized in a variety of ways, such as through an outright sale to another company, or even via the distribution of free shares to members of the public. However, privatizations are often effected via an IPO, with the original shareholders (the government) selling shares to the public and, on occasions, raising additional finance for the company at the same time. Hence privatizations are an important subset of total IPOs, although they are sometimes differentiated from private-sector flotations in that governments may have particular, frequently conflicting, objectives that they want to achieve through privatization (such as encouraging individual share ownership). We consider, in the third part of the book, evidence on how different privatization programmes have been executed and what constitutes best practice in privatization.

We also attempt to draw general policy conclusions for all IPOs based upon our survey of the theory and international evidence. There is a surprising degree of heterogeneity in the way companies go public in different countries, and it is possible to identify some 'models'—in the sense of rules, regulations, and institutions—that work much better than others. We also consider some important ways in which the IPO market is changing, including the use of the internet to disintermediate the IPO process, and the possibility of using auction mechanisms to set prices for IPOs.

In the remainder of this introductory chapter, we briefly discuss the various steps involved in an IPO, and use this framework to describe the different methods of taking companies public that are observed in various countries.

1.1 How to Go Public

1.1.1 *The choice of market*

There are various steps involved in going public. The first step is typically making sure that the company can satisfy the regulations imposed by stock exchanges and regulatory bodies. It is important to note that the act of going public involves two separate procedures. First, investors have to be found who are prepared to buy the shares being offered. Second, the shares have to be admitted to a stock exchange, so that the investors are able to trade the shares. In the past, this distinction may have mattered very little. Companies in a particular country would almost always choose to have their shares traded on their domestic stock exchange (which itself was often a monopoly) and would abide by the rules regarding IPOs imposed by that exchange. However, major changes have taken place in recent years that make this distinction between the sale of shares in the company and the trading platform increasingly important.

Considering the trading platform first, the traditional stock exchanges have been subject to increasing competition. Some of this competition has been from other traditional exchanges, as companies have increasingly been free to choose where to have their shares quoted. One manifestation of this competition has been the trend towards national exchanges merging or forming joint ventures to create larger—hopefully more liquid—markets. This process of consolidation has been particularly noticeable within the EU, where a number of coalitions of exchanges have formed, all with a view to creating the dominant European trading platform. Increasingly, therefore, trading platforms will no longer be defined by national boundaries. Rather, they will be defined by their rules and regulations and their liquidity.

The increasing irrelevance of national boundaries has also had consequences for the governance and ownership of exchanges themselves. In the past many exchanges were essentially mutual organizations, owned by the institutions that were active participants on that particular exchange. As the spread of electronic trading has made those national, or geographical, links virtually irrelevant, so the traditional ownership structures have become ill-suited to the task of competing against rival exchanges. Hence, many exchanges are de-mutualizing, and are becoming companies in their own right, and some are themselves conducting initial public offerings. These changes in ownership and governance will further accelerate the trend towards major structural changes in the organization of exchanges.

A further manifestation of this increased competition has been the creation of segmented markets. Many traditional exchanges have created new markets aimed, in particular, at young firms with high growth potential. This tendency has been particularly pronounced in Europe, where the new markets include EASDAQ, the Neuer Markt in Germany, the Nieuwe Markt in the Netherlands, the Nouveau Marché in Paris, the Nuovo Mercato in Italy, and Euro.NM in Belgium. These new markets have the common feature that companies face less stringent entry requirements than the traditional markets in terms of age, size, or the requirement for a record of profitability. These lower entry requirements may be 'formal' in the sense of different rules, or more 'informal' in terms of the interpretation of existing rules. On the other hand, each of these six new markets has stricter rules regarding information disclosure and transparency than the traditional markets in their countries.

However, not all the new market segments that have been created impose stricter disclosure. For example, the London Stock Exchange currently comprises three markets: the main market (also known as the Official List), the alternative investment market (AIM) designed for smaller, growing companies, and techMARK, designed for high-technology companies. The rules governing these markets differ. In order to gain admission to the main market for listed securities, it is necessary to be admitted to the Official List by the UK Listing Authority (a division of the Financial Services Authority) and also to be admitted to trading by the London Stock Exchange. In contrast, companies seeking admission to AIM or techMARK are not bound by the UK Listing Authority's listing rules, and are generally subject to less regulation.

This example illustrates a further feature of the process of going public: in most countries the sale and trading of securities to the public is subject to careful regulation. The bodies charged with such regulation differ somewhat across countries, but typically involve the regulators of the financial sector—such as the Securities and Exchange Commission (SEC) in the USA, or the Financial Services Authority in the UK—and/or particular stock exchanges. In the past, when in many countries there was a single national stock exchange, the regulation of the admission of new companies was often undertaken by the stock exchange itself. However, the advent of considerable competition between existing exchanges and the development of many new exchanges have tended to result in a separation of general rules regarding the offering of securities to the public, and the rules required by a particular exchange. Typically, a public body will define rules and regulations regarding the admission of companies to 'official' markets. Companies will have to satisfy these rules and those imposed by any particular official exchange in that country. In contrast, 'unofficial' markets are not subject to regulation by public bodies, with the markets themselves setting the rules for admission. In the UK example, the fact that the responsibility for regulating which companies can be listed no longer resides with the London Stock Exchange (since 1999) reflects the fact that competition for companies from rival trading platforms has emerged in a significant way.

To summarize, one of the first key decisions for a company going public is the choice of market upon which the shares will be traded. Increasingly, choices are no longer constrained by national boundaries. Having decided which exchange(s) to list on, the next stage is to produce the information required for the initial prospectus. The process of producing a prospectus typically involves a number of intermediaries such as auditors, lawyers, and investment banks. In the next section we focus on the various roles played by investment banks in the process of going public.

1.1.2   *Producing a prospectus*

There are a number of phases involved in an IPO. First, there is an initial information-gathering phase, during which the investment bank that has been chosen as the lead manager (in some cases a number of banks are designated co-lead managers) works closely with the firm going public to perform the due diligence investigations and to produce the information required to satisfy the appropriate regulatory authorities (both the securities regulators and the chosen exchanges). A key decision in the offering will clearly be the issue price, and during the initial information-gathering stage the analysts from the lead manager will form some initial views as to the likely market value of the company using a variety of techniques. Two of the most commonly employed valuation techniques include discounted cash flow analysis and peer group analysis. In many cases the lead manager(s) will produce a research report, drawing on the work of their analysts, which can then be used as a briefing document for investors, before the preliminary prospectus is produced.

Investment banks may also conduct some pre-marketing, during which analysts distribute briefing documents to institutional investors as a way of introducing the company. There will often follow a large number of meetings and telephone calls with the potential investors during which they will be encouraged to air any concerns they might have (for example regarding the strength of management, or the markets in which they operate). In some cases institutional investors are invited to submit feedback forms to the lead manager.

During this period the lead managers may, in some countries, put together a syndicate of other banks that will underwrite and/or market the issue to investors. Underwriting and marketing are, of course, quite distinct functions. In some countries banks are engaged in a pure underwriting role, with marketing being conducted solely by the lead investment bank (perhaps in conjunction with advertising). In other cases the role of the syndicate is almost entirely to bring the new issue to the attention of its investor clients, with little (or no) underwriting role. These differences will be explored later in this section when we describe some of the main techniques that are used in different countries.

The culmination of the initial information-gathering phase is the publication of an initial prospectus. In the USA initial prospectuses are referred to as *red herrings* and in other countries they are often called *preliminary* or *pathfinder prospectuses*. In many countries this prospectus will include an initial price range for the shares, which represents a first 'best guess' at the value of the company drawing on the valuations produced by the investment bank's analysts and the feedback from the pre-marketing. Initial price ranges can typically be changed, and are designed to produce a frame for the views of the investors. These views are sought during the marketing and pricing phases that follow. Only when the final price for the issue is fixed is the official prospectus produced.

However, some techniques for taking companies public essentially fix the price before formally inviting investors to bid for the shares (in which case the pricing phase is incorporated into the initial information-gathering phase). In these cases it may not be necessary to produce an initial prospectus and then a final prospectus, as the price is fixed earlier in the process (in particular before the marketing phase). The distinction between those issue methods that condition the offer price on the indications of demand received during the marketing phase and those that set the price prior to formal marketing is an important one, and we shall give some examples of how such methods work later in this chapter.

1.1.3 *Marketing*

Having produced a (preliminary or final) prospectus, the second main stage, during which the issue is marketed to investors, takes place. This marketing can take a variety of forms. Many companies are encouraged by their investment bank advisers to undertake 'road shows', whereby the senior managers make presentations in a number of locations, typically those with a high concentration of institutional investors. For example, when Germany's telecommunications company Debitel prepared to go public in 1999, two separate road show teams, led by the CEO and the CFO, respectively, made presentations to institutional investors in 20 cities in nine countries, including Frankfurt, London, Milan, Paris, Zurich, New York, and Boston, over a twelve-day period. At the same time, all the investment banks in the marketing syndicate (if one has been formed) will contact their clients in various ways to bring the impending offer to their attention. Other important forms of marketing can include press briefings, which can be especially important when the involvement of retail investors is desired, internet alerting services, and advertising.

Contrary to popular belief, road shows are not usually intended to provide investors with additional information about the company. In many jurisdictions, issuers are not in fact allowed to divulge any information not contained in the (preliminary) prospectus when meeting potential investors, and if they do they are required to file amendments with market regulators, thereby making the information available to investors at large. In Microsoft's road shows, for instance, Bill Gates was told by his lawyers not to 'say anything that deviated from the prospectus or added new information'[1]. Road show presentations that we have seen confirm that management's formal presentations merely reiterate fairly general information already contained in the prospectus. Perhaps surprisingly, road shows may instead be a way for the investment banker to gather information from investors, about their views of the company and its valuation.

In offerings where the price has already been fixed, the main purpose of the marketing stage is to elicit bids from investors (at the fixed price). These bids would then be fed into the final stage, whereby the shares are allocated to the investors, which we discuss below. In some cases the bids received during the marketing stage are legally binding (for example those from retail investors), but in the case of institutional investors the bids are more normally not. However, in practice, even though such institutional bids may not be legally binding, there is a strong presumption that investors should be prepared to honour their bids (except where some new information has come to light). As we shall discuss, investment banks, which repeatedly manage IPOs, can to some extent encourage good

---

[1] Bro Uttal, 'Inside the deal that made Bill Gates $350,000,000', *Fortune*, 21 July 1986.

behaviour from investors provided they have some discretion over the final allocation of shares.

For those issues where only an initial indicative price range has been set, the marketing phase is designed to produce expressions of interest from the various investors, which will be fed through the lead manager and/or the marketing syndicate. The marketing phase thus generates a lot of additional information regarding the reaction of the potential investors to the offer, which can be fed into the next stage of the process when the final price is set. This raises an interesting problem for the investment bank: investors may have incentives to withhold information regarding the issue if they think that the information will be used to their disadvantage. This problem is likely to be particularly acute in cases where (i) information is costly to acquire and (ii) the information, if revealed, would lead to a revision of the issue price. For example, if a certain investor is particularly skilled at valuing companies in a given sector, and if these skills are expensive to acquire and replicate, then at the margin the views of this investor will be very informative to those charged with arriving at an appropriate issue price. But if this investor were to report very strong demand for the shares during the marketing phase, this might result in an upward revision of the offer price and hence would amount to the investor bidding the price up against himself. This problem has been the subject of considerable research, which we review in Part II. The main implication is that it may be necessary to use the pricing and allocation decisions to overcome the natural reluctance of informed investors to reveal their views regarding a particular IPO.

1.1.4 *Pricing and allocation*

Having produced a large volume of information about the company, as published in the prospectus, and marketed the company to potential investors, the final stage involves the pricing and/or allocation of the shares.

In those cases where the price has already been fixed, the only remaining decision is the allocation of shares. When the issue is undersubscribed, all bids can be met in full with the underwriters taking up any unallocated shares. However, when the issue is over-subscribed, then some allocation rule is necessary. Of course, in the case of fixed-price offerings, it has not been possible to change the price in response to excess demand or supply, and so heavy over (or under)-subscription is more likely. In practice, a number of allocation methods are observed in fixed-price offerings, which reflect the regulations imposed by the securities regulators or the stock exchanges on which listing is sought.

Many countries have 'fair' allocation rules, which require all bids to be scaled down pro rata until supply equals demand. However, such rules can result in strategic behaviour by investors if it becomes clear that an issue is going to be extremely 'hot'. In such circumstances the rational response to a pro rata allocation rule is to submit inflated bids for shares, in the hope of gaining a higher allocation. Clearly, everyone has the same incentives and so offers can become, on the face of it, hugely over-subscribed. In practice, however, there may be practical limits to such strategies. For example, in some countries investors have to send a cheque for the number of shares they have bid for. This cheque is then cashed before the final allocation is made. Once the allocation of shares has been decided, the investors receive refunds of the unsuccessful part of their bids. Such rules tend to limit the extent of strategic overbidding.

However, pro rata allocation rules are certainly not always enforced. Many countries allow discrimination in favour of particular types of investor, most typically small retail investors. Such rules can provide another mechanism for avoiding strategic overbidding, as the allocation rules can be skewed in favour of investors who bid for a limited number of shares. It is also possible in many countries to use random allocation rules, where the investors are essentially chosen by lottery. In general, there has been a tendency in a number of countries that tend to use fixed-price methods to impose more regulations on the allocation process. This has been prompted by a number of high-profile scandals involving the preferential allocation of heavily over-subscribed shares to politicians and others in positions of influence.

While fixed price methods continue to be used in a number of countries, there has been a strong trend towards techniques that fix the issue price only after expressions of demand have been elicited from investors. By far the most popular method is that of book-building, and we will discuss this first before considering other methods that condition the final offer price on revealed demand.

Book-building consists of three main steps. (See Benveniste and Spindt 1989; Benveniste and Wilhelm 1990; and Sherman and Titman 2000 for interesting analysis of the book-building approach.) The first step involves the investment bank determining which investors will be invited to participate. In most cases small retail investors are not included in book-building efforts, although a tranche of shares may be reserved for retail investors who then pay the price resulting from the book-building exercise. The reasons for excluding retail investors are mainly the infeasibility of inviting bids and discussing the issue with a large number of small investors, although it is probably also true that retail investors may typically be less informed as to the value of the company than professional investors. Increasingly, companies are choosing to market their shares to overseas as well as domestic investors. Such investors may be particularly valuable if they have experience of investing in, and valuing, similar companies. One key role of the syndicate of investment banks is to provide access to a set of well informed investors who will be involved in determining the appropriate issue price.

The second stage involves the investors who are invited to participate in the book-building submitting their indications of demand. These indications can take a number of forms. Least informative are strike bids. *A strike bid* simply means that the bidder is prepared to buy a given number of shares at any price within the initial price range. In other words, the bidder presents the investment bank with a completely inelastic demand curve, leaving it to others to set the price. More informative are *limit bids*, where the bidder submits a price–quantity combination. A single investor might submit a number of limit bids—sometimes known as *step-bids*—which amounts to revealing that investor's demand curve as a step function to the investment bank. Generally, investors can submit bids at any time until the book closes, and are free to revise, or even cancel, their bids. Hence the book-building process, which typically takes eight to ten working days, is dynamic, with the investors and investment bank both getting a feel for the state of demand and with investors revising their bids as the process evolves.

To begin with, bids will generally be submitted within the initial price range specified by the investment bank in the preliminary prospectus. However, if during the book-building it becomes clear that demand is either very strong or weak, the price range can be revised and new bids invited from investors. In practice, it will usually be necessary to submit the revised price range to the regulatory authorities, who may require the new information to be published in various ways. Thus, very late revisions to the price range could result in a delay to the IPO timetable, and hence the investment bank will need to judge whether a revision is likely reasonably early in the book-building.

At the end of the book-building phase, the investment bank running the book essentially has a demand curve for the issue. As well as the final demand curve, the investment bank also has information on when bids were submitted and revised. This information is then used during the third phase of the book-building, during which the final price and allocations of shares are determined. It is important to note that the investment bank, in consultation with the issuing company, retains considerable discretion over the issue price and allocation of shares. Despite having a good idea of the demand for the shares on offer, the final price will not be determined by a mechanistic crossing of demand and supply. Relatively little is known about how investment banks use the information in the book to determine the final price as they tend to keep their books firmly shut to outsiders (including academic researchers). One exception is the work of Cornelli and Goldreich (2000), who provide an interesting view inside the book-building process for 23 IPOs. In general, investment banks will frequently state that one of their aims in pricing is to produce modest returns for the initial investors. In part, such underpricing can be rationalized as a reward to those taking part in the book-building for providing valuable information. However, in practice, as we shall see in the next chapter, the out-turn returns are frequently far from modest. Thus, there is an important distinction between book-building and formal auctions, as in the latter the price and allocations will tend to be determined by a predetermined rule.

Once the final issue price has been set, the allocations to the investors are determined. The sorts of non-discrimination rules that often apply to fixed price offerings do not apply to book-building efforts: the investment bank, in consultation with the issuing company, will have complete discretion over who is allocated shares. This discretion over allocation is one of the controversial aspects of book-building, in part because not all investors are able to take part in the book-building in the first place. However, such discretionary allocations can be rationalized, as we will discuss in Part II of this book, if they are directed in favour of those investors who submitted particularly informative bids during the book-building phase. For example, bids received early in the book-building process and those that revealed the price sensitivity of the bidder are both more informative than, say, a late strike bid.

The final allocation of shares may also reflect the preferences of the issuing company regarding the types of initial investor it wants. Indeed, some investment banks produce 'quality' rankings of investors according to how closely they are perceived to match the preferences of the issuing company. This information may then be fed into both the pricing and allocation decisions.

Once the final allocations have been decided, the investors who participated in the book-building are contacted to confirm their bids; up until this point the bids are typically not legally binding. The final prospectus, including the issue price, will then be printed, and the shares will normally start trading within a couple of days.

An obvious alternative to the book-building method of pricing and distribution discussed above would be to conduct a formal auction in order to set the price and allocation. While book-building has similarities to an auction—in that the offer price is conditioned on indications of demand—there are some important differences. In particular, as the previous paragraphs should have made clear, book-building is a heavily intermediated process. In other words, the investment banking syndicate collects together all the bids and then makes the pricing and allocation decision according to its own set of (generally unknown) criteria. In contrast, auctions have the potential to be conducted as entirely disintermediated processes. A set of rules can be announced *ex ante* that determine the pricing and allocation decisions, and these rules can often be executed by computer (as seen in many internet-based auction mechanisms). There are clearly many different auction models—such as single-price auctions (where each successful bidder pays the same price) or discriminatory-price auctions (where you pay what you bid)—and these differences may significantly affect the outcome of the auction.

Until the mid-1980s, auctions were frequently used to conduct IPOs in the UK. For example, in 1983, 15 of the 24 public IPOs (which excludes the large number of placings, for which the public cannot generally subscribe) in that year were conducted by auctions (known at that time as offers for sale by tender). However, no private-sector IPOs by auction have taken place in the UK since 1986, although part of the British Airports Authority (BAA) privatization in 1987 was conducted via an auction. Indeed, this latter issue had an interesting feature in that it was a discriminatory price auction, where investors paid what they bid for the shares, rather than the more normal procedure of a single strike price being set once all bids have been received. The reasons for the demise of auctions in the UK are unclear; certainly no regulatory impediments have been introduced.

While auctions have fallen out of favour in the UK, they continue to be used in a few countries. In Japan regulatory changes in the wake of the Recruit Cosmos scandal (see Chapter 2) made auctions compulsory for IPOs between 1990 and 1997. The Japanese system is interesting in that a formal auction is used for a portion of the issue, and the price determined by the auction is then used to fix the price of the remaining shares. Within the auction investors pay the price they bid, as in the BAA example above, with shares being allotted to the highest bidders until the auction issue becomes fully allocated. The price used to sell the remainder of the shares is then set at the weighted average of the successful bid prices from the auction.

Kaneko and Pettway (1994) document how initial underpricing has fallen significantly since these regulatory changes were introduced, from around 70 per cent in the mid-1980s to 12 per cent in the early 1990s. In France, book-building co-exists alongside an auction-type mechanism—known as the *offre à prix minimal*—although in the case of French auctions the price is not set automatically by the bids, as the authorities do not allow certain 'extreme' bids to influence the price. Finally, in Israel, where Walrasian uniform price auctions are often used to set the price, Kandel, Sarig and Wohl (1999) still observe underpricing. Biais and Faugeron-Crouzet (1998) claim this may be because of tacit collusion between investors. Such collusion may be more likely when the auction mechanism creates a strong reaction of price to demand, as is the case with Walrasian auctions. The design of appropriate auction mechanisms, which elicit information from informed investors and are immune from tacit collusion by investors, is likely to be an important area of academic research, and commercial initiatives, in the future.

As will be clear from this section, many alternative methods are employed to determine the price and allocations of IPOs. Although book-building has been growing enormously in popularity in many countries during the 1990s, in many countries more traditional approaches—such as fixed price offers—are still employed. In part this may reflect the relative costs of the different methods, which we return to below. But in part the diversity of approach also reflects important differences in institutional characteristics of the financial system and the regulation of capital markets.

1.1.5 *After the IPO*

Once the final pricing and allocation decisions have been made, trading in the shares usually starts within a couple of days. In some countries the role of the investment bank essentially finishes at this stage, thus making the IPO a distinct event, quite separate from the subsequent trading. However, in other countries the investment banks that conduct IPOs provide further services to the company for some period after trading begins.

An important additional service that is supplied in some countries is to stabilize the price of the shares once they start trading in the after-market. Essentially, the investment banking syndicate stands prepared to buy shares in the after-market in the event of pressure for the share price to fall (in particular below the issue price) and to sell more shares (either at the time of the IPO or in the after-market) in the event of high levels of excess demand for the shares. This support is usually linked with the granting of an *over-allotment option* to the investment banking syndicate. The purpose of the over-allotment option is as follows. If there is healthy demand for the shares at the time of the IPO, the sponsor can sell more shares than were allotted in the original offer, thus creating a short position. If prices in the after-market stay above the issue price, then no action is taken by the sponsor and the short position is covered by exercising the over-allotment option. Typically, the size of such options is 10–15 per cent of the issue size, although any sized option could be granted. However, the real purpose of the option is to reduce downward pressure on prices in the after-market. If the market price falls below the issue price, the sponsor will buy shares to partially, or fully, cover the short position. If the sponsor purchases shares only at or below the offer price, covering the short position in this way is actually profitable. The ability of the sponsor to stabilize prices is limited by the size of the over-allotment option and the length of time over which the option is granted. A typical over-allotment may last for 30 days, although, if the sponsor is confident that the share price will not fall, the option may be exercised within this period.

When the price stabilization is terminated, the book is closed on the deal and the syndicate breaks up, which typically occurs within a week or so of the listing. While such schemes introduce uncertainty into the final sum raised through an IPO, they allow a more accurate balance of supply and demand at the price that is fixed for the issue.

While price stabilization has been popular in the USA for many years, and has increasingly been adopted in other countries, the activity has yet to be sanctioned by the stock exchanges or the securities regulators. In practice, the activities of the investment banking syndicate are rarely transparent to regulators (see Aggarwal 2000*a*), and this raises certain public policy concerns. It seems likely that price stabilization practices will be the subject of continuing debate both in the USA and in those countries that are considering whether to sanction price stabilization.

There are various other services that members of the investment banking syndicate may provide in the after-market. First, they may commit to making markets in the stock to ensure liquidity. Second, and importantly, they may provide continued analyst coverage of the company after its IPO. This can be important in ensuring a steady flow of information about the company, which should tend to promote liquidity. Although such commitments are usually not an explicit component of the investment banks' contract with the firm going public, there is often an implicit understanding that this service will be provided. Good analysts are clearly expensive, and so this implicit guarantee of their continued coverage of the company may to some extent be reflected in fees charged at the IPO. Finally, the investment bank conducting the IPO is often involved in helping the company to raise additional finance in the future. The performance at the IPO (and in the after-market) will clearly affect the reputations of both the investment bank and the company, and will influence the ease with which additional funds can be raised from the capital markets.

1.2   IPO Methods

The previous sections have described the various stages in conducting an IPO in, for the most part, quite generic terms, rather than focusing on a particular country. This is quite deliberate. IPO methods have been changing considerably in many countries, and many of the distinctions between the various methods have become increasingly blurred as investment banks increasingly compete for business on a global basis.

For example, a distinction is often drawn between IPOs conducted on a fixed-price basis and those conducted using book-building. However, to understand the distinction between the two approaches it is necessary to know how the fixed price was arrived at in the first place. Did the investment bank do much pre-IPO marketing of the issue, asking potential investors (informally) for their views about the appropriate price? Clearly, the revelation of demand by investors is quite a formal process in a book-building exercise, but it may be that fixed-price methods are gathering similar information on a less formal basis. However, as we shall discuss in detail in Chapter 3, one important issue is whether the investment bank that attempts to gather this information is able to induce investors to reveal it. This will depend crucially upon whether the bank is able to discriminate in favour of those who reveal particularly useful information, either by preferential allocations of the issue or by preferential prices.

For example, consider UK IPOs conducting via *placings*. This is one of the most popular methods for taking companies public in the UK, in particular for smaller IPOs. In many countries (although, interestingly not in the UK) such methods would be called *private placements*, as a key feature is that the issue is sold to a particular set of clients—

rather than the public at large—of the investment bank conducting the IPO. During a placing the issuing bank, effectively, underwrites the whole issue at an agreed—and fixed—price. However, the issuing bank will immediately arrange to place the shares with investors, although typically this task will be delegated to a specialist broker. In practice, the placing of the shares will normally be achieved on the day the placing agreement is signed, often within a couple of hours. The role of the issuing bank in this case is principally to arrange for the distribution of the shares rather than to bear risk.

Clearly, there is an important distinction between placings and more public offering methods in terms of which groups of investors are able to subscribe to the issue. However, there be may much less of a clear distinction in terms of how the price is set. Increasingly, investment banks conduct placings by issuing a pathfinder prospectus, marketing the issue to institutional clients, and discussing their views about prices. They may not publish an initial price range and then undertake a book-building process to set the final price, but they will none the less be gathering information regarding the demand curves of institutional investors that will influence their choice of final price. Crucially, the investment bank retains a large degree of discretion in the allocation of the issue, thus allowing the potential for rewarding those investors that provided useful information earlier in the process. So, in practice, the distinction between a formal book-building and a placing—in terms of price-setting—may be relatively fine.

On the other hand, some 'fixed-price' methods of issuing, such as fixed-price public offers, afford the investment bank little discretion in the allocation of the issue, and this may undermine their ability to reward investors. Examples include public offers in the UK and *offres à prix fermé* in France, both of which require 'even-handed' allocations, typically pro rata.

The investment bank is always faced with the issue of judging demand for an IPO, and so the important question is really whether certain issue techniques—in particular the methods of gathering this information and involving investors—are less efficient in terms of pricing accuracy and the direct costs of the process. We will give some evidence on the direct costs in the next section, but the issue of whether different issuing techniques result in systematically superior outcomes for the issuing firm has only recently become the subject of research (see e.g. Ljungqvist *et al.* 2000).

We would argue, and we return to this issue in the final chapter, that an interesting distinction between issue methods is likely, in the future, to be the extent to which the IPO process involves intermediaries—in particular investment banks—in the pricing and allocation decisions. The increasing use of the internet for all sorts of transactions, including many financial transactions, is likely to have important implications for the way IPOs are conducted. There are already a number of internet sites that are dedicated to selling IPOs, where investors essentially take part in an auction for the shares. Interestingly, despite the relevant technology having been readily available for a couple of years, at the time of writing there have been surprisingly few IPOs whose pricing and allocation have been completed via an internet auction. Equally, it is surprising that many of the auction mechanisms that have been introduced still allow the issuing firm some discretion in the setting of the final price. Applying auction theory to IPOs raises all sorts of interesting questions, and commercial opportunities, that are likely to be the focus of much attention in the future. (See Biais and Faugeron-Crouzet 1998 for an interesting discussion.)

1.3 The Costs of Going Public

The previous sections have documented the various stages involved in going public, and the different techniques that can be used. In this section we briefly consider the implications of the issue method on the cost of an IPO. Many of the costs associated with conducting an IPO are essentially fixed—the costs of marketing, legal and auditing work, etc.—which tends to result in significant economies of scale. Other costs, such as selling commissions or underwriting fees, are often proportional to the sums raised, although for large issues it is frequently possible to negotiate proportionately lower fees. Consequently, the costs of going public, expressed as a percentage of the funds raised, tend to fall with the size of issue.

The costs of going public can be split into two broad groups. First there are the costs borne by the company in preparing for the IPO.

These would include fees paid to auditors and lawyers, the cost of conducting a marketing road show, and the (opportunity) cost of management time. It is difficult to get consistent estimates of these costs, and so empirical analysis of the costs of going public tends to focus on the fees charged by investment banks, which are generally revealed in prospectuses and/or to regulatory authorities. These are usually expressed in percentage terms as a gross spread charged by the investment bank.

Analysis of the costs of IPOs across countries requires care, however. First, the average size of IPOs differs considerably across countries. Given the economies of scale in conducting an IPO, it is clearly necessary to control for such size differences. Second, there are some big differences in the costs of the different IPO techniques. In general, conducting an IPO using book-building is more expensive than those methods that fix the price without a book-building. It is therefore also necessary to control for the issue technique when estimating the cost of going public.

None the less, once these factors are controlled for, some clear trends emerge. Starting with the USA, where book-building tends to be used for almost all IPOs, there is a heavy clustering of gross spreads at around 7 per cent. Indeed, the frequency with which the '7 per cent solution' (to use the title of a recent paper by Chen and Ritter 2000) is observed, has raised questions about the competitiveness of the investment banking industry in the USA. For example, Chen and Ritter (2000) report that over 90 per cent of all IPOs raising between $20 million and $80 million have gross spreads of *exactly* 7 per cent. The gross spreads observed on larger IPOs are much less clustered, and (on a value weighted basis) in recent years have typically averaged between 5 and 6 per cent.

Looking outside the USA, Ljungqvist *et al.* (2000) analyse the gross spreads of around 1,000 book-building efforts and 600 fixed-price offers for 65 countries. Considering the sample as a whole, and therefore not controlling for different issue sizes, they report average gross spreads of 4.6 per cent for book-building efforts and 2.2 per cent for fixed-price offerings. Given that in many countries book-building efforts tend to be more frequently used for larger issues, this would suggest that the increased costs associated with book-building are actually somewhat larger than these raw averages suggest. However, the authors point to various other complications that should be taken into account before arriving at such a conclusion. In particular, there has been an increasing tendency to market IPOs on an international basis (rather than just in the country of origin) and also to obtain listings in more than one country. Marketing and listing are clearly linked, although there are many companies that choose to market globally but list only in their home market. Not surprisingly, there are additional costs associated with marketing and listing in more than one market, and, given that the USA is by far the most popular market for companies to target, there is a strong correlation between the incidence of book-building and those companies that choose to market and/or list overseas.

What Ljungqvist *et al.* find is that, once all these factors—size, US listings, US marketing, and specific country fixed effects—are controlled for, book-building efforts cost about 1.3 per cent more than fixed-price offers. Listing in the USA adds around 1.4 per cent on average to the costs, and marketing in the USA adds a further 0.4 per cent to the gross spread. Interestingly, although on first sight the average cost of book-built IPOs looks lower than the 7 per cent typically found for small to medium-sized US issues, the lower average costs observed outside the USA are the result of the considerably larger average size of non-US IPOs (which therefore benefit more from economies of scale). For a comparable sample of IPOs that fall within the $20 million to $80 million range considered by Chen and Ritter, US banks also seem to charge around 7 per cent on average to non-US companies that are marketed in the USA.

Looking at the cost differences across countries, one also has to be careful to control for differences in issue method, issue size, etc. The general results found by Ljungqvist *et al.* are that the 'Anglo' capital markets—including the UK, Singapore, Malaysia, and South Africa—have significantly lower costs than average, while the costs of IPOs in Germany, Sweden, Italy, Japan, Canada, and Israel are significantly higher than average. These differences are likely driven by the state of competition among the various financial intermediaries, which will itself in part be a function of the regulatory and legal environment. As capital markets—both investors and intermediaries—become increasingly global in outlook, these institutional differences between countries in terms of company law, stock exchange rules, and securities regulation are likely to increasingly determine the relative cost of going public in different countries.

1.4   Summary

This chapter has introduced the main stages involved in conducting an IPO. In many respects the choices facing companies conducting an IPO have increased in the last few years. National boundaries have increasingly become less relevant. Companies now actively *choose* which exchange(s) to have their shares traded on, which investors to market the issue to, what technique to employ for pricing and distribution, etc. Our intention throughout has been to focus on the generic steps involved in conducting an IPO, rather than on the specific approaches taken in particular countries. Having said this, there have been some clear trends across countries in recent years, with an increasing use of book-building methods and an increased tendency to market IPOs internationally.

In summary, the performance of IPOs is of considerable interest to all parties involved in equity markets: to investors, to issuers, to investment banks, to policy-makers, and of course to academics. If anything, the interest in the performance and efficiency of the IPO process has increased further since the first edition of this book was written—with the enormous increase in the number of IPOs conducted in Europe, the entry of international investment banks into the IPO market in many countries, and, not least, the extraordinary underpricing that has been observed in many countries in recent years. These factors, and others, have resulted in many new theoretical and empirical analyses of the IPO process, which we survey in Part II of the book. Before that, in the next chapter we consider the international evidence on initial underpricing and long-run underperformance. Then in Part III we discuss the lessons from two decades of privatization—which constitutes a particular type of IPO—in the UK and elsewhere, and speculate on the possible research and policy agenda for the next few years.

CHAPTER 2

Stylized Facts

2.1 Introduction

2.1.1 *The new issue market*

While the USA and the UK have had vibrant primary equity markets for a long time, IPOs have made a significant appearance in much of continental Europe and the liberalizing economies in Latin America and Asia only since the 1980s. In some countries private-sector firms have gone public in the wake of large-scale government privatization programmes, as in Chile and Mexico, while in others tax changes, deregulation of investment restrictions on institutional and foreign investors, and generational change have prompted entrepreneurs to seek fresh funds from the stock exchange or to liquidate share holdings by selling to a dispersed group of investors. Some stock exchanges, beginning to view listings as a source of revenue, have pro-actively lowered listing requirements or established new market segments aimed at small, high-growth ventures in an attempt to entice firms to float. Until 1997, for instance, firms floating on the Spanish markets were required to have made a profit sufficient to pay a dividend of at least 6 per cent of capital in the previous two consecutive years, or in three non-consecutive years within the previous five years. In 1997 this was replaced with a requirement that companies must be able to 'prove' they will reach sufficient profit levels in future. The number of IPOs subsequently doubled. However, the change was insufficient to allow JazzTel, an upstart broad-band telecoms provider, to raise money in Madrid. In December 1999 JazzTel instead opted for a dual listing on NASDAQ and EASDAQ.

One way to illustrate the recent popularity of initial public offerings is to compare the numbers of listed domestic companies in the early 1980s and the late 1990s. Since the change in this number is net of delistings, such a comparison will tend to understate the occurrence of flotations. The diagrams in Figure 2.1 graph the percentage increase in listings for 18 industrialized and 36 emerging stock markets. All but 12 of these have many more listed firms now than they did in the early 1980s. The number of quoted firms increased the most in emerging markets. It more than doubled in 15 countries—rising 34-fold in Indonesia and nine-fold in Egypt—and increased by 243 per cent on average. At the same time, the number of listings fell in nine emerging markets, predominantly in Latin America. The largest fall occurred in Uruguay, from 50 firms in 1981 to 16 in 1997. In part, this is no doubt related to the financial and currency crises besetting the region in the late 1990s, but in part it also reflects the increasing tendency of issuers to bypass their local capital markets and access the US capital markets directly, often via American Depository Receipts. In the industrialized world, all but three countries saw substantial increases in the number of listed firms. The largest increase occurred in Finland, where the total number of listings jumped from 48 in 1983 to 147 in 1999. The three exceptions are the UK (down 11 per cent), New Zealand (down 20 per cent), and Belgium (down 27 per cent). In the case of the UK, the fall in the number of listings does not reflect an illiquid IPO market: on the contrary, we estimate that more than 80 British firms on average go public every year. The overall fall in the number of British listings thus reflects an offsetting, and higher, rate of delistings caused by mergers, buy-outs, or financial distress.

Detailed data on the actual number of flotations are available for a handful of the above markets. Figure 2.2, which is based on data compiled by Ljungqvist and Wilhelm (2001), illustrates the 1990s 'Going Public boom' in the 15 countries of the EU. The annual number of IPOs in the EU has varied from a low of 65 in 1992 to a high of 540 in 1999, with a marked upward trend beginning in 1995. To put this in perspective, during the 1990s there were 510 IPOs per year in the USA and 110 in Japan, compared with 265 from the EU. Over the decade as a whole, 5,103 American firms went public (almost exclusively in the USA), compared with 2,654 companies from the EU (some of which floated outside their home country, such as in the

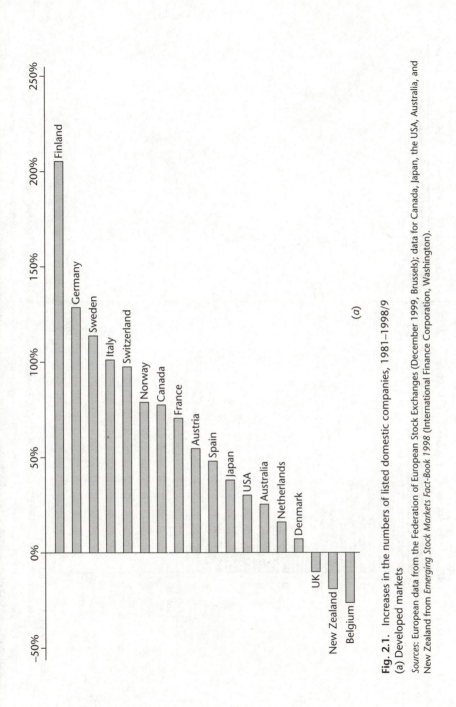

Fig. 2.1. Increases in the numbers of listed domestic companies, 1981–1998/9
(a) Developed markets

Sources: European data from the Federation of European Stock Exchanges (December 1999, Brussels); data for Canada, Japan, the USA, Australia, and New Zealand from *Emerging Stock Markets Fact-Book 1998* (International Finance Corporation, Washington).

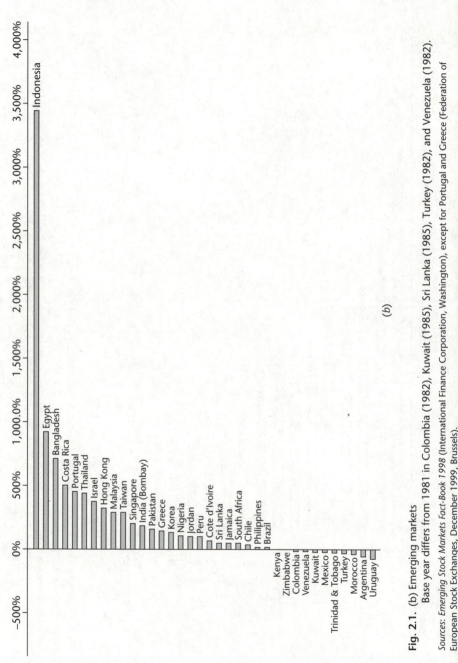

Fig. 2.1. (b) Emerging markets

Base year differs from 1981 in Colombia (1982), Kuwait (1985), Sri Lanka (1985), Turkey (1982), and Venezuela (1982).

Sources: Emerging Stock Markets Fact-Book 1998 (International Finance Corporation, Washington), except for Portugal and Greece (Federation of European Stock Exchanges, December 1999, Brussels).

USA) and 992 Japanese firms (since 1991). In 1998 and 1999, more European companies went public than American ones, which we believe is unprecedented (though good comparative data for the nineteenth and early twentieth centuries are not available).

Germany and France in particular have developed very active IPO markets, and in 1999 overtook the UK as the most active IPO markets in Europe. This can be explained largely by the success of the Neuer Markt in Frankfurt and the Nouveau Marché in Paris. Similar new market segments were created in Milan (Nuovo Mercato), Brussels (Euro.NM Belgium), and Amsterdam (Nieuwe Markt), which until 31 December 2000 operated an alliance with the Paris Bourse and the Deutsche Börse AG under the Euro.NM banner. EASDAQ was set up to compete with the established exchanges and their new creations, but, as Figure 2.3 shows, it could not match the explosive growth in listings seen on the Euro.NM markets. The London Stock Exchange established the Alternative Investment Market (AIM) in June 1995 and techMARK in November 1999, neither of which have proved as successful as the Euro.NM markets. In October 2000, following the collapse of its merger plans with Deutsche Börse, the London Stock Exchange announced its intention to create a new, pan-European competitor to the Neuer Markt.

2.1.2 *International differences and convergence in the use of initial public offerings*

Until the recent IPO boom, continental European IPOs were quite a different breed from their US and UK cousins. (Many Asian IPO markets have long resembled those in the USA and the UK.) First, they typically involved mostly old, large, well established companies rather than start-up ventures in risky new industries. In the first edition of this monograph, we estimated that the median age among continental European offerings was 50 years, many times that of the typical US or UK IPO firm, which tends to be less than ten years old when taken public. Second, machine tool manufacturers, banks, and other such traditional industries dominated most continental European new issue markets, while IPOs in the USA and the UK have long been a popular way for start-up enterprises in new industries to attract risk capital or for venture capitalists to exit investments in

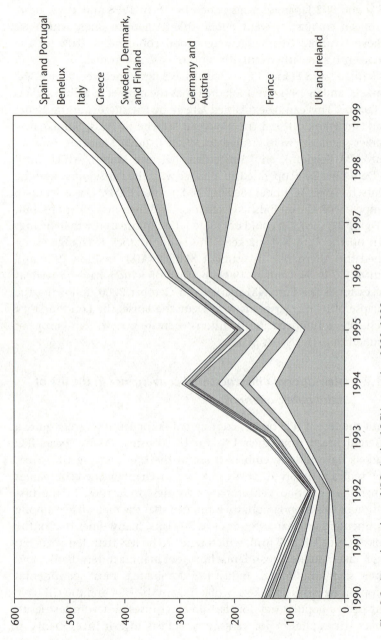

Fig. 2.2. Annual numbers of IPOs in the 15 EU countries, 1990–1999

Source: Ljungqvist and Wilhelm (2001).

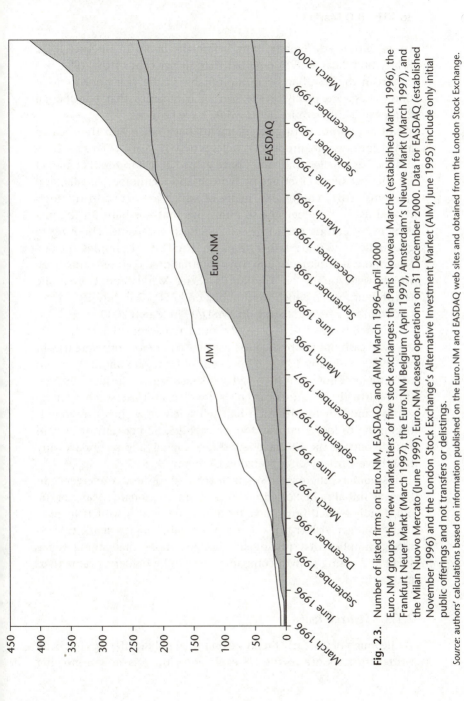

Fig. 2.3. Number of listed firms on Euro.NM, EASDAQ, and AIM, March 1996–April 2000

Euro.NM groups the 'new market tiers' of five stock exchanges: the Paris Nouveau Marché (established March 1996), the Frankfurt Neuer Markt (March 1997), the Euro.NM Belgium (April 1997), Amsterdam's Nieuwe Markt (March 1997), and the Milan Nuovo Mercato (June 1999). Euro.NM ceased operations on 31 December 2000. Data for EASDAQ (established November 1996) and the London Stock Exchange's Alternative Investment Market (AIM, June 1995) include only initial public offerings and not transfers or delistings.

Source: authors' calculations based on information published on the Euro.NM and EASDAQ web sites and obtained from the London Stock Exchange.

young businesses. Finally, long before the boom in internet IPOs, Beatty and Zajac (1995) reported that 58 per cent of the 1984 IPO cohort in the USA had been unprofitable in the year prior to flotation. These are precisely the sort of companies that continental European listing requirements would have kept out.

Not any more. Listing requirements have fallen and the median age in continental Europe IPO circles is now 12 years. Offer sizes have dropped as smaller companies have gained access to the IPO market for the first time. Offerings by biotech and technology, media, and telecoms (TMT) companies, many of which are active in internet-related fields, have become so numerous that—perhaps for the first time ever—Europe has witnessed American companies choosing to go public in Europe rather than on NASDAQ. Examples include Macropore Inc (biotech) and Toys International.com (e-commerce), which went public on Frankfurt's Neuer Markt, and Uproar Inc (e-entertainment), which went public on EASDAQ in July 1999 prior to obtaining a second listing on NASDAQ in March 2000.

It used to be the case in parts of continental Europe that an IPO was a way to cash out as opposed to raise new equity for corporate use. In the 1980s and early 1990s, 67 per cent of Portugal's and 23 per cent of Germany's flotations involved *only* shares sold by insiders. By contrast, virtually all American IPOs involve at least some primary equity, and usually around a half sell solely new shares. Europe is beginning to look that way too. Since 1995, 82 per cent of IPOs in Europe outside the UK have raised new capital, and secondary-only IPOs have virtually disappeared in Germany.

In summary, there is now a distinct trend towards convergence in the way initial public offerings are used internationally. Many of the old, family-owned firms have by now gone public, so it is increasingly younger, riskier firms that tap the public equity markets. This change implies that pricing has become more challenging, since small and young growth companies tend to be harder to value than mature firms.

2.1.3   *Stylized facts*

While much of the early literature on initial public offerings has been written in response to the US experience, there is now a growing body of international research which has confirmed the main styl-ized facts previously found in the American new issue market. As out-lined in the previous chapter, the most extensively documented empirical regularity is the initial underpricing phenomenon: first-day trading prices typically exceed the price at which the shares were offered to investors. A second stylized fact—which we discuss below —concerns the time-series behaviour of first-day returns and IPO volume: there are cycles in both the extent of underpricing and the number of firms coming to market. Lastly, a more recent empirical anomaly is the poor long-run performance of initial public offerings. The following three sections will present the empirical evidence on each of these. The availability of international research presents an opportunity to assess the robustness of the proposed theoretical models which try to rationalize the new issue phenomena. As we mentioned in the previous chapter, these explanations are almost exclusively predicated on an analysis of the US IPO market and thus may fail to explain why, despite differences in institutional and other conditions across countries, IPOs are underpriced and seem to perform poorly in the after-market in almost every country.

2.2 Underpricing

2.2.1 *The international evidence*

Probably the earliest empirical regularity in the new issue market to have attracted attention is the fact that companies apparently under-price their shares when going public. This implies on the one hand a handsome profit for those investors lucky (or privileged) enough to obtain stock in the offering, and on the other an opportunity cost of going public to the company's old owners. Table 2.1 lists comparative evidence of IPO underpricing from a large number of countries. Most evidence comes from the USA, while studies on other countries are more recent, reflecting the higher rate of flotations from the 1980s onwards. The first-day premium that investors experience is positive in virtually every country, and typically averages more than 15 per cent in industrialized countries and around 60 per cent in emerging markets, measured between subscription and the first day of trading.

Table 2.1. Comparative evidence of IPO underpricing

Country [a]	Study	Sample period	Sample size	Initial return (%)[b]
USA	Ibbotson et al. (1994)	1960–92	10,626	15.3
USA	Ritter (1987)[c]	1977–82	664	14.8
USA	Ritter (1987)[d]	1977–82	364	47.8
Australia	Finn and Higham (1988)	1966–78	93	29.2
Australia	Lee et al. (1996)	1976–89	266	11.9
Australia	Woo (2000)	1990–95	115	12.4
Austria	Aussenegg (1999)	1984–99	76	6.5
Belgium	Manigart and Rogiers (1992)	1984–90	28	13.7
Canada	Jog and Srivastava (1996)	1971–92	254	7.4
Canada	Kryzanowski and Rakita (1999)	1993–99	242	7.2
Denmark	Jakobsen and Sorensen	1984–98	117	5.4
Finland	Keloharju (1993a)	1984–92	91	14.4
France	Jacquillat (1986)[e]	1972–86	87	4.8
Germany	Ljungqvist (1997)	1970–93	180	9.2
Great Britain	Jenkinson and Mayer (1988)[f]	1983–86	143	10.7
Great Britain	Jenkinson and Mayer (1988)[g]	1983–86	68	4.7
Great Britain	Jenkinson and Mayer (1988)[h]	1983–86	26	-2.2
Italy	Cherubini and Ratti (1992)	1985–91	75	29.7
Japan	Jenkinson (1990)	1986–88	48	54.7
Japan	Kaneko and Pettway (1994)[i]	1989–93	37	12.0
Netherlands	Buijs and Eijgenhuijsen (1993)	1982–91	72	7.4
New Zealand	Vos and Cheung (1992)	1979–91	149	28.8
Norway	Emilsen et al. (1997)	1984–96	68	12.5
Spain	Fernandez et al. (1992)	1985–90	71	35.4
Sweden	Rydqvist (1993)	1970–91	213	39.0
Switzerland	Kunz and Aggarwal (1994)	1983–89	42	35.8
Brazil	Aggarwal et al. (1993)	1979–90	62	78.5
Chile	Aggarwal et al. (1993)	1982–90	19	16.3
China	Mok and Hui (1998)[j]	1990–93	87	289.2
China	Mok and Hui (1998)[k]	1990–93	22	26.0
Greece	Kazantzis and Thomas (1996)	1987–94	129	50.9
Hong Kong	McGuinness (1992)	1980–90	80	17.6
Israel	Kandel et al. (1999)	1993–94	28	4.5
Korea	Dhatt et al. (1993)	1980–90	347	78.1
Malaysia	Dawson (1987)	1978–83	21	166.6
Mexico	Aggarwal et al. (1993)	1987–90	37	33.0
Nigeria	Ikoku (1995)	1989–93	63	19.1
Philippines	Sullivan and Unite (1998)	1987–97	104	22.7
Poland	Aussenegg (2000)	1991–98	149	35.6
Portugal	Alphao (1989)	1986–87	62	54.4
Singapore	Koh and Walter (1989)	1973–87	66	27.0
Taiwan	Chen (1992)	1971–90	168	45.0
Thailand	Wethyavivorn and Koo-smith (1991)	1988–89	32	58.1
Turkey	Ozer (1997)	1989–94	89	12.2

These averages hide some cases of enormous underpricing; in Malaysia, for instance, the average new issue between 1978 and 1983 started trading at a 167 per cent premium over its offer price.

There are several reasons why emerging-market IPOs are so much more underpriced than US or European ones. Political and bureaucratic meddling is one of them. While countries such as Taiwan and Korea have recently liberalized the way in which issuers and underwriters can determine the flotation price, the evidence summarized in the table mostly pre-dates such regulatory reform and hence reflects the effect of administrative fiat. For instance, prior to the 1988 partial deregulation, Korean firms had to price their shares at book value, while until 1993 Taiwanese offering prices were calculated using a formula based on the price–earnings ratio and other characteristics of three supposedly 'comparable' firms.

Favouritism is another form of political interference that has been rife in many countries, both emerging and developed. In Malaysia new issues have been used not only to aid ethnic policy, but also (or so it has been alleged) to line the pockets of the politically influential: while the law requires ethnic Malays (as opposed to ethnic Chinese) to be allocated a minimum of 30 per cent of shares in equity offerings, generous allocations of deeply discounted stock have allegedly found

[a] The table presents results for three groups of countries: the USA, other developed countries, and emerging markets. The classification into developed and emerging markets follows the financial indicators section in *The Economist*.

[b] Initial returns may be measured between the (first) subscription day and the first trading day, or some day soon after trading starts. They may be gross or net of the concurrent market return. Generally, results are robust to market-return adjustments and the choice of time frame. Averages are calculated using equal weights. Apart from in the USA, capitalization-weighted or gross-proceeds weighted averages would not be significantly different.

[c] Firm commitment offerings only.

[d] Best efforts offerings only.

[e] Tender offers only.

[f] Placings.

[g] Fixed-price offers.

[h] Tender offers.

[i] Auctions, compulsory since 1989.

[j] A-shares in Shanghai, reserved for domestic Chinese.

[k] B-shares in Shanghai, reserved for foreign investors.

Source: the Danish numbers are from Jan Jacobsen and Ole Sørensen at Copenhagen Business School.

their way into the hands of a privileged few, in spite of an otherwise ostensibly fair pro rata allocation system modelled on the UK example. More notoriously, the Japanese Recruit Cosmos scandal has become a byword for corruption: in April 1989 Japan's prime minister Noboru Takeshita was forced to resign when it was revealed that the Recruit Company had attempted to buy political influence via targeted allocations of highly underpriced shares in its spun-off Cosmos subsidiary. Thus, in some countries offer prices are set on the basis not only of who you are, but also of whom you want to please. In the wake of Recruit Cosmos, Japan relaxed regulations concerning the pricing of IPOs while tightening allocation rules. The move to letting offering prices be determined by auction has substantially reduced average underpricing, from about 70 per cent to 12 per cent. Similar effects of deregulation are evident in Korea and other liberalizing countries.

As in Japan after 1989, auction-like offering mechanisms such as tenders in the UK, the Netherlands and Belgium, or *offres à prix minimal* in France, are generally associated with low levels of underpricing. Most Chilean IPOs have also used auctions, and have been modestly underpriced, at least by emerging-market standards. This is not particularly surprising, given that, unlike fixed-price offers, tenders allow market demand at least partly to influence the issue price.[1] What is curious, though, is that we do not observe a shift towards greater use of auctions: tenders are rare in most European countries (Finland, Germany, Italy, Sweden, Switzerland) despite the absence of regulatory restrictions on the way firms price their shares. Moreover, they have become increasingly uncommon in the Netherlands and have disappeared altogether in the UK. In Japan, where bookbuilding has been permitted since 1997, auctions have fallen into disuse. France is now the only European country where IPOs are frequently sold by auction.

In the USA, underpricing also varies systematically with the choice of offering mechanism: *ex post* discounts are markedly lower in firm-commitment than in best-efforts offerings. This is not surprising:

---

[1] However, there is a danger of comparing apples and oranges. We will argue in Ch. 3 that auctions are not very good at generating valuation-relevant information, compared with book-building efforts. This raises the possibility that auctions are chosen by issuers who are easier to value to begin with, while issuers whose values are more uncertain use book-building. We should then not be surprised to see auction IPOs experiencing lower underpricing.

exceptionally risky firms may find it both difficult and expensive to obtain underwriting cover and hence typically may turn to best-efforts contracts instead. (However, best-efforts offerings have become much rarer in the USA, and such arguably high-risk companies as one-year-old internet companies have gone public in firm-commitment IPOs.)

2.2.2 Discussion

Economists studying the underpricing phenomenon long used to term it a puzzling anomaly. In an efficient and perfect market, theory suggests, companies should not 'leave money on the table', certainly not in such large quantities. While the evidence from some emerging markets and from pre-Recruit Japan could easily be dismissed as the none-too-surprising outcome of corruption or bureaucratic pricing mechanisms almost deliberately designed to obstruct market forces, the same cannot presumably be said of the US or European experience.

In trying to explain why firms are floated at too low a price, economists have generated a large theoretical and empirical literature, whose main line of attack is the assumption of market perfection and efficiency. Depending on the approach, underpricing becomes an efficient form of compensation for investors, induces underwriters to exert optimal selling effort, or serves as insurance against future potential litigation by disaffected shareholders. Part II of this book will review these contributions in some detail. Almost invariably, underpricing is seen as involuntary but unfortunately necessary, even in the signalling approach, which assumes that high-quality firms use underpricing as a signal to lower their cost of capital in subsequent funding exercises: if there were a cheaper way to signal quality, presumably firms would choose not to underprice their offerings.

However, few theories can account for the fact that practitioners view a discounted flotation as a *success* which will tend to get the firm a good press. When Sock Shop International went public on the London Stock Exchange in 1987, its chief executive pronounced herself 'ecstatic' at the flotation being underpriced by 65 per cent.[2] To

---

[2] *Financial Times*, 15 May 1987. Loughran and Ritter (2001) argue that issuers do not care about leaving so much money on the table because the states in which underpricing ends up

an economist this is extraordinary: selling an asset at well below its market value is not usually cause for celebration. Consider selling your house for 100,000, only to see it sold on immediately for 115,000! This raises two questions: who stands to lose from underpricing, and are there benefits to discounting one's IPO?

The main cost is borne by the original owners. This is obviously true if the original owners participate in the IPO by offering some of their existing shares. In that case, underpricing implies that they will fail to realize the full value of their investments in the company. But even if they do not participate in the IPO—that is, if all shares on offer are primary—the old owners have to dilute their stakes more the more highly underpriced the offering: for a given funding need, the lower the offer price, the greater the number of shares that need to be sold. It is worth noting, however, that the traditional measures of underpricing reported in Table 2.1 greatly overstate the original shareholders' wealth losses. Only a shareholder who sold her entire stake would experience the headline underpricing loss, whereas if she retained at least some shares the opportunity of selling in the after-market would remain. In Germany, for instance, IPOs are underpriced by 10 per cent on average, but the old owners lose a much lower 4 per cent of the pre-flotation value of the company (Ljungqvist 1995a).[3] None the less, 4 per cent of, say, a 100 million enterprise is still a sizeable amount of money to leave on the table. Habib and Ljungqvist (2001) estimate that the average issuer in the USA between 1991 and 1995 suffered underpricing-related wealth losses of US$6.5 million.

Counteracting these costs are a number of potential benefits. Underpriced offers are typically heavily oversubscribed. Whether the publicity generated by having to ration investors, or even turn them away, outweighs the underpricing cost is an open question, but many practitioners seem to interpret the extent of excess demand as an indicator of a flotation's success. For example, when broadcast.com, an internet company, went public in July 1998, the company *requested* that Morgan Stanley Dean Witter, its underwriter, under-

---

being high tend to be the states when issuers learn that they are much richer than they had expected. This, of course, assumes that such issuers did not sell all their shares at the IPO.

[3] Owner-related losses are lower than investor-related underpricing would suggest, partly because a great number of new issues involve no insider sales, and partly because retention rates when insiders do participate in the offering tend to be high, in Germany and elsewhere.

price its shares substantially. It went public at $18 a share and closed 249 per cent up at $62¾, creating considerable media interest in what was then 'the hottest IPO ever'.

Another, more readily acceptable, benefit is the insurance against under-subscription that underpricing provides. It could be argued that the disutility associated with one's offering being left with the underwriters greatly exceeds the reduction in utility arising from greater dilution or lower realized gains. The 4 per cent figure for Germany would suggest that such an insurance policy is not all that expensive for the original owners.

In some countries, underpricing may be a tax-efficient way to remunerate employees. Rydqvist (1997) argues that the relatively lower tax on capital gains compared with employment income encouraged Swedish companies to underprice more than they would otherwise have done. Following tax reform in 1990, which removed the tax advantage of underpricing, average initial discounts dropped from 41 per cent to 8 per cent.

Lastly, while underpricing may lead to the financial dilution of the insiders' retained stakes, it may also, perversely perhaps, ensure that their control is *not* diluted. The point is that excess demand affords the issuer the opportunity to choose a shareholder base of its liking. Since underpriced flotations almost invariably have to be rationed, the greater is underpricing, the smaller is the average pro rata allocation and thus the less is the likelihood of future challenges to the old owners' control.

On balance, therefore, underpricing need not be simply a cost of going public, variously rationalized in the early literature on the subject as an involuntary but necessary compensation, signalling or insurance device: it may also have desirable side-effects which compensate for the costs of forgone capital gains and dilution.

2.3 Cycles in IPO Volume and Initial Returns

2.3.1 *When do firms go public?*

The received wisdom in finance textbooks is that issuing corporate securities in an efficient market should not be a positive net present

value (NPV) transaction, meaning that the timing of a financing decision should not matter since any offering will be fairly priced.[4] It
might be tempting, therefore, to conclude that IPOs occur randomly
over time. However, this is not what we observe in practice. As Figure
2.2 showed, the number of firms coming to market is far from
random, with IPO volume rising and falling at the same time in different countries. Figure 2.4 takes a closer look at the USA, for which a
long time series, going back to 1960, is available. There are clear signs
of positive autocorrelation: periods of high IPO volume are likely to
be followed by further heavy IPO activity.[5] Often, it is a narrow set of
industries that drive the volume increase. To illustrate this, Figure 2.5
plots the percentage of aggregate monthly IPO gross proceeds raised
by oil and gas companies (SIC code 131) in the USA between January
1970 and July 1999. The high-volume periods that show up as spikes
coincide with the oil price hikes of 1973/4, 1979/80, and 1990/1.
Another obvious example of industry clustering is the 1999 boom in
IPOs by internet-related companies in the USA and in Europe.

How can we square these patterns with the textbook paradigm?
Unlike a bond issue, say, or some other form of financing decision,
going public is a much less reversible step which has implications far
beyond simply raising funds. Even if we accept the tenet that the sale
of shares to investors is a zero-NPV transaction, such that firms
cannot take advantage of the market by selling overpriced shares (on
average), the decision to go public in the first place presumably needs
to be a positive-NPV proposition. Hence, the flow of companies
coming to market should depend on factors that determine the trade-
off between the costs and benefits of a stock market listing. When
these factors vary over time, so will the number of firms seeking a
quotation. These factors are clearly related to the determinants of
private companies' demand for outside equity capital, and the
market's willingness to supply such capital.

Listing and other requirements imposed by a stock exchange can
affect the costs of going public both directly and indirectly. For
instance, a reduction in listing fees or publicity and compliance

---

[4] See e.g. Brealey and Myers (1991: 289).
[5] In the USA, for instance, Ibbotson and Jaffe (1975) report autocorrelations in the region of
75 per cent in monthly IPO volume during the 1960s.

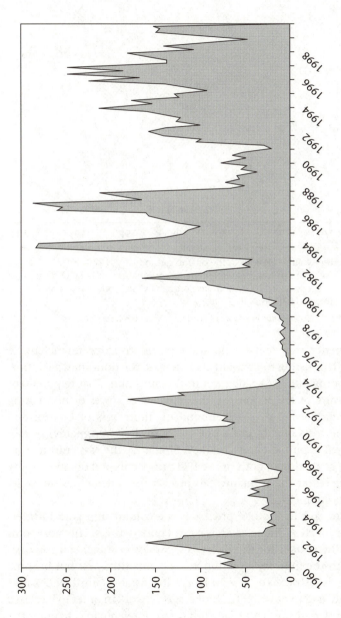

Fig. 2.4. Quarterly IPO volume in the USA, 1960–1999.
IPO volume is the number of companies going public per quarter.

Source: authors' calculations using data from Jay Ritter, available at http://bear.cba.ufl.edu/ritter/ipoall.htm

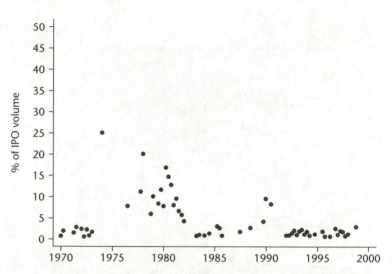

Fig. 2.5. High-volume periods in the oil and gas industry, 1970–1999
The figure shows the percentage of aggregate monthly IPO gross
proceeds raised by oil and gas companies (SIC code 131) between
January 1970 and July 1999.

Source: authors' calculations using data obtained from Securities Data Company.

requirements may make a flotation more attractive financially. A
relaxation of listing rules could also increase the non-financial attraction of going public. A reduction in the minimum float requirement
or an easing of restrictions on the issuance of lower or non-voting
stock might decrease the likelihood of future loss of control and
hence the costs of subjecting one's firm to the (presumably) greater
scrutiny of a public equity market. Similarly, the less information
needs to be disclosed, both in the IPO prospectus and on an ongoing
basis, the better the company can protect its strategic position relative to its competitors.

A major cost in the IPO process is the commission paid to intermediaries, such as financial advisers and underwriters. The more competitive the market for these services, the lower in general the cost.
Entry into the industry would increase competitiveness but in some
countries is restricted by law. In Japan, for instance, until 1997 banks
effectively had to have a retail brokerage network in order to be active
in IPO underwriting. This made it hard for foreign banks to enter the

market. In the USA the loosening, and subsequent repeal, of the Glass–Steagall Act during the 1990s has resulted in some leading commercial banks (including Citicorp, NationsBank, Bank of America) entering the IPO underwriting market and quickly winning substantial market share. However, there appears to be no evidence that they have tended to compete on the fees they charge issuers for their services: Hansen (2001) shows that most commercial bank underwriters charge 7 per cent of gross proceeds in most deals, just like the long-established investment banks (cf. Chen and Ritter 2000). However, the underwriting fee is obviously not the only dimension in which underwriters might compete; another is the offer price that banks promise potential issuers.[6] Evidence reported in Ljungqvist *et al.* (2000) suggests that issuers outside the USA trade off higher fees against higher offer prices.

If the original owners care about dilution of control, they will tend to take their firms public in periods of high stock market valuations, since for a given funding need a higher offer price implies less dilution. Thus, IPO volume should be related to the stock market climate. It should also vary with the availability of investment opportunities and hence the business cycle, since funding needs should be greatest when there are many projects to finance.

On the benefit side, the availability of alternative sources of funding will affect the attractiveness of going public in many ways. At high levels of gearing, for example, a firm may find it increasingly expensive and difficult to raise bank loans, and may balk at the corporate control implications of tighter loan covenants or more intrusive bank monitoring. As the amount of retained earnings varies over the business cycle, a flotation therefore becomes increasingly tempting in an economic upswing, when earnings are still low. Regime changes, such as a reduction in capital gains taxes or a more liberal attitude to the tax deductibility of going-public-related costs, will also increase the net benefit the original owners receive from a flotation. Chemmanur and Fulghieri (1999) specifically model IPO volume by contrasting the relative costs of going public and of raising private equity from venture capitalists. In their model, hot markets occur when favourable

---

[6] Gande *et al.* (1999) find that commercial banks' entry into the underwriting of debt offerings has lowered spreads and increased offer prices.

profitability shocks induce more investors to produce information about companies in certain industries, which in turn makes going public more attractive.

The available evidence generally supports these considerations. Högholm and Rydqvist (1995) link the European 'IPO boom' of the 1980s to rising share prices and deregulation, while Ljungqvist (1995*b*) provides evidence that in Germany the number of flotations changes over time in line with the business cycle, stock market conditions, and the gradual increase in competitiveness of the underwriter market.

2.3.2   *Predictability of underpricing*

Like IPO volume, the extent of underpricing also tends to vary over time in most markets. Figures 2.6 and 2.7 illustrate this for the USA and Germany, respectively. The 'hot issue' market of the late 1990s is clearly visible, with initial returns averaging 95 per cent in the USA in the final quarter of 1999 and 55 per cent in Germany in 1998. This hot issue market was not unprecedented. In the USA similar conditions prevailed in 1961, 1967–8, and 1980. Germany experienced a hot issue market in 1985. (The spikes in the 1960s represent low IPO volume.) Note how rare periods of overpricing are. In Germany there has never been a year when IPOs were overpriced on average. In the USA only 15 of the 160 quarters between 1960 and 1999 saw the average company open below its offer price, and these have tended to be the quarters when relatively fewer companies were floated. This suggests that a 'stagging' or 'flipping' strategy—investing indiscriminately in all IPOs and selling as soon as trading commences—has little downside risk, though note that all our figures show equally weighted averages: the profitability of stagging could look different if the investor ended up with relatively more of the overpriced than of the underpriced offerings.

Another striking feature of the graphs is the relatively high persistence in initial returns. Periods of high initial returns frequently last for several months, which suggests that underpricing is highly positively autocorrelated.[7] From the stag's point of view this is good

---

[7] For US evidence on this, see Ibbotson *et al.* (1994).

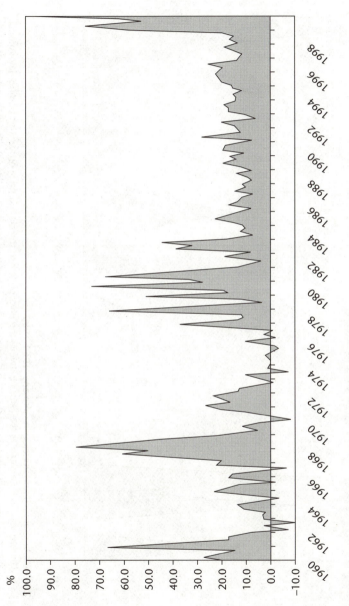

Fig. 2.6. Average quarterly underpricing in the USA, 1960–1999
Underpricing is computed as the return between the offer price and the closing price on the first trading day. Quarterly averages are equally weighted and are given in percentages.

Source: authors' calculations using data from Jay Ritter.

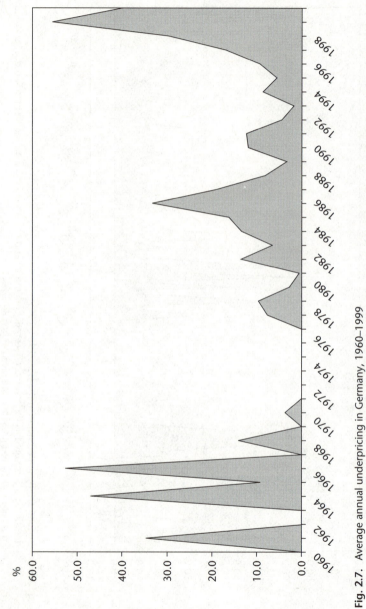

Fig. 2.7. Average annual underpricing in Germany, 1960–1999
Underpricing is computed as the return between the offer price and the closing price on the first trading day. Annual averages are equally weighted and shown in percentages. The annual numbers of IPOs in the 1960s were in single digits. There were no IPOs in 1960, 1962, 1963, 1967, 1969, 1971, 1974–6, and 1980.

news, since it implies that future (average) initial returns are predictable with a considerable degree of accuracy. To the economist, it presents a challenge: if underpricing is worrying *per se* from an efficient markets point of view, its predictability is even more worrying since it implies that a yet more profitable trading rule than *indiscriminate* stagging exists.

Forecasts of future initial returns can be made considerably more precise if factors other than past underpricing are considered. There is overwhelming evidence that underpricing is higher in buoyant stock markets: Davis and Yeomans (1976) (UK), Reilly (1977) (USA), McGuinness (1992) (Hong Kong), and Rydqvist (1993) (Sweden) all show that initial returns tend to be higher following periods of high returns on the market index. In Germany IPOs are more heavily underpriced not only when the market is performing well, but also in macroeconomic upswings, when already-listed firms issue historically large amounts of seasoned equity, and when stock market volatility is low (Ljungqvist 1997).

Explanations for the link between the incidence of hot issue periods and stock market and business cycle conditions are much thinner on the ground. Conceptually, the magnitude of initial returns will vary when the fundamental parameters identified in theoretical underpricing models change. For instance, if underpricing serves to insure against litigation, greater underpricing will become necessary as the likelihood of future lawsuits increases. However, as yet there has been no convincing effort to endogenize how and why these parameters change with macroeconomic and stock market conditions: why, for instance, would litigation risk increase in buoyant markets?

Another approach is to argue that, as the costs of going public are lower and the benefits greater in certain periods, a flotation could become so attractive that a firm would be willing to accept higher than usual underpricing in order to take advantage of a good IPO climate. This takes us back to the earlier discussion of cycles in IPO volume: buoyant stock markets and economic upswings are good times to go public and hence may induce a greater tolerance of underpricing.

An alternative explanation, favoured by investment bankers, relates to the availability of funds. When a particularly large number of companies tap the equity market, as for instance when there are a large number of privatization offers, a greater enticement in the form of underpricing must be offered for investors to be willing to sub-scribe for shares. However, this rings somewhat hollow. Most devel-oped economies should be assumed to have deep enough financial markets to absorb large amounts of new stock on a bait of, say, a 'mere' 10 per cent underpricing discount. In emerging markets, the often enormous over-subscription ratios—factors of 100 and more are not uncommon in Asia—even in times of heavy IPO activity indicate that investors will be more than willing to buy even if offer prices are set higher. It thus seems unlikely that the supply of investable funds is highly sensitive to the number of offerings.

2.3.3   *Underpricing as a leading indicator of IPO activity*

Typically, the underpricing and IPO volume cycles are not perfectly synchronized. Rather, 'hot issue' markets seem to be followed by periods of high new issue volume, as in the USA, where Ibbotson *et al.* (1994) document that initial returns lead volume by 6–12 months; for instance, the very high initial returns seen in the USA in 1980 and 1981 were followed by a doubling of quarterly IPO volume. Following the increase in IPO volume, initial returns tend to return to normal. Similar lead–lag relationships are also evident in Australia (Lee *et al.* 1996) and Germany and Sweden (Ljungqvist 1995*b*).

Why more companies go public after periods of sustained under-pricing is not entirely clear. In the first edition of this monograph we speculated that higher underpricing might act as a signal of investors' appetite for new offerings, thereby enticing firms to go public. Lowry and Schwert (2000) develop this idea: higher-than-expected under-pricing may suggest that investors value IPO companies more highly than the companies and their advisers had expected. In terms of the fundamental cost–benefit trade-off referred to earlier, this would tend to spur more companies into floating, and pricing their IPOs more aggressively, leading to higher IPO volume and lower underpricing. An alternative hypothesis, proposed by Lowry and Schwert, is based on variation over time in the degree of market power that underwrit-ers enjoy. As their market power increases at a certain point in time (for reasons that are not further illuminated), underwriters find it easier to underprice without losing market share. Banks benefit from underpricing since the lower is the required marketing effort, the lower is the offer price. The exogenous increase in market power has therefore made underwriting more profitable. This in turn may prompt banks to seek out more companies to take public, thus leading to higher subsequent IPO volume.

If an increase in initial returns signals an unexpectedly responsive IPO market, we would expect to see firms and their underwriters responding in one of three possible ways. More private firms should register their IPO with the listing authorities; firms already in registration should speed up their process through the regulatory hoops; and fewer IPOs should be cancelled. This increase in IPO activity should lower investors' costs in evaluating the IPOs, which in turn could lead to lower required underpricing.

Using US data to distinguish between the two hypotheses, Lowry and Schwert conclude that the empirical evidence is consistent with the notion that initial returns are informative about the demands of IPO investors, but not with the notion that banks enjoy market power.

2.4   Long-Run Performance and the 'New Issues Puzzle'

2.4.1   *The evidence*

The underpricing literature has traditionally assumed an investment strategy where the IPO investor sells her allotted shares in the early after-market, thus profiting from the discount at which the shares were offered. A natural question to ask is how those investors fare who buy from the initial IPO investors when trading starts. The efficient markets hypothesis would suggest that IPOs perform neutrally, in accordance with asset pricing theories, thus yielding neither abnormal profits nor excess losses. Early studies investigated this question by looking at the first few months of trading of IPOs. The fact that no abnormal performance could be detected was construed as evidence that the stock market efficiently values IPO shares once trading begins, and that no further abnormal returns—beyond the underpricing premium—can be earned.

However, a seminal study by Ritter (1991) found evidence of substantial negative abnormal returns over longer time horizons: a comprehensive sample of 1,526 US companies that came to market between 1975 and 1984 underperformed control firms of a similar size and in the same industries by some 29 per cent after three years of trading. Perhaps for this reason, Wall Street brokers used to joke that IPO stands for 'It's Probably Overpriced'.

Ritter's paper spawned several other studies of IPO long-run performance in other countries and time periods, which are summarized in Table 2.2. Underperformance appears not to be a recent phenomenon: even in the 1920s American IPOs underperformed the market. Nor does it appear to be confined to the USA: with the notable exceptions of Malaysia, Singapore, Sweden, and Turkey, work in other countries has shown that long-run market-adjusted returns, typically measured over a three-year investment horizon, are negative.[8] In Australia, Brazil, and Canada, first-day buyers fare particularly badly. These findings suggest that, while new issues are a profitable investment opportunity if bought at flotation, they should not be held much beyond the first few weeks or months of trading, and if possible should be shorted to profit from the negative return drift.

Astonishingly, seasoned equity offerings (SEOs) appear to share the poor long-term performance of IPOs: Loughran and Ritter (1995) and Affleck-Graves and Spiess (1995) both document wealth losses—of a similar magnitude to those experienced in IPOs—over three- and five-year holding periods in large samples of US seasoned equity issues. Levis (1995) reports a similar pattern for the UK. Hertzel *et al.* (1999) show that listed US companies underperformed spectacularly following *private* sales of seasoned equity. And even firms that withdrew previously announced seasoned equity offerings subsequently underperformed, according to Alderson and Betker (1997). One possible objection to these various findings is that they may be driven by the IPO underperformance phenomenon: since newly listed companies have a high propensity to return to the primary market within a

---

[8] Korea, too, appears to be an exception: Kim *et al.* (1995) show that a sample of 99 IPOs earned excess returns averaging 91.6 per cent over the first three years of trading. However, as Jay Ritter has suggested to us, this may be the artefact of daily price limits. To the extent that the first-day price is not an equilibrium price, the initial underpricing return will erroneously be incorporated into the long-run return measurement.

Table 2.2. Comparative evidence of IPO long-run performance.

Country	Study	Sample period	Sample size	Window (years)[a]	Return (%)[b]
Australia	Lee *et al.* (1996)	1976–89	266	3	–51.0
Brazil	Aggarwal *et al.* (1993)	1980–90	62	3	–47.0
Canada	Shaw (1971)	1956–63	105	5	–32.3
Chile	Aggarwal *et al.* (1993)	1982–90	28	3	–23.7
Finland	Keloharju (1993*b*)	1984–89	79	3	–21.1
Germany	Schlag and Wodrich (2000)	1884–1914	163	5	–7.8
Germany	Ljungqvist (1997)	1970–90	145	3	–12.1
Great Britain	Levis (1993*a*)	1980–88	712	3	–8.1
Hong Kong	McGuinness (1993*b*)	1980–90	72	2	–18.3
Italy	Giudici and Paleari (1999)	1985–95	84	3	–2.6
Japan	Cai and Wei (1997)	1971–92	180	5	–26.0
Korea	Kim *et al.* (1995)	1985–88	99	3	+91.6
Malaysia	Paudyal *et al.* (1998)	1984–94	62	3	+9.0
New Zealand	Firth (1997)	1979–87	143	5	–17.9
Singapore	Lee *et al.* (1996)	1973–92	132	3	+0.8
Sweden	Loughran *et al.* (1994)	1980–90	162	3	+1.2
Switzerland	Kunz and Aggarwal (1994)	1983–89	34	3	–6.1
Turkey	Kiymaz (1998)	1990–95	138	3	+44.1
United States	Stigler (1964*a,b*)	1923–28	70	5	–37.7
United States	Simon (1989)[c]	1926–33	35	5	–39.0
United States	Simon (1989)[d]	1934–40	20	5	+6.2
United States	Stigler (1964*a,b*)	1949–55	46	5	–25.1
United States	Cusatis *et al.* (1993)[e]	1965–88	146	3	+33.6
United States	Loughran (1993)	1967–87	3656	6	–33.3
United States	Loughran and Ritter (1995)	1970–90	4753	5	–30.0
United States	Ritter (1991)	1975–84	1526	3	–29.1

[a] 'Window' is the number of years over which after-market returns are recorded.

[b] Returns are calculated over the investment window and are not annualized, exclude the initial underpricing return, and are generally market-adjusted, but not risk-adjusted. Some authors use a range of benchmarks; in these cases, a representative result is shown. Computation methodologies vary.

[c] IPOs on regional exchanges only; a sample of 18 NYSE stocks performed neutrally (average cumulative abnormal return: –1.16 % after 5 years).

[d] Aggregated NYSE and non-NYSE long-run IPO returns, reported in Simon (1989): table B4.

[e] Subsidiaries of listed companies that were spun off in an initial public offering. The positive returns are driven by a subsample of spin-offs that were targets of take-over bids.

few years of going public, IPO firms are over-represented in any SEO sample. However, it turns out that following an issue of common shares, long-seasoned firms underperform by just as much as recent IPOs. Hence poor post-issue performance seems to afflict both firms that have recently gone public and those that have been trading for a long time. Moreover, Ikenberry *et al.* (1995) document the mirror image of issuing firms' underperformance for companies repurchasing their own shares: buy-backs are followed by several years of outperforming the market.

Studies focusing on long-run operating performance confirm the results found in share price studies. Jain and Kini (1994) report significant declines in operating returns on assets, as well as operating cash flows deflated by total assets, over the first three to five years after flotation among a large sample of US IPOs, both in absolute terms and relative to a matched control sample. Again, the same pattern holds for seasoned equity offerings: according to Loughran and Ritter (1997), operating performance peaks at about the time of the offering and declines significantly over the following four years, relative to a matched control sample of non-issuers; once more, this is not driven by the subset of recent IPO firms that reissue.

Summarizing these various phenomena, Loughran and Ritter (1995) label the poor operating and share price performance of firms that go public or issue seasoned equity the 'new issues puzzle'.

2.4.2 *Theoretical explanations*

Equilibrium explanations for this curious evidence are less than abundant. The very existence of profitable trading rules, which is implied by the systematic long-run underperformance of new equity issues, suggests a potential violation of the informational efficiency of stock markets and thus continues to defy theoretical modelling efforts based on the paradigm of rational behaviour.

However, there are some simple interpretations. First, it is possible that the widespread practice by underwriters of supporting an issue's trading price in the after-market spuriously leads to observations of abnormally low returns: flotations that are initially supported might well underperform if measured from the first trading day—when prices are artificially high—but might perform neutrally if measured from the date when support is withdrawn. Second, it is difficult at the best of times to control correctly for risk over long time horizons. The problems are more daunting in the case of IPOs since, owing to the automatic absence of pre-flotation share prices, no simple estimates of systematic risk are available. Hence the available evidence should probably be taken with a pinch of salt: maybe the poor returns are less marked if adjusted for true risk. Indeed, recent work reviewed in Chapter 6 questions whether there is a 'new issues puzzle' at all, suggesting instead that the results in Table 2.2 are a 'methodological illusion'. At this juncture, it is unclear whether the stylized fact of IPO underperformance will survive or will find its way onto the scrapheap of scientific history.

Methodological issues aside, part of the literature has focused on fads and irrational investor behaviour to explain poor long-run performance. A typical argument runs like this. The evidence on operating performance indicates that firms go public after periods of fast growth in earnings that are not sustained post-flotation; in fact, there is some evidence suggesting that companies even massage their accounts prior to going public. Investors then pay over the odds when trading starts—thus leading to first-day underpricing price jumps—but are consistently surprised by the decline in operating performance and therefore mark down share prices in response to worse-than-expected earnings reports—thereby leading to negative after-market returns.

A variation on this theme suggests that investors are only periodically (rather than permanently) over-optimistic about the prospects of firms coming to market. If companies could 'time' their flotations to coincide with periods of faddishly high expectations among investors, we would at once have an explanation not only for the long-run underperformance, but also for the clustering of IPO volume: firms are simply taking advantage of windows of opportunity.

However, to us it seems unlikely that investors can be consistently fooled in this manner (though recent events surrounding IPOs by firms in the internet space are hard to rationalize). Any explanation that is predicated on persistent misvaluation raises as many questions as it purports to answer: above all, why do investors not learn from past experience? After all, IPOs seem to have been performing poorly for many decades, at least in the USA, so one would reasonably expect investors to discount glowing earnings reports when deciding how much to pay for newly floated shares. Moreover, the 'timing' argument rests on the unrealistic assumption that firms can tell when investors are excessively optimistic: surely, if they could, they would not merely go public but instead would go short on equities, wait until investor sentiment had returned to normal, then cover their short positions and make an enormous arbitrage profit in the process.

In summary, while the air is thick with conjecture, economists do not yet know what (if anything) causes initial public offerings to perform poorly in the long run. The evidence, if correct, is disturbing. With initial underpricing, at least there is an element of arbitrariness in setting the offer price, and thus we can think of reasons why one might want to set the price below its expected after-market value. But for a certain type of firm (those recently listed) to perform worse than expected consistently and persistently, something must be amiss either with the way we measure risk and performance, or with the asset-pricing theories we use to form expected returns, or with the rationality of market participants.

2.5 Summary

Since the early 1980s, initial public offerings have enjoyed increasing popularity in many economies that have not traditionally relied much on public equity markets for the funding needs of their corporate sector. Almost without exception, these countries have experienced the same empirical phenomena to which the more developed Anglo-Saxon primary markets have long been prone: flotations are significantly underpriced initially but seem to perform poorly over the first few years of trading. These stylized facts of initial underpricing and long-run underperformance, and to a lesser extent the time series behaviour of initial returns and IPO volume, have for some time occupied a central place on the theoretical and empirical research agenda, and this book is devoted to assessing the state of this literature.

While few countries have escaped an underpricing study, less hard evidence is available about the long-run performance of newly floated firms. The USA apart, most studies look at relatively short and recent sampling periods, concentrating mostly on the 1980s and using relatively simplistic methodologies. There is thus a great need for further international research to assess the robustness of the extant findings, with respect to both different countries and other sampling periods.[9]

The long-run performance evidence is still exploratory also in another respect. Not knowing what the true expected return on a stock should be, researchers resort to asserting certain benchmarks, for instance using asset pricing models such as the CAPM or the Fama–French (1992) three-factor model. Should the observed return turn out to be lower than the derived expectation, the firm is deemed to be underperforming. Obviously, this procedure is only as good as the benchmark one uses—a choice that in the case of IPOs is made more difficult in a number of ways, for example how to estimate systematic risk when there is no pre-flotation share price history, and what benchmark to use if, as in Finland, twice as many firms have gone public as were initially listed? There is now an emerging consensus that the resolution of these methodological issues is sufficient to explain the apparently anomalous share price behaviour of IPOs in the USA. Whether the same is true in other countries remains to be seen.

What is astonishing is that underpricing, and perhaps long-run underperformance, are such consistent phenomena across countries with very different company populations, corporate control mechanisms ('bank-based' *v.* 'market-based'), and institutional, legal, taxation, regulatory, historical, and cultural frameworks. This calls for theoretical explanations that are equally applicable to any country whose IPOs experience abnormal performance, whatever its particular framework.

Few, if any, available theoretical models fit this bill. Most are phrased with the US new issue market in mind, but various features of the US framework that are purportedly driving the results are conspicuously absent in other countries, the more recent convergence in the use of book-building notwithstanding. The next part of this book will outline the main theoretical explanations that have been advanced in the academic literature, evaluate them against the

---

[9] In the first edition of this monograph we noted that Germany had a lively IPO market before the First World War and wondered whether these flotations underperformed as well. The answer is yes: Schlag and Wodrich (2000) show that German IPOs in 1884–1914 underperformed the index by 7.8 per cent.

available evidence, and discuss their general applicability in the light of cross-country institutional differences. Despite a multitude of models, we feel that no single explanation can claim universal acceptance, and that some of the more popular models sound less than plausible once one looks beyond US horizons.

Part II

THEORY
AND EVIDENCE

CHAPTER 3

Asymmetric Information

3.1 Adverse Selection Models: The Winner's Curse

Perhaps the best-known asymmetric information model of initial underpricing is Rock's (1986) winner's curse. Rock assumes that both the issuing firm and its underwriting bank are completely uninformed about the true value of the shares on offer, whereas some—but not all—investors are perfectly informed. To justify these assumptions, he alludes to the notion that the market in the aggregate has better information than any one player, including the issuer itself. Since issuer and bank are assumed to have the same information, the model also abstracts from agency problems: the bank acts in the firm's best interest.

Informed investors bid only for attractively priced IPOs, whereas the uninformed bid indiscriminately. This imposes a 'winner's curse' on an uninformed investor: in unattractive offerings, she receives all the shares she bids for, while in attractive offerings, she faces competition for shares from the informed. For such an uninformed investor, the simple averages of underpricing returns shown in Chapter 2 are meaningless, because across many offerings she receives an average return that is weighted towards overpriced offerings. In the extreme case, she is rationed completely in every underpriced IPO and receives 100 per cent allocations in every overpriced IPO, resulting in average returns that are negative!

If this is the outcome the investor expects, she will withdraw from the market and we will be left with an IPO market populated with equally informed investors.[1] Rock now assumes that the primary market is dependent on the continued participation of uninformed investors, in the sense that informed demand is insufficient to take up all shares on offer even in attractive offerings. Therefore, something needs to be done to help the uninformed at least break even. The solution is to deliberately underprice every offering (in expectation). This does not remove the allocation bias against the uninformed—they will still be crowded out by informed investors in the most underpriced offerings—but they will no longer (expect to) make losses on average, even after adjusting for rationing.

Note that it is not rationing *per se* that necessitates underpricing; it is instead the bias in rationing, with expected conditional allocation probabilities being smaller in good than in bad offerings. This is a variation on Akerlof's (1970) 'lemons' problem in the used car market: uninformed buyers will withdraw from a market if their informational disadvantage results in their being presented with an adverse selection from the quality distribution of goods.

Going public is, for the most part, a one-off event in a firm's history. Dynamically, the primary market is under threat from Rock's winner's curse, but no individual firm gains much from contributing to its continued viability when coming to market. This leads to a free-rider problem: collectively, all current and future issuers benefit from a reduction in the winner's curse, but, because part of the benefit from underpricing accrues to other issuers, firms individually have a sub-optimal incentive to underprice. Indeed, it would be individually optimal to let someone else 'bribe' uninformed investors into the market but to overprice one's own flotation.

Enter the underwriters: as repeat players, banks do have an incentive to ensure that new issues are underpriced lest they lose under-

---

[1] Or will we? A situation where everyone is informed is not in fact an equilibrium. Imagine that all remaining investors are informed. Only attractively priced IPOs will succeed and all others will fail for lack of buyers. But then, assuming that becoming informed is costly, this creates an incentive to cease becoming informed and to free-ride on the information of the other investors instead. The investor would simply bid for IPO shares indiscriminately, receiving shares in the attractive IPOs but not in the unattractive ones (which will still fail)—clearly a profitable strategy. Since every investor faces the same incentive, no one would choose to become informed, so unattractive offerings would no longer fail. But if no one is informed, there is an incentive to become informed, in order to avoid the unattractive IPOs. So a situation in which no one is informed is not an equilibrium either.

writing commissions in the future, as Beatty and Ritter (1986) show. Banks' activities are kept in check by the vigilance of issuers on the one hand and investors on the other: underwriters that underprice too much (too little) should subsequently lose business from issuers (investors). Nanda and Yun (1997) and Dunbar (2000) investigate the hypothesis that mispricing hurts an investment bank's reputation capital. Consistent with Beatty and Ritter's claim, Nanda and Yun find that overpricing (but not high levels of underpricing) lead to a decrease in the lead underwriter's own stock market value, whereas moderate levels of underpricing are associated with an increase in stock market value, perhaps indicating that underwriters can extract *quid pro quo* benefits from investors to whom they allocate moderately underpriced shares. Interestingly, in jointly managed IPOs it is the lead manager, not the co-managers, who suffers as a result of mispricing. Dunbar finds that banks subsequently lose IPO market share if they either underprice or overprice too much, squarely supporting Beatty and Ritter's claim.

3.1.1 *Testable implications and evidence*

Implicit in the winner's curse model is the notion that, if properly adjusted for rationing, uninformed investors' abnormal returns are zero, on average—that is, just enough to ensure their continued participation in the market. (See Table 3.1, which lists the testable implications of the winner's curse model alongside the available empirical evidence.) Similarly, the informed investors' conditional underpricing return should just provide a normal return on their information production. While the former is potentially testable, the latter is not, not least because informed and uninformed investors cannot in practice be distinguished. Moreover, very few markets publish enough allocation data to allow underpricing returns to be adjusted for rationing. The evidence, from countries that use(d) fixed-price rather than book-building mechanisms, mostly supports the presence of a winner's curse: in Singapore, the UK, and Finland initial returns do indeed tend to zero when adjusted for rationing.

As underpricing represents an involuntary cost to the issuer, there are clear incentives to reduce the information asymmetry and the resulting adverse selection problem between informed and

Table 3.1. The winner's curse explanation of IPO underpricing

	Result	Source	Empirical evidence	
1	In order to avoid the 'lemons' problem of adverse selection, issuers rationally underprice, in an informational environment in which (i) some investors are perfectly informed, and (ii) all other investors, issuers, and underwriters have no information about 'true' firm value. Underpricing returns then tend to the riskless rate when ration-adjusted.	Rock (1986) Beatty and Ritter (1986)	Yes: Koh and Walter (1989) Levis (1990) Keloharju (1993b)	[Singapore] [UK] [Finland]
			No: McGuinness (1993a) Cheung et al. (1993)	[Hong Kong] [Hong Kong]
2	Underpricing decreases as heterogeneity of information decreases (e.g. in offerings geared towards 'informed' investors, usually assumed to be institutional investors).	Michaely and Shaw (1994)	Yes: Michaely and Shaw (1994)	[USA]
			No: Jenkinson (1990) Tinic (1988)	[UK] [USA]
3	To cut the underpricing cost, the informational asymmetry can be reduced by choosing a reputable underwriter (certification): more prestigious underwriters (i) are associated with less risky IPOs, and (ii) thus underprice less in expectation.	Carter and Manaster (1990) Booth and Smith (1986)	Yes: Carter and Manaster (1990) Johnson and Miller (1988 Megginson and Weiss (1991) Michaely and Shaw (1994) La Chapelle and Neuberger (1983) Kim et al. (1993) Habib and Ljungqvist (2001)	[USA] [USA] [USA] [USA] [USA] [Korea] [USA]
			No: James and Wier (1990) Beatty and Welch (1996) McGuinness (1992) Ljungqvist (1995a)	[USA] [USA] [Hong Kong] [Germany]

#	Statement	Theory	Evidence	Country
3′	(ditto) for other agents.	Titman and Trueman (1986) *auditors*	Yes: Barry *et al.* (1990) Megginson and Weiss (1991) Lin and Smith (1998) *venture capitalists* Balvers *et al.* (1988) Beatty (1989) *auditors*	[USA] [USA] [USA] [USA] [USA]
			No: Gompers and Lerner (1997) Hamao *et al.* (2000) *venture capitalists* McGuinness (1992) *auditors*	[USA] [Japan] [Hong Kong]
4	Issuers take costly actions to reduce underpricing up to the point where their underpricing-related wealth losses are minimized.	Habib and Ljungqvist (2001)	Yes: Habib and Ljungqvist (2001)	[USA]
5	Underwriters who underprice too much (little) will lose business from issuers (investors).	Beatty and Ritter (1986)	Yes: Beatty and Ritter (1986) James (1992) Dunbar (2000)	[USA] [USA] [USA]
6	Underpricing is greater when the underwriter exercises the 'over-allotment option' (to issue up to 15% more stock).	Rock (1986)	*see* Table 3.2.	
7	The greater is *ex ante* uncertainty, the higher is expected underpricing.	Ritter (1984) Beatty and Ritter (1986)		
8	'Hot issue' periods are characterized by a higher level of *ex ante* uncertainty, necessitating higher underpricing.	Ritter (1984)	No: Ritter (1984)	[USA]

uninformed investors. One solution is to market a flotation solely to one or the other of these categories, but not to both. This typically happens in UK private placings—where brokers contact only their regular (institutional) investors; interestingly, however, these are no less underpriced than offers sold to the public at large. Another way to reduce the asymmetry in information is to retain a reputable underwriter (or other agent, such as auditor); by agreeing to sponsor an offering, the prestigious intermediary certifies the quality of the issue. If reputation capital is valuable, prestigious banks will refrain from underwriting low-quality issuers. The information content of the firm's choice of intermediaries may therefore reduce investors' incentives to produce their own information, which in turn will militate against the winner's curse. Broadly speaking, this certification hypothesis seems to hold in the USA, but not in some other countries (cf. Table 3.1).

Habib and Ljungqvist (2001) generalize the notion that issuers have an incentive to reduce underpricing and model their optimal behaviour. They argue that, *if* issuers can take costly actions (such as hiring a reputable underwriter) that reduce underpricing, they will do so up to the point where the marginal cost of reducing underpricing further equals the marginal benefit. This marginal benefit is measured not by underpricing itself, but by the reduction in the issuer's wealth that underpricing implies. Wealth losses and underpricing are not the same. Compare an issuer that floats a single share with one that floats the entire company. Clearly, the latter's wealth would suffer much more from underpricing, giving it a much stronger incentive to take costly actions to reduce underpricing. Using data for a large sample of US IPOs, Habib and Ljungqvist find that issuers do optimize, in the sense that spending one dollar more on reducing underpricing would increase wealth losses by 98 cents at the margin.

3.1.2 *Underpricing and* ex ante *uncertainty*

A key empirical implication, due to Ritter (1984) and formalized in Beatty and Ritter (1986), is that underpricing should increase in the *ex ante* uncertainty surrounding an issue. Beatty and Ritter provide an interesting intuition for this result. An investor who decides to engage in information production implicitly invests in a call option on the IPO, which she will exercise if the 'true' price exceeds the strike price, the price at which the shares are offered to the public. The value of this option increases in the extent of valuation uncertainty, so more investors will become informed. This raises the required underpricing, since an increase in the number of informed traders aggravates the winner's curse problem—although, of course, if enough people become informed, the winner's curse would presumably disappear.

Table 3.2 lists the various studies that have looked at the relationship between numerous proxies for *ex ante* uncertainty and initial underpricing. We have grouped the proxies into five categories: company characteristics, offering characteristics, prospectus disclosure, certification, and after-market variables. Since the degree of valuation uncertainty will vary over the various stages of the IPO process, we expect some of these categories to be more informative than others. For instance, uncertainty should be highest when a prospective issuing firm approaches potential investment banks, but should be much lower after a bank's due diligence and book-building. Using company characteristics such as age or turnover to measure *ex ante* uncertainty therefore ignores the information production that takes place in the IPO market. Conversely, using after-market variables such as trading volume or volatility would rely on information that was not in fact available at the time of the IPO. The three intermediate categories therefore seem more plausible.

Among offering characteristics, the most popular proxy for valuation uncertainty is gross proceeds. However, Habib and Ljungqvist (1998) show that, as a matter of identities, underpricing is strictly decreasing in gross proceeds *even when holding uncertainty constant*.[2] This clearly makes it unsuitable as a proxy for valuation uncertainty. A more suitable proxy may be the width of the price range. Most IPOs in the USA, and increasingly outside the USA as well, fix an indicative price range at the start of book-building. This range is not binding, and in the 1990s about a half of US IPOs were ultimately priced outside the range. None the less, it seems plausible to assume that issues

---

[2] Essentially, this follows because IPO proceeds are positively correlated with the number of newly issued shares, whereas the post-IPO share price is negatively correlated with that number because of dilution.

Table 3.2. Evidence on the relationship between *ex ante* uncertainty and underpricing[a,b]

Proxy	Study	Country
Company characteristics		
Age	Ritter (1984)	USA
	Megginson and Weiss (1991)	USA
	Ritter (1991)	USA
Sales	Ritter (1984)	USA
Relistings *v.* truly new listings	Muscarella and Vetsuypens (1989*b*)	USA
Offering characteristics		
Inverse gross proceeds	Beatty and Ritter (1986)	USA
	McGuinness (1992) *	Hong Kong
	Prabhala and Puri (1998)	USA
% width of filing price range	Hanley (1993)	USA
	Prabhala and Puri (1998)	USA
Offer price	Tinic (1988)	USA
	Prabhala and Puri (1998)	USA
	Brennan and Hughes (1991)	USA
	Beatty and Welch (1996) *	USA
Underwriting fee	Habib and Ljungqvist (2001)	USA
	Prabhala and Puri (1998)	USA
	Bloch (1989)	USA
Disclosure		
Is earnings forecast included in prospectus?	Clarkson and Merkley (1994)	Canada
Log (1 + number of uses of IPO proceeds)	Beatty and Ritter (1986)	USA
	McGuinness (1992) *	Hong Kong
Log (1 + number of risk factors)	Beatty and Welch (1996)	USA
Certification		
Established credit relationships	James and Wier (1990)	USA
	Slovin and Young (1990)	USA
Venture-backing	Megginson and Weiss (1991)	USA
	Barry *et al.* (1990)	USA
	Lin and Smith (1998)	USA
	Gompers and Lerner (1997) *	USA
	Hamao *et al.* (2000) *	Japan
Reputation of underwriter	Megginson and Weiss (1991)	USA
	Carter and Manaster (1990)	USA
	Habib and Ljungqvist (2001)	USA
	Beatty and Welch (1996) *	USA

Proxy	Study	Country
After-market variables		
Standard deviation of daily after-market returns	Ritter (1984, 1987)	USA
	Clarkson and Merkley (1994)	Canada
	Finn and Higham (1988)	Australia
	Prabhala and Puri (1998)	USA
	Wasserfallen and Wittleder (1994)	Germany
Daily trade volume in early after-market	Miller and Reilly (1987)	USA
	Prabhala and Puri (1998)	USA
	Göppl and Sauer (1990)	Germany

[a] Most underpricing models predict that the greater is *ex ante* uncertainty about the 'true' value of an initial public offering, the higher must be underpricing. The table summarizes the international evidence on this proposition for a variety of uncertainty proxies.

[b] All but the studies marked with * find support for the hypothesized relationship.

for which valuation uncertainty is greater are marketed with a wider price range (see e.g. Hanley 1993). Prabhala and Puri (1998), however, point out that the time between setting the price range and setting the final price varies across companies. Timeliness and informativeness of this variable could thus vary in a cross-section of issues. We might add that the information content of the price range *at the time of pricing the IPO* could be very low, since the book-building phase may have produced new information leading the underwriter to change its prior assessment of valuation uncertainty over the book-building phase.

The final offering characteristic that has been put forward is the offer price itself. This variable is more timely than the indicative range, since it is mostly fixed at the last moment, after the book-building exercise. Brennan and Hughes's (1991) model implies that firms can encourage analysts to produce information by means of stock splits to lower the share price. This is because fractional trading commissions decrease in the share price level. Applied to the IPO context, issuers might choose to set a low price to encourage information production, which would presumably take place in the after-market. However, this would imply that the information production stage carries over into the after-market, rather than being completed at the final pricing.

Risk proxies based on what is disclosed in the prospectus are, to some extent, endogenous to offering characteristics. For instance, the number of uses of IPO proceeds as disclosed in the prospectus is a function of the size of the offering and of the split between primary (new) and secondary (old) shares sold. This is because firms raising no, or only little, fresh capital physically have no, or fewer, *corporate* uses for the cash to report in their prospectuses. This is not to argue that the *nature* of the disclosed uses might not be informative (though this remains to be investigated empirically): issuers might plan to use IPO proceeds for R&D, rather than to pay down debt, with different implications for valuation uncertainty. The number of risk factors listed in the prospectus suffers from similar drawbacks, in that more risk factors are disclosed the more new capital is being raised. In addition, valuation uncertainty and legal uncertainty are not necessarily the same: some risk factors might be included in a prospectus for legal reasons only, while shedding little light on the problem of valuation. An obvious example is the routine mentioning of the fact that 'no prior public market has existed' for the company's stock, which must by definition be true for all IPOs but isn't always explicitly stated.[3] Similarly, some companies state only specific risk factors while others include a large number of generic ones, such as 'Competition could harm our business' or 'A failure to manage our internal operating and financial functions could adversely affect our business'.[4] Unless the propensity to state the obvious correlates with underlying valuation uncertainty, a simple count of risk factors is unlikely to be informative cross-sectionally.

The fourth group of uncertainty proxies builds on certification arguments. One argument holds that agents that participate in the IPO market repeatedly, such as venture capitalists or underwriters, can build up reputation capital to certify that an issue is priced 'fairly'. This might reduce the extent of the winner's curse, resulting in lower required underpricing. However, valuation uncertainty and the extent of the winner's curse are not the same. Nor is it obviously true that more prestigious investment banks will underwrite less uncertain offerings. Why? Prestigious underwriters presumably have access to better information production mechanisms (such as a network of better informed investors) and charge higher fees. If so, the marginal benefit of using a more prestigious underwriter will be greater, the

---

[3] We randomly examined ten American S-1 registrations backed by Goldman Sachs in June 1999, precisely half of which mentioned 'no prior market' among their risk factors.

[4] Both examples are taken from the S-1 registration of 1-800-FLOWERS.COM, 21 May 1999.

greater is valuation uncertainty: why pay Goldman Sachs's high fees if you are a 50-year-old window manufacturer with stable profits and few growth opportunities?[5]

Even though Beatty and Ritter's hypothesis receives overwhelming empirical support, as Table 3.2 shows, the fact that almost every underpricing theory worth its salt also predicts a positive relationship between risk and return (see below) renders it unsuitable as evidence in favour of Rock's model. It can be used as an indirect test, however. Ritter (1984), in trying to square underpricing cycles with the winner's curse, argues that, if the winner's curse is the sole reason why IPOs are underpriced, then changes in the extent of the winner's curse—say, arising from changes in *ex ante* uncertainty—should be the sole reason why underpricing varies over time. However, he finds that it is industry-specific events, rather than changes in the risk composition of IPO cohorts, that drive changes in initial returns.

3.1.3 *Discussion*

While the winner's curse model rests on a deceptively simple and rather intuitive observation—that more heavily underpriced flotations will be more heavily rationed, making a mockery of simple measures of underpricing which are based on an equally weighted average—there are some serious grounds for scepticism. How realistic is the assumption that issuers must pay for the uninformed investors' participation in an offering? If, as Rock asserts, the resources of the informed are limited, the uninformed could simply invest through the informed investors, in exchange for a fee, to avoid the mistake of subscribing to overpriced issues. (Renaissance Capital Corporation, for instance, manages a mutual fund called 'IPO Plus Aftermarket Fund'.) This is one of the reasons why investment funds exist in the first place: there are economies of scale in becoming informed.

How severe is the allocation bias in practice? The answer depends on who is informed and who is not, a distinction that mostly defies empirical testing. Several studies have looked at institutional versus retail investors. Needless to say, we cannot rule out that the information

---

[5] It is true that there is little variation in the fees underwriters charge in the USA (cf. Chen and Ritter 2000). Outside the USA, on the other hand, top American banks charge higher fees compared with 'local' banks, holding issue size constant (cf. Ljungqvist *et al.* 2000).

asymmetry is most severe *within* groups, rather than between institutional and retail investors.[6] Nevertheless, this approach has yielded some interesting insights. The Securities and Exchange Commission (1971) looked into the treatment of US institutional investors in stock market flotations. The findings are surprising: institutions did *not* receive preferential treatment in the form of favourably sized allocations of oversubscribed issues; on the contrary, oversubscribed issues were typically severely rationed. Since information production is undoubtedly costly, would the rather small per-firm allocations really justify becoming informed? More recent evidence by Hanley and Wilhelm (1995) extends this observation: no doubt institutions do benefit greatly from underpriced IPOs, but, remarkably, there is no difference in the size of allocations that institutions receive in underpriced and overpriced issues.[7]

This finding is significant in two respects. First, it suggests that institutions cannot engage in 'cream-skimming', that is using their information advantage to avoid overpriced flotations. Second, institutions do not impose a winner's curse on retail investors. Later in this chapter we will discuss a model due to Benveniste and Spindt (1989), which accurately predicts that institutions cannot refuse to participate in less attractive offerings, as the underwriters would strike them off their distribution lists in future IPOs. Again, doubters may point to the unobserved distribution of information across and within these investor categories; but in our view, at least a modicum of doubt regarding the winner's curse is appropriate.

Underpricing theories essentially come in one of two forms: either underpricing is thought to be the involuntary but necessary response to some underlying information or other problem, or it is regarded as

---

[6] Are institutional investors informed? If they are, they ought to be able to invest selectively in better performing IPOs. While Hanley and Wilhelm (1995) can find no evidence in support of this conjecture, Field (1995) shows that IPO firms perform better relative to matched seasoned firms, the greater their institutional shareholdings. However, this does not prove that institutions are informed: even the flotations with the greatest institutional stakes underperform broad stock market indices. In Japan, underperformance is unrelated to shareholder structure (Cai and Wei 1997).

[7] Krigman *et al.* (1999) argue that block traders systematically 'flip' their IPO allocations on the first day in precisely those issues that subsequently underperform the market. This leads to differences in institutional ownership a few months after the offering. Such differences were documented by Field (1995).

a deliberate action chosen by the issuing firm in the pursuit of some wealth-maximizing objective. As the winner's curse model falls into the former category, one would expect firms to be keen on any change to the allocation mechanism that takes account of the private information among investors and thus necessitates no (or lower) underpricing. The most notable example of such an alternative mechanism is the auction or tender offer. Yet tender offers have proved unpopular with issuers in countries where there is a choice of offering method, except in France.[8] This implies that underpricing is not necessarily as involuntary as the winner's curse suggests. We next turn to a theory that ascribes a value to underpricing.

3.2   Underpricing as a Signal of Firm Quality

Another strand of the theoretical literature reverses Rock's assumption regarding the informational asymmetry between issuing firms and investors. If companies have better information about the present value and risk of their future cash flows than do investors, underpricing may become a means of convincing potential buyers of the 'true' high value of the firm. Allen and Faulhaber (1989), Grinblatt and Hwang (1989), and Welch (1989, 1996) have contributed theories with this feature. These models are variations on the signalling theme first introduced into economics by Spence (1974) in the context of labour markets. In this section, we will first discuss the workings of signalling in general, then show how signalling might work in the IPO context in particular, and finally consider the testable implications and empirical evidence.

3.2.1   *Signalling models*

Suppose that in a proposed transaction one party has superior information about vital characteristics—quality, longevity, resale value—of the good to be transacted. For instance, Spence (1974) assumes

---

[8] Wimmers (1988) reports survey evidence that 76% of his respondents (German IPO firms in 1978–87) would not have wished to use a tender instead of a fixed-price offering. Tenders seem to have disappeared altogether in the UK since 1986; cf. Jenkinson (1990). For similar evidence from the Netherlands, cf. Wessels (1989).

that job candidates are better informed about their own ability than are potential employers. Similarly, a used car dealer is better informed about the quality of cars on his forecourt than are potential buyers; and—in our context—issuing firms may be better informed about their risks and future prospects than are potential IPO investors. These are further instances of the adverse selection problem we discussed in the previous section, though here it is the seller (or issuer in the IPO context) who has the informational advantage, rather than fellow buyers (the informed IPO investors in Rock's model).

Using the used car market as an illustration, Akerlof (1970) showed that, as long as buyers cannot observe the quality of cars on offer at the time of purchase, adverse selection will cause the market to fail in the sense that only low-quality cars will be offered for sale. Why? Because buyers will never pay fair value for a supposedly high-quality car given the chance that it might not in fact be of high quality. Sellers of high-quality cars will therefore withdraw from the market.

What can the owners of high-quality cars do to persuade buyers to pay a price commensurate with the true quality? A look at what is done in practice is instructive. Sellers can offer product warranties or money-back guarantees; they can allow potential buyers to have the product checked by an independent expert (a common practice in used car sales in the UK); and they can build a reputation for selling quality cars over time, which would require 'underpricing' high-quality cars in early transactions and recouping this expense once buyers have been persuaded to put their trust in a dealer's reputation. Note that these are all costly actions. What sellers cannot do is simply *claim* that their cars are high-quality—because of the obvious incentives to lie—or offer direct disclosure of any car's service records and accident reports—because of the obvious incentives to cheat (what economists call 'moral hazard').

More generally, the informed party cannot simply announce the type, but rather must take some action to 'signal' it—in the spirit of 'actions speak louder than words'. The uninformed party then transacts with the informed party, making the terms of transaction depend on the observed signal. For instance, employers might offer a wage contract which depends on a worker's education level, or used car buyers might bid different prices depending on the length and comprehensiveness of the seller's warranty.

In general, there are two types of equilibrium in signalling models: pooling and separating equilibria. In a pooling equilibrium all types send the same signal, so the receiver cannot infer the unobserved characteristic and thus cannot distinguish between the various types. In Spence's model, every worker is paid the expected marginal product, implying that high-ability workers are underpaid and low-ability ones are overpaid. In a separating equilibrium, on the other hand, different types send different signals, on the basis of which the receiver can tell them apart. For instance, higher-ability workers signal their type by choosing a higher level of education, allowing employers to offer high-ability workers a higher wage.

For a separating equilibrium to exist, (i) there must be signalling costs, which (ii) differ across types.[9] Consider Spence's labour example. In a separating equilibrium, low-ability workers have a clear incentive to mimic high-ability workers, as this would raise their pay. For a separating equilibrium to come about, therefore, it must be incentive-compatible for the low-ability workers not to adopt the high-ability workers' choice of signal, which will be the case if the signal is costlier, at the margin, for low-ability than for high-ability workers. By the same token, high-ability types will choose to separate only if the associated cost is outweighed by the benefit, i.e. the higher wage rate. So, there are two incentive-compatibility constraints. If they are not met, a pooling equilibrium will result.[10]

It is a feature of separating equilibria that the type that is forced to signal is strictly worse off than in a first-best full-information world (or if her type could credibly and verifiably be announced). This is because—while she *will* receive the fair terms of transaction conditional upon the signal fully revealing her type, as she would in the absence of the informational asymmetry—she has to engage in costly signalling. Low types, on the other hand, receive the same benefit as they would in a first-best world, while not incurring the signalling cost.

The required ingredients of a signalling model thus are: differential signalling cost, and a mechanism for reaping the benefit of the costly signal.

---

[9] These two conditions form what is called the *single-crossing property.*

[10] In addition, there are two participation constraints, stating that in equilibrium each party has to be at least as well off as it would be if it withdrew from the market.

3.2.2 *Signalling with underpricing*

The differences between the IPO signalling models are fewer than the similarities. The key informational assumption states that the issuing firm is better informed about the present value of its future cash flows than are investors or underwriters (the latter not having any explicit role in these models). Another key but hidden assumption is that firms go public in order to transfer ownership and control fully to new shareholders—which may not necessarily be the case in reality. Under this assumption, entrepreneurs are assumed to maximize the expected proceeds (or expected utility of the proceeds) of a two-stage sale: they sell a fraction α of the firm at flotation and the remainder in a later open market sale.

Signalling true value is beneficial to a high-value company as it allows a higher price to be fetched at the second-stage sale if separation is achieved. In the words of Ibbotson (1975), who is credited with the original intuition for the IPO signalling literature, issuers underprice in order to 'leave a good taste in investors' mouths'. With some positive probability, a firm's true type is revealed before the post-IPO financing stage, introducing the risk to low-quality issuers that any cheating on their part will be detected before they can reap the benefit from the signal. This makes separation possible, in that it decreases the expected benefit from signalling to low-value firms and thus drives a wedge between high-value and low-value firms' marginal signalling cost.

The signal is the initial offering price. Provided the implied reduction in IPO proceeds and the risks of detection are sufficiently great to deter low-value firms from mimicking high-value ones, by floating at a lower price and thus underpricing, a high-value firm can influence investors' after-market beliefs about its value, which in turn determine the amount raised in the final sell-off. High-value firms thus face a trade-off between costly signalling and greater subsequent proceeds.

While the signalling models are *consistent* with 'hot issue' periods if some exogenous shock changes the fundamental parameters, thus causing many firms simultaneously to switch from a pooling to an underpricing equilibrium, we see no economically compelling reason why the costs of or benefits from signalling should change much over time. Moreover, because the required switch would be exogenous to the model, the signalling literature can shed no light on *why* 'hot issue' markets might occur.

Table 3.3 summarizes the key differences between the three pioneering IPO signalling models by Allen and Faulhaber (1989), Grinblatt and Hwang (1989), and Welch (1989). Of these, Grinblatt and Hwang's is the richest. Here, investors are uncertain not only about the present value of the firms' future cash flows, but also about their variance. Risk-averse entrepreneurs therefore employ *two* signals—their retention rate and the level of underpricing—to signal these two unobservable attributes. The model generalizes Leland and Pyle's (1977) well-known insight that owners can reveal their knowledge of high future cash flows by retaining a larger fraction of equity in the firm, as the implied under-diversification is costlier to the owners of high-variance firms than to those of low-variance ones.

While the signalling models are technically elegant and perhaps intuitively appealing, there are several grounds for scepticism. Much depends on the empirical question of whether companies do indeed follow two-stage selling strategies, as they must in signalling models in order to recoup the cost of the signal. And even if they do, the form that the second-stage financing round takes is important. In countries where shareholders enjoy pre-emption rights to seasoned offerings of primary equity, there would be no benefit to signalling: it is a well-known fact that the pricing of a rights issue is wealth-neutral. Welch's model, which relies on high-value firms separating to receive more favourable terms in subsequent equity offers, thus cannot account for the observed underpricing in Germany, the UK, and any other country whose investors enjoy pre-emptive rights. (This criticism does not apply to subsequent secondary sales by insiders, to which outside shareholders do not have pre-emption rights.)

Other countries require the original owners to abstain from selling further shares in the after-market for a specified period. For instance, the 'lock-in' period in the USA is typically 180 days, though it can be as short as 90 days and as long as two years. The longer the 'lock-in' period, the greater the chance that exogenous events will come to dominate whatever goodwill the underpricing signal may have created initially.

The signalling models need to assume that IPO companies must meet some minimum capital requirement at flotation—otherwise, a

Table 3.3. A comparison of IPO signalling models

	Assumptions	Signal	Signalling cost	Benefit of signalling to high-value firms	Revelation of type
Allen and Faulhaber (1989)	2 firm types; risk-neutral firms	Initial offering price (P_0)	Forgone funds at IPO; cost greater to low-value firms	Owners sell remaining stake (1-α) in the after-market	Endogenous: Bayesian learning based on dividends that noisily reveal true type
Grinblatt and Hwang (1989)	Continuum of firm types; risk-averse entrepreneurs	Initial offering price and fraction of equity floated (P_0,α)	(i) Forgone funds at IPO (ii) Under-diversification	Owners later sell remaining stake (1-α) at a higher price and achieve portfolio diversification	Exogenous: nature may reveal type according to some probability
Welch (1989)		Initial offering price (P_0)	Direct imitation cost borne by low-value firms; if insufficient to deter mimicking, underpricing becomes additional wedge leading to separating equilibrium	Subsequent equity offering on behalf of the firm	Exogenous: nature may reveal type according to some probability

firm could 'signal' by infinitely underpricing a single share, and subsequently raising its required funds in the after-market. The cost of
such a signalling strategy would be zero, which would violate the
single-crossing condition. The models were originally formulated
with the US primary market in mind, where flotations typically
concern young start-up companies. However, outside the USA and
the UK, issuers have traditionally been large, well established firms
which consequently do not conform to the minimum-capital
assumption. Moreover, as discussed in Chapter 2, many European
IPOs have traditionally involved sales by existing owners and managers, rather than capital-raising exercises by the firm. How sensible a
minimum capital constraint is in the European context then depends
on whether the original owners are sufficiently risk-averse to prefer a
certain (since underwritten) amount of cash at flotation to an uncertain, but probably higher (since not underpriced) amount if selling
into the after-market.

Finally, there is the question of the optimality of signalling: would
firms really choose the underpricing signal if they had a wider range
of actions to choose from? Such a range could include the choice of
particularly reputable underwriters (Booth and Smith 1986), auditors
(Titman and Trueman 1986), or venture capitalists, each of whom
would perform a certification-of-quality role; the quality of the board
of directors, and in particular the choice of non-executive directors,
who similarly would put their reputation on the line; and direct disclosure of information to IPO investors, backed by a mechanism
designed to deter fraudulent disclosure (Hughes 1986). Unless signalling via underpricing proves to be the most cost-effective way to
persuade potential investors of the high quality of an IPO—which
seems at least doubtful—the existence of alternatives dents the credibility of the signalling models.

In this context, it is worth mentioning a final variation on the signalling theme. Chemmanur's (1993) model of information production shares the informational and multiple-sale assumptions of the
signalling literature, but does not view underpricing as an effective
signalling device. Assume that none of the above signals—including
underpricing—can bring about a separation equilibrium. In that case,
high-quality issuers may attempt to tackle the root of the problem
directly: the information asymmetry between themselves and market

participants. This could be reduced by encouraging the latter to engage in information production about the firm. Underpricing is the compensation that high-quality firms offer to investors for their costly information production.

3.2.3   *Testable implications and evidence*

The signalling models generate a rich set of empirical implications concerning the relationship between underpricing and the probability, size, speed, and announcement effect of subsequent equity sales. Table 3.4 lists the more important of these. Rather than discuss each of them in detail, we will focus on the generic (rather than model-specific) hypotheses which we deem most crucial to the credibility of the signalling approach.

If firms do underprice to condition investors favourably for later equity offerings, we would expect reissuing companies to have experienced greater underpricing. However, the evidence on this is mixed, as Table 3.4 shows: although supported in Finland and Hong Kong, the hypothesis is rejected in the USA—both for insider sales and for primary equity offers. Nor is it true in general that more underpriced offerings increase the probability that a company will return to the market, except in Finland.

Clearly, signalling models would be of little practical importance if companies did *not* follow a multiple-stage sale policy of an initial flotation followed by subsequent equity offerings or insider sales. The evidence is hardly supportive. While Welch (1989) reports that about a quarter of US flotations in 1977–82 returned to the market within three years of going public, raising significant amounts of money in relation to their IPO proceeds, the absence of a benchmark for what is a 'normal' level of equity issuance makes the interpretation of these figures difficult. Helwege and Liang (1996*a*) provide quite different numbers. They track the 1983 IPO cohort in the USA and find that, in any of the following ten years, fewer than 4 per cent of firms return to the equity market: instead, the marked increase in investment expenditure that this cohort saw over its first decade of listing was financed mainly by retained earnings and private debt.

It is certainly true that these results, based as they are on observed outcomes, may fail to reflect companies' initial intentions at flotation

Table 3.4. The signalling explanation of IPO underpricing

	Result	Source	Empirical evidence	
1	In order to signal firm quality so that they can subsequently issue seasoned equity or sell the owners' retained stakes at more favourable prices, high-quality issuers rationally underprice, in an informational environment in which: (i) issuers are perfectly informed, and (ii) investors have no information about firm value; therefore, companies that reissue have higher underpricing than those that don't.	Ibbotson (1975) Allen and Faulhaber (1989) Grinblatt and Hwang (1989) Welch (1989)	Yes: Keloharju (1993a) McGuinness (1992) No: Jenkinson (1990) Garfinkel (1993) James (1992) Michaely and Shaw (1992) Ruud (1990) Spiess and Pettway (1997)	[Finland] [Hong Kong] [UK] [USA] [USA] [USA] [USA] [USA]
2	Companies for which there is no informational asymmetry, and thus no need to signal, do not underprice.	Allen and Faulhaber (1989)		
3	Positive relationship between underpricing and probability of seasoned equity offering (SEO) or open-market insider sales.	Jegadeesh et al. (1993)	Yes: Keloharju (1993a) Jegadeesh et al. (1993) *weak evidence* No: Michaely and Shaw (1994) Garfinkel (1993) Levis (1995)	[Finland] [USA] [USA] [USA] [UK]
4	Positive relationship between underpricing and amount of SEO or open-market insider sales (underpricing is costly, so high-quality firms minimize amount raised at IPO).	Welch (1989) Jegadeesh et al. (1993)	Yes: Jegadeesh et al. (1993) *weak evidence* No: Michaely and Shaw (1994) Keloharju (1993a)	[USA] [USA] [Finland]

Table 3.4. (cont.)

	Result	Source	Empirical evidence	
5	Positive relationship between underpricing and speed of SEO or open-market insider sales (the higher the underpricing, the shorter the interval between IPO and SEO).	Jegadeesh et al. (1993)	Yes: Levis (1995) Jegadeesh et al. (1993) weak evidence	[UK] [USA]
			No: Keloharju (1993a)	[Finland]
5′	Negative relationship between underpricing and speed of SEO or open-market insider sales (the higher the underpricing, the longer the interval between IPO and SEO).	Welch (1996)	Yes: Welch (1996)	[USA]
6	Less unfavourable price reaction to SEO announcement for firms with higher underpricing.	Welch (1989) Jegadeesh et al. (1993)	Yes: Jegadeesh et al. (1993) Slovin et al. (1994) caveat: The implied benefit at the SEO does not outweigh the underpricing cost.	[USA] [USA]
			No: Michaely and Shaw (1994) Garfinkel (1993) Ruud (1990)	[USA] [USA] [USA]
7	Positive relationship between underpricing and subsequent earnings performance and dividend policy.	Allen and Faulhaber (1989)	No: Michaely and Shaw (1994)	[USA]

8 More favourable price reaction to dividend announcement by firms that underprice more.	Allen and Faulhaber (1989)	No: Michaely and Shaw (1994)	[USA]
9 Positive relationship between underpricing and insider holdings for given level of variance.	Grinblatt and Hwang (1989)	Yes: Firth and Liau-Tan (1997)	[Singapore]
10 Positive relationship between underpricing and firm value for given fraction of insider holdings.	Grinblatt and Hwang (1989)	No: Michaely and Shaw (1994) James and Wier (1990) Yes: Koh et al. (1992)	[USA] [USA] [Singapore]
11 Positive relationship between underpricing and firm value for given level of variance	Grinblatt and Hwang (1989)	No: Michaely and Shaw (1994) No: Michaely and Shaw (1994)	[USA] [USA]
12 positive relationship between underpricing and post-issue operating performance.	Jain and Kini (1994)	No: Jain and Kini (1994)	[USA]
13 The greater is ex ante uncertainty, the higher must be expected underpricing.	Grinblatt and Hwang (1989) Welch (1989)	See Table 3.2	

and thus could be prone to bias. However, a third key implication receives no empirical support either. If underpricing does function as a signal of firm quality, subsequent cash flows should, on average, prove the signal right: whether or not it subsequently cashes in on the signal, the higher a company's underpricing, the higher its subsequent cash flows. Jain and Kini's (1994) study of post-flotation operating performance rejects this hypothesis.

The one implication that the evidence supports almost unequivocally is the positive relationship between *ex ante* uncertainty and initial returns, already familiar from the winner's curse. This relationship is implied by the models, since a noisier environment increases the extent of underpricing that is necessary to achieve separation.

3.3   Principal–Agent Models

None of the models discussed so far has accorded investment banks any particular role. In the winner's curse model, banks are assumed to be as ignorant about a firm's value as the firm itself, and in the signalling models banks are simply passive distributors of shares to the public. We now turn to a third set of models, which focuses on potential agency problems between the investment bank managing the flotation and the issuing firm. The scope for such problems seems immense: in many countries, the underwriter market is far from competitive, and the question arises whether banks have market power which they can exercise at the expense of issuers.

Even in a well-developed capital market such as in the USA, banks may be assumed to be better informed about investor demand than issuers. In an imperfectly competitive underwriter market, this may allow banks to earn information rents, for instance in the form of sub-optimal selling effort. If effort is not perfectly observable or cannot be verified in court, banks find themselves in a moral hazard situation when acting as the issuers' agents in selling an IPO.

Conceptually, underwriters have conflicting incentives regarding the pricing of a flotation. On the one hand, underpricing lowers both the risk of failing to place all available stock with investors, and their unobservable effort costs in marketing and distributing an issue. On the other hand, since underwriting fees are typically proportional to gross flotation proceeds, and thus inversely related to underpricing, investment banks should also have an incentive to minimize underpricing. It is conceivable that the resulting trade-off between underwriters' costs and benefits from underpricing involves some positive initial returns in equilibrium.

Baron and Holmström (1980) and Baron (1982) construct a screening model which focuses on the lead manager's benefit from underpricing. In a screening model, the uninformed party offers a menu or schedule of contracts, from which the informed party selects the one that is optimal given her unobserved type and/or hidden action. The contract schedule is designed to optimize the uninformed party's objective, which, given his informational disadvantage, will not be first-best optimal. An example is the various combinations of premium and excess that a car insurer may offer in order to price-discriminate between different risks (unobservable type) or to induce safe driving (moral hazard).

To induce optimal use of the underwriter's superior information about investor demand, the issuer delegates the pricing decision to the bank. Given his information, the underwriter self-selects a contract from a menu of combinations of IPO prices and underwriting spreads; if likely demand is low, he selects a high spread and a low price, and *vice versa* if demand is high.[11] This optimizes the underwriter's unobservable selling effort by making it dependent on market demand. Compared with the first-best solution under symmetric information, the second-best incentive-compatible contract involves underpricing in equilibrium, essentially since his informational advantage allows the underwriter to capture positive rents in the form of below-first-best effort costs. The more uncertain the value of the firm, the greater the asymmetry of information between issuer and underwriter, and thus the more valuable the latter's services become, resulting in greater underpricing. This is a further rationalization for the empirical observation that underpricing and proxies for *ex ante* uncertainty are positively related.

Models focusing on the role of underwriters are potentially very powerful in explaining the time variation in underpricing. The

---

[11] There is empirical support for the notion of a menu of compensation contracts. Dunbar (1995) shows that issuers successfully offer underwriters a menu that minimizes offering costs by inducing self-selection.

Baron–Holmström model implies non-stationary underpricing if the extent of informational asymmetry, and hence the level of agency costs, changes over time. For instance, an increase in competition may lower the scope for discretionary underpricing, by increasing the possibilities for yardstick competition or, more directly, via banks competing for IPO mandates by offering higher flotation proceeds.

Table 3.5 outlines the model's testable hypotheses and the empirical evidence. A potentially powerful way to test the model would be to investigate the underpricing experience of flotations that have little or no informational asymmetry between issuer and bank, as when the underwriter has an equity stake in the company or the issuer cuts out the intermediary by going public without underwriting. Some limited evidence along these lines is available for the USA. Empirically, self-underwritten offerings are no less underpriced than traditional IPOs, a finding that, importantly, holds true for a set of self-underwritten bank offerings studied by Muscarella and Vetsuypens (1989a). It should be noted, though, that their results are based on a very small sample (38 banks), which cautions against drawing firm conclusions. Moreover, banks are not monolithic institutions, implying that there may still be inter-departmental moral hazard problems.

While the final judgement should, in our view, await further testing, the literature has, by and large, interpreted Muscarella and Vetsuypens's findings as a refutation of the Baron–Holmström model. Given the institutional and market power of banks in some countries—Germany being an obvious example—the model has immediate intuitive appeal in explaining the existence and evolution of underpricing, and thus, we feel, should not be abandoned lightly. A set of models that explore the role of intermediaries further will be discussed next.

3.4   Information Revelation Theories

3.4.1   *The Benveniste–Spindt Model*

Benveniste and Spindt (1989) suggest that a key function of the investment bank that takes a company public is to elicit information

Table 3.5. The principal–agent explanation of IPO underpricing

	Result	Source	Empirical evidence	
1	In order to compensate underwriters for the use of their superior information, issuers rationally let underwriters underprice, in an informational environment in which: (i) underwriters have superior information about the demand for the new shares, and (ii) their marketing efforts are unobservable/unverifiable.	Baron (1982) Baron and Holmström (1980)	No: Muscarella and Vetsuypens (1989a) *Banks underwriting own IPOs also underprice.* Barry et al. (1990) *Banks with equity stakes in firms also underprice.*	[USA] [USA]
2	Self-marketed IPOs should be less underpriced, as there is no asymmetry of information.	Muscarella and Vetsuypens (1989a)	No: Muscarella and Vetsuypens (1989a)	[USA]
3	The greater is *ex ante* uncertainty, the higher is expected underpricing.	Baron (1982)	See Table 3.2	
4	Larger offerings require greater distribution effort by the underwriter, and thus greater underpricing.	Michaely and Shaw (1994)	Yes: Michaely and Shaw (1994)	[USA]

from better informed investors. This may seem odd (though it is the same assumption that underlies the Rock model): surely it is issuers who have the informational advantage in that they know more about their strengths and weaknesses and their future prospects. This is the type of asymmetric information familiar from the signalling models discussed earlier. However, it also seems plausible that there is a second asymmetry of information running in the other direction. Institutional investors may know more than the issuer about the prospects for the company's competitors or the economy as a whole. Also, because they are exposed to the flow of IPOs on a continuous basis, institutional investors may know more about the strength of the IPO market in general or deals by similar companies already in the pipeline. And finally, even the least well informed investor knows something the issuer doesn't: her own demand for the shares. So, while issuers know their own particular piece of the jigsaw better than anyone else, investors hold other pieces of the same jigsaw which when put together give a clearer picture of the value of the company. The task of the underwriter is then to acquire as many jigsaw pieces as possible before setting the offer price.

But why would investors cooperate and reveal their information, especially when the information is positive? After all, by not disclosing their information, they could subscribe at the incomplete-information price and sell, in the after-market, at the higher full-information price.[12] Moreover, there is an obvious incentive not only to withhold but to misrepresent positive information—that is, to claim that the issuer's future looks bleak when it doesn't—for this might induce the underwriter to set a lower offer price. The challenge for the underwriter is therefore to design a mechanism that induces investors to reveal their information truthfully, by making it in their best interest to do so.

Benveniste and Spindt (1989) show that book-building can, under certain conditions, be such a mechanism. As explained in Chapter 1, the book contains investors' indications of interest (which can take the form of price–quantity bids, unlimited bids, or 'soft' information such as 'give me what you've got'). These indications of interest can

---

[12] This assumes that, once trading starts, prices will fully reveal all available information—in other words, that the market is informationally efficient.

communicate the various jigsaw pieces the investors hold. To make sure that they do, the underwriter offers a stick and a carrot. The stick is that any investor who claims that her jigsaw piece looks unfavourable is allocated no or only very few shares. This mitigates the incentive to misrepresent positive information. The carrot is that any investor who claims her jigsaw piece looks favourable (for instance via an aggressive indication of interest, such as bidding for a large quantity at a high price) is rewarded with a disproportionately high allocation of shares. Taken together, the stick and the carrot can ensure that an investor is never better off claiming bad news when the news is in fact good.

To make this mechanism work, the underwriter underprices the issue. Effectively, an investor's monetary reward for truthful reporting equals the number of shares allocated times dollar underpricing (the difference between the after-market and the offer prices). If the underwriter is doing his job well, each investor's reward will just reflect the marginal value of her private information. It follows that underpricing increases in the marginal value of private information. Consider the case where an investor's private information suggests the IPO is 'red-hot'. The underwriter's task, as before, is to ensure that the investor is no better off lying than telling the truth. However, in a 'red-hot' IPO the value of lying is particularly high, so the underwriter is forced to offer a correspondingly greater reward for truth-telling. Since the reward equals the product of shares allocated and dollar underpricing, he should first increase the investor's allocation. However, if this is insufficient to ensure truthful reporting, the underwriter will have to increase dollar underpricing as well.

Despite their deliberately leaving money on the table, Benveniste and Spindt show that issuers are better off. A numerical example may help to make the point. Imagine the underwriter's best estimate indicates that the value of the company lies within the range of $9–$11 a share. If no information is forthcoming, the issue will be priced at $10 a share. The investor knows the company is in fact worth $20 a share. She could sound keen, but not too keen, causing the underwriter to price at the upper end of the range and yielding the investor a profit of $9 per share allocated. Note that the issuer is $1 per share sold better off than if no information is reported. But the underwriter can do better. By increasing the investor's allocation, the underwriter can induce her to bid more aggressively and reveal the full extent of her positive information. The final outcome might be that the IPO is priced at $15 per share, leaving $5 per share on the table but also leaving the issuer better off than had the offer price been set at $10 or $11. While this implies that investors enjoy high underpricing returns, the issuer benefits from being able to float at a price in excess of the underwriter's initial best estimate. In other words, successful book-building is unlikely to eliminate underpricing altogether, but it can reduce it relative to what it would have been in the absence of information acquisition. Empirically, this is a demanding benchmark, since the counterfactual is not observed.

Many underwriters and institutional investors deal with each other repeatedly in the IPO market. This gives the underwriter an additional stick: the threat to strike an investor off the distribution list in future flotations if she withholds or misrepresents her information. So in this repeated game, the investor must weigh the one-off gain from lying against the probability and size of her allocation not only in the current but also in all future IPOs. This implies that underwriters that are more active in the IPO market carry a bigger stick: their larger IPO deal flow should allow them to obtain investors' cooperation more easily (and more cheaply) than less active underwriters could. Repeated interaction benefits issuers in another way too. Active underwriters can effectively bundle offerings across time. Waving their stick, they can induce investors to buy into poorly received IPOs from time to time. Regular investors will play ball as long as the loss they suffer in any given IPO is no greater than the expected present value of future rents they will derive from doing business with the underwriter. This in turn reduces the investor's incentive to lie: downplaying one's information will occasionally result in being asked to buy IPO shares at a loss, making lying less attractive to begin with. The upshot is that the required reward for not lying is smaller, which means lower underpricing and higher gross proceeds for the issuer.

There are two final implications of allowing repeated interaction. First, underwriters may treat regular investors more favourably than occasional investors even when the latter bid more aggressively into the book than the former. This follows because the value of the bank's underwriting activities depends more on the future cooperation of regular investors than on being able to price any given IPO more fully. Second, the ability to bundle IPOs across time gives book-building an edge over auctions. While auctions can be designed to induce truthful revelation of private information, the fact that bidders usually remain anonymous prevents underwriters from establishing relationships with them, so that every auction is *de facto* a stand-alone event.

3.4.2 *Extensions*

In a closely related paper, Benveniste and Wilhelm (1990) point out that underpricing is a relatively inefficient way to acquire information as it benefits successful IPO subscribers indiscriminately. It would be more efficient—that is, less costly to the issuer—to focus the reward on those investors who contribute the most to the price-finding process. Imagine in the earlier example that the underwriter could offer the informed investor an exclusive discount: in return for revealing the $20 per share valuation, the investor would be entitled to purchase the shares at $11. This would remove her incentive to downplay her information. The remaining shares could be offered at something closer to the full-information value of $20, resulting in higher gross proceeds to the issuer, or equivalently in less money left on the table overall.

Unfortunately, most countries impose pricing restrictions to the effect that underwriters are prohibited from price-discriminating between investors.[13] Examples include the USA, where the National Association of Securities Dealers' Rules of Fair Practice require uniform pricing. Benveniste and Wilhelm's analysis suggests that such uniform-pricing rules diminish the efficiency of book-building. In addition to constraining pricing decisions, some countries also constrain allocation decisions to be 'fair' or 'even-handed'. Many countries with British legal foundations, for instance, impose a pro rata allocation rule requiring uniform rationing across all investors or within each size band of bids. Ruling out discretionary allocation prevents underwriters from forming valuable long-term relationships

---

[13] Pay-as-you-bid auctions are extremely rare. The Taiwanese experience is discussed in Liaw *et al.* (2000).

with informed investors in the spirit of Benveniste and Spindt's model, implying a sub-optimally and needlessly high level of underpricing. Hybrid offerings, which combine a book-building exercise aimed at institutional investors with a fixed-price offering aimed at retail investors, similarly reduce the underwriter's allocation discretion and so increase required underpricing.

In countries where both price and allocation discrimination are banned, information acquisition cannot occur as the underwriter has no way of rewarding information reporting. Pricing consequently will be less efficient. Perhaps surprisingly, discretion increases the efficiency of the IPO market.

Benveniste and Wilhelm (1990) also investigate the interaction of information acquisition and the winner's curse. Book-building is essentially a two-step process: first, price discovery takes place in the pre-market or book-building phase, and then this is followed by the distribution of the securities to the investors who took part in the pre-market, as well as to retail investors. If book-building succeeds in revealing the informed investors' private information, the informational asymmetry between them and retail investors is reduced. This implies that book-building offers issuers an additional benefit: it can reduce the winner's curse and thus result in lower required underpricing. Regulatory constraints on pricing and/or allocation decisions will reduce the effectiveness of book-building, which in turn weakens the underwriter's ability to reduce the winner's curse.[14] Outside the USA, we often find retail investors being offered shares at a discount to the price set for institutions. This is consistent with the presence of a winner's curse.

Benveniste, Busaba, and Wilhelm (1996, 2000) suggest two ways to reduce the cost of information acquisition. The argument of Benvenistge, Busaba, and Wilhelm (1996) turns on the idea that underpricing is relatively inefficient because (in the absence of price discrimination) it cannot be targeted at investors who reveal their private information. They suggest that price support may be easier to target and so may be a more efficient form of compensation. We discuss this point more fully in the next chapter, but in brief consider the sit-

---

[14] Note that here the *existence* of underpricing is due to asymmetric information and a winner's curse, while institutional factors affect the level/extent of underpricing.

uation where some but not all regular investors have indicated positive information. The challenge for the underwriter is to persuade the
more sceptical investors to bear the increase in the offer price, reflecting the positive information the other investors have revealed. This
requires trust, for the underwriter has an obvious incentive to overstate investor demand: his fees increase in the offer price. To counteract this incentive, he can offer to buy back shares in the after-market
at the offer price, which insures investors against price falls. It would
be unnecessary to offer such price support to all investors, so it seems
natural that underwriters should discriminate in favour of regular
investors. In the next chapter we will discuss how penalty bids can be
used to exclude retail investors from the benefits of price support.

Benveniste *et al.* (2001) show that underwriters can reduce required
underpricing if the issuer has a credible option to withdraw the offering. Downplaying positive information increases the likelihood that
the issuer will withdraw, which reduces an investor's gain from lying.
This in turn reduces the reward required to induce truthful revelation. Consistent with this prediction, James and Wier (1990) find
that companies that have secured lines of credit before their IPOs
(and thus have a more credible threat to withdraw) experience lower
underpricing.

From the discussion so far, it may seem that book-building will
always be preferred to fixed-price offerings, but this need not be the
case. Benveniste and Busaba (1997) investigate the issuer's choice
between the two. In their model, the expected offer price following a
book-building exercise is higher than in a fixed-price offer. The reason
is related to the idea of 'cascades'. Welch (1992) shows that information cascades can develop in fixed-price offerings if IPO investors
make their subscription decisions sequentially: later investors can
condition their bids on the bids of earlier investors, and demand
can then either snowball or remain low over time. This gives market
power to early investors who can 'demand' more underpricing in
return for committing to the IPO and thus starting a positive cascade.
In book-building, cascades do not develop because the underwriter
can maintain secrecy over the development of demand in the book.
Less underpricing is therefore required. Book-building also offers the
issuer the valuable option to increase the offer size if demand turns
out to be high (either unconditionally, by issuing more shares, or

conditionally, by giving the underwriter an overallotment option). Benveniste and Busaba show that the additional shares can be sold at their full marginal value, that is that the amount of money 'left on the table' is unaffected by the decision to sell more shares. Why? Because total dollar underpricing is determined by the total value of investors' private information, not by the size of the offering. Increasing the number of shares on offer allows the underwriter to reduce percentage underpricing, leaving total dollar underpricing the same.

Despite these advantages, book-building does not necessarily dominate fixed-price offers. The issuer's proceeds are uncertain in a book-building IPO, while they are known in a fixed-price offering. Benveniste and Busaba suggest that the issuer's choice then depends on her risk tolerance regarding the uncertain proceeds and the inherent riskiness of her IPO. This may help explain why book-building and fixed-price offerings co-exist in some countries, such as France and Sweden.

Sherman and Titman (2000) extend the Benveniste–Spindt framework to consider *costly* information production. They note that Benveniste and Spindt assume the number of informed investors to be fixed. In that case, investors receive relatively larger allocations in the 'bad' states of the world (or else the issue fails) than they would if the number of investors could be increased. Selling to an exclusive pool of investors therefore increases the gain from downplaying good information, which in turn increases the underpricing required to induce truthful reporting. If exclusivity is costly, it is puzzling why underwriters maintain it. The contribution in Sherman and Titman is to explain the trade-off that determines the number of investors who are invited to participate in the pre-market. In their setup, a larger pool of investors increases the accuracy with which the IPO is priced. Accuracy is not the same as underpricing, but instead denotes how informative the price will be in the early after-market. This departs from Benveniste and Spindt's assumption that the after-market price will always be fully revealing, whatever happens in the pre-market. Lower accuracy could lead to greater share price volatility (as price discovery continues into the after-market) or lower after-market liquidity (as investors fear competing with better informed traders). An issuer will then care about pricing accuracy to the extent that greater volatility or lower liquidity are undesirable. For instance, if the issuer hopes to obtain feedback from the secondary market about the expected profitability of planned corporate investments, a more accurate price will be desirable so a larger investor pool is targeted. On the other side of the trade-off, a larger pool requires greater underpricing if we assume that information production is costly. This contrasts with Benveniste and Spindt's prediction that an increase in the size of the pool reduces underpricing. Benveniste and Spindt assume that information production is costless, so an increase in the size of the pool always reduces the incentive to lie as outlined earlier.

The upshot is that the underwriter can induce different levels of information production, using the issue price and allocations, on the basis of the cost to investors of producing information and the value of this information to the issuer. The question then is not merely *whether* the underwriter induces information revelation, but what the efficient amount of information collection is.

One interesting implication of this model is that investors who choose to become informed do not necessarily earn excess returns. When the demand for accuracy is relatively low, few investors are targeted and underpricing is chosen to just cover the cost of their information production. Only when a relatively high degree of pricing accuracy is required, and a very large pool of informed investors is targeted, will total dollar underpricing exceed information production costs. This implies that only in certain circumstances will repeated interaction with regular investors allow the underwriter to reduce underpricing, for there is normally no rent to claw back from them in the first place.

There is a second case in which investors will earn rents: namely if regulations impose a minimum number of IPO investors or a maximum number of shares that each IPO investor may purchase.[15] In either case, the size of the investor pool must be larger, which can lead to inefficiently high levels of information production. To counteract this, the underwriter can allocate shares to uninformed investors. However, uninformed investors earn excess returns because, under uniform pricing, they enjoy the benefit of underpricing but do not

[15] In July 1994, for instance, the Thai Securities and Exchange Commission imposed the following rules: a minimum of 30% of shares to be allocated to retail investors; up to 60% to be allocated at the underwriter's discretion but with no more than 0.5% allocated to any one investor; and up to 10% to be allocated according to the issuer's wishes.

bear the costs of information production. Sherman (2000) develops this argument further. Repeated interactions allow the underwriter to reduce the uninformed investors' excess returns. As in Benveniste and Spindt's model the underwriter can bundle good and bad deals over time, using the threat of striking uninformed regulars off their distribution list in future.

The idea of costly information production is further developed in a model by Benveniste, Wilhelm and Yu (2000) which links the underwriter's capacity to 'bundle' IPOs over time to the empirical observation that IPOs tend to occur in waves. The central idea is that the valuation uncertainty is composed of a firm-specific and an industry component. Obtaining information about the industry component allows investors to evaluate other offerings in that industry more cheaply. In other words, some pieces of the valuation jigsaw may be correlated across securities being priced simultaneously or in short succession, leading to economies of scale in information production. This would be the case if a buyside analyst finds it cheaper to value two companies with similar value drivers going public in short succession than two companies either with different value drivers or going public at different points in time. These information spillovers could lead to too few firms going public, because the first firm to do so must compensate investors for their whole valuation effort, while later firms can 'free-ride' on the information production.[16]

By establishing networks of regular investors, underwriters may be able to reduce this negative externality. To do so, they compensate investors for their information costs across a *sequence* of offerings. Consistent with this prediction, we observe investment banks specializing in particular industries, and taking companies public in industry-specific 'waves'. In 1980 and 1981, for instance, a disproportionate number of the firms going public in the USA were oil and gas

---

[16] The idea that information spillovers can cause IPO clustering is explored in three papers that are not based on the Benveniste–Spindt information-acquisition story. Booth and Chua (1996) point out that, when many companies come to market, the marginal cost of information production is lower, so average underpricing falls. This explanation is consistent with Lowry and Schwert's (2000) evidence discussed in Ch. 2. Mauer and Senbet (1992) argue that IPO companies which start trading in the secondary market may reduce the valuation uncertainty surrounding companies with similar technologies which are in the process of going public. Stoughton *et al.* (2000) develop a model in which one firm's IPO provides information about industry prospects, thus causing many similar companies to go public soon after.

exploration companies. Similarly, in the USA and in Europe, the majority of issuers in 1998 and 1999 were active in internet-related industries. Of course, the fact that an underwriter spreads the information cost across several issues is equivalent to a tax on later issuers, or a subsidy for the first issuer. However, overall economic welfare increases because 'bundling' prevents a first-mover's value-creating IPO from being abandoned. Note that to force later issuers to share in the information production cost requires some degree of market power among underwriters: otherwise, a new bank could enter the underwriting industry and offer to take second-movers public at better prices. There is plenty of circumstantial evidence of market power. The underwriting industry is highly concentrated in many countries. In the USA, for instance, we calculate that the three most active underwriters have lead-managed between 49 and 64 per cent of IPOs by value in 1995–9, between 36 and 53 per cent in 1990–4, and between 37 and 71 per cent in 1985–9. The composition of this top tier has also been remarkably stable. Goldman Sachs and Merrill Lynch have ranked in the top three in 14 and 11 years, respectively, between 1985 and 1999, and Goldman Sachs has been the most active underwriter in 11 out of the 15 years. Moreover, Chen and Ritter (2000) document that the vast majority of US mid-sized issuers paid their underwriters gross spreads of *exactly* 7 per cent. This finding has led to a lawsuit alleging that 27 securities firms conspired to 'fix and maintain' the share of IPO proceeds that go to underwriters (*Wall Street Journal*, 5 November 1998), filed in Manhattan federal court shortly after the release of Chen and Ritter's paper to the business press.

3.4.3 *Evidence*

The book-building literature has grown tremendously in the past few years, generating a rich set of empirical predictions. We list these in Table 3.6, following roughly the order of our above discussion. The challenge facing empiricists in testing the Benveniste–Spindt model is two-fold: first, we need detailed data on each investor's bids and allocations, and second, we need a way of identifying whether an investor is informed or uninformed, and whether she is a regular or occasional client of the underwriter's. Bid and allocation data are

Table 3.6. The marketing explanation of IPO underpricing

	Result	Source	Empirical evidence	
1	Underwriters can entice 'informed' investors to truthfully reveal their superior information pre-sale through their allocation and pricing decisions; underpricing serves to compensate informed investors for truthful reporting. In particular, underwriters give allocation priority to investors who indicate positive information.	Benveniste and Spindt (1989) Sternberg (1989)	Yes: Cornelli and Goldreich (1999)	[various]
2	Underpricing is positively related to the *ex ante* marginal value of investors' private information.	Benveniste and Spindt (1989)		
3	Investment banks give priority to regular investors (those they deal with repeatedly over time); doing so minimizes underpricing; regular investors will, from time to time, help underwriters by taking up any slack in under-subscribed offers.	Benveniste and Spindt (1989)	Yes: Hanley and Wilhelm (1995) Aggarwal (2000b) Cornelli and Goldreich (1999) No: Keloharju (1996) Tinic (1988)	[USA] [USA] [various] [Finland] [USA]
4	Underwriters with higher IPO deal flow can reduce underpricing more	Sherman (2000)		
5	Flotations for which positive information is revealed will be priced towards or beyond the upper end of the initial price range; however, the final price will be set below the full-information price to allow regular investors to be compensated via underpricing.	Benveniste and Spindt (1989) Hanley (1993)	Yes: Hanley (1993)	[USA]

#	Description			
6	Similarly, the number of shares to be issued is more frequently increased above the initially proposed level, the greater the final offer price in relation to the initial range.	Hanley (1993)	Yes: Hanley (1993)	[USA]
7	Underpricing is positively related to the level of interest in the pre-market; in particular, issues eventually priced in the upper part of the offer price range are more underpriced ('partial adjustment phenomenon').	Benveniste and Spindt (1989)	Yes: Hanley (1993) Sternberg (1989)	[USA] [USA]
8	Underpricing increases in the allocations to investors who indicate low interest; increasing the number of investors targeted reduces the likelihood that such allocations have to be made, resulting in lower underpricing.	Benveniste and Spindt (1989)	Yes: Ljungqvist et al. (2000)	[65 countries]
9	In firm-commitment offerings, underwriters have an incentive to 'presell' an issue as much as possible before trading begins, leading to inefficiently large allocations to investors who indicate low interest; therefore, underpricing is higher the more the issue is presold.	Benveniste and Spindt (1989)	Yes: Welch (1991)	[USA]
10	Underpricing is higher in countries with binding restrictions on allocation and/or pricing, than in countries with no such restrictions; it is highest in countries that require both 'even-handed' allocation and non-discriminatory pricing.	Benveniste and Wilhelm (1990)	Yes: Ljunqvist and Wilhelm (2001) No: Loughran et al. (1994)	[4 countries] [25 countries]
11	Underwriters can reduce underpricing by offering price support selectively to investors who cooperate in the price-finding process.	Benveniste et al. (1996)	Yes: Benveniste et al. (1998)	[USA]

Table 3.6. (cont.)

Result	Source	Empirical evidence	
12 Issuers who possess a credible threat to withdraw their offerings can induce truthful information reporting at lower levels of underpricing.	Benveniste et al. (2001)	Yes: Benveniste et al. (2001) James and Wier (1990)	[USA] [USA]
13 Book-building leads to a higher offer price than fixed-price offerings but also to more uncertain proceeds; after-market volatility in fixed-price offerings is relatively greater.	Benveniste and Busaba (1997)		
14 If information production is costly but can increase pricing accuracy, underwriters determine the optimal size of the investor pool by trading off information costs and the benefits of accurate pricing. To induce more information production, the underwriter must increase underpricing. The following types of issuers may have higher demands for accuracy and therefore experience higher underpricing: (i) riskier companies, (ii) smaller firms whose shares are likely to be less liquid, and (iii) firms with high expected future capital needs.	Sherman and Titman (2000)		
15 As information production costs fall, both the optimal size of the investor pool and underpricing of 'hot' IPOs increase.	Sherman and Titman (2000)		
16 As the value of information increases, the optimal size of the investor pool and expected underpricing increases.	Sherman and Titman (2000)		

17 As the accuracy of investors' information increases, the size of the pool increases for low starting levels of accuracy and decreases for high starting levels of accuracy, while underpricing decreases in either case.	Sherman and Titman (2000)
18 If regulations impose a minimum number of IPO investors or a maximum number of shares each IPO investor may purchase, both the size of the investor pool and expected underpricing increase.	Sherman and Titman (2000)
19 Restrictions on the minimum number of investors are more likely to bind in smaller offerings, so smaller offerings are more likely to be underpriced than larger offerings.	Sherman and Titman (2000)
20 Restrictions on the maximum number of shares bought are more likely to bind in larger offerings, so larger offerings are more likely to be underpriced than smaller offerings.	Sherman and Titman (2000)
21 Where such restrictions exist, the underwriter can reduce underpricing by allocating some shares to uninformed investors—who, however, earn rents (they do not incur the information production cost).	Sherman and Titman (2000)
22 By bundling offerings over time, the underwriter can reduce uninformed investors' rents.	Sherman (2000)
23 Underwriters 'bundle' IPOs in the same industry, thereby spreading information production costs and enabling more companies to go public. The extent of learning (information production) about common valuation factors diminishes over a sequence of IPOs in the same industry.	Benveniste, Busaba and Wilhelm (2000) Yes: Benveniste, Wilhelm and Yu (2000) [USA]

usually kept confidential, but in recent years some data have become available. Cornelli and Goldreich (1999, 2000) have access to the books of one European investment bank active in 23 international (non-US) IPOs. They classify an investor as informed if she submits price-limited as opposed to strike (market) orders, arguing that the price limit is more informative to the underwriter than a mere quantity order. The empirical patterns in the underwriter's allocation and pricing decisions are strongly consistent with the Benveniste–Spindt model: the underwriter favours both investors who submit price-limited orders and regular investors with better allocation-to-bid ratios. The final offer price is closely related to the limit orders in the book, in particular those submitted by large and by frequent bidders.

Whether these results can be generalized depends on how representative this European bank is. Ljungqvist *et al.* (2000) provide evidence from 65 countries that the quality of book-building—as measured by the underpricing cost of inducing truthful information reporting—heavily depends on whether a US bank lead-manages the issue and on whether US-based investors are targeted. Indeed, book-building by non-US banks targeted at their domestic clients appears to provide no pricing advantage over fixed-price offerings. This is consistent with the prediction that access to informed (US) investors and high expected future IPO deal flow favours certain US investment banks.

Short of detailed bid and allocation data, there are other predictions that can be tested using publicly available data. Revisions in the offer price and the number of shares offered in the pre-market are likely to reflect investors' level of interest and the aggregate nature of their information. A flotation for which positive information is revealed should be priced towards the upper limit of the range, or—if the information is particularly positive—above the range, whereas a less well received offering should be priced towards the lower limit. Benveniste and Spindt's model suggests that underpricing should be concentrated among the offerings drawing the highest level of pre-market interest. In other words, even though the underwriter adjusts the price upwards, he does so only partially, in order to leave enough money on the table to compensate informed investors for their truthful revelation. Hanley (1993) provides empirical evidence of this 'partial adjustment' phenomenon. The less well received offerings can be fairly priced or overpriced, depending on the underwriter's ability to 'bundle' deals over time. Hanley and Wilhelm (1995) find support for 'bundling'. Using the relative allocations of institutions and retail investors in 38 US IPOs conducted by a leading investment bank over the period 1983–8, they show that institutions are more favoured over retail investors, the stronger is an offering's reception in the premarket. At the same time, however, institutions are given similar allocations in overpriced as in underpriced deals.

Internationally, Benveniste and Wilhelm (1990) predict lower underpricing in more 'permissive' capital markets. The institutional framework in the UK, for example, which typically forbids both discretionary allocation and pricing,[17] would hence engender greater underpricing than that in the USA, which merely restricts pricing. Similarly, underpricing in Singapore should have fallen following the liberalization of price and quantity restrictions in 1992—a proposition that remains to be tested. Loughran *et al.* (1994) offer a bird's-eye perspective on the influence of allocation discretion by consolidating measures of average underpricing calculated in 25 country-specific studies. Although their 'meta-analytic' approach sheds some light on how underpricing varies depending on whether information is collected prior to pricing and on whether the underwriter maintains allocation discretion, the results are far from clear-cut, perhaps because of other cross-country differences which they do not control for, such as company size or *ex ante* uncertainty. Disturbingly, however, they claim that uniform pricing tends to be the norm even in countries that have no legal, regulatory, or other requirement to that effect.

3.4.4 *Discussion*

The evidence is broadly consistent with the central insights of Benveniste and Spindt. This allows us to investigate the often-heard claim that book-building is inherently 'unfair' because it favours institutions over retail investors. The Benveniste–Spindt model sug-

---

[17] With the recent introduction of book-building techniques in the UK, it has become possible to discriminate between those investors—typically, institutions—that participate in the international tender offers. However, there remains a requirement that shares allocated to public offers be allocated fairly.

gests that such favouritism is in fact efficient: if book-building is about information acquisition, then it is the informed investors who need to be rewarded for revealing their information. Most retail investors will know little more than their own demand, whereas some institutional investors may hold other valuable jigsaw pieces. Fairness would be violated if *all* institutional investors were favoured relative to retail investors, irrespective of the value of their information. This follows because in the Benveniste–Spindt model it is those institutions that are both informed and cooperative that should be rewarded. Indeed, some of the evidence that we reviewed above suggests that institutions are *not* treated equally, but instead are given allocations that reflect their contribution to the price-finding process. A final implication of this analysis is that IPO underwriting is an industry with relatively high barriers to entry: the quality of a book-building exercise depends crucially on the bank's access to a network of informed investors and its ability to induce these investors to reveal their information truthfully. This will favour established underwriters and banks with larger IPO deal flow: history and size do matter. Barriers to entry in turn imply that successful underwriters will earn rents. The extraordinary profitability of the top underwriters attests to this.[18]

3.5 Summary

Before turning to more explicitly institutional reasons why firms may wish, or be forced, to underprice their initial public offerings, it is worthwhile to summarize the asymmetric information literature. While we have no doubt that simple averages of underpricing returns, computed across a large number of firms, are unrealistic in ignoring the effects of rationing, and perhaps even an informational allocation bias, we do not think that such a winner's curse should necessitate underpricing unless the issuer expressly desired the participation of uninformed investors, a point we will return to in Chapter 7 when discussing governments' objectives in encouraging wider share

[18] According to Bloomberg, the IPO underwriting revenue of the top 25 investment banks in the USA in 1999 totalled US$3.6 billion (see A. Levy, 'Club', *Bloomberg Magazine*, May 2000: 27–35).

ownership. Similarly, the notion of initial underpricing as a deliberate signal of quality does not seem convincing—outside, perhaps, the USA—for reasons of logic and institutional differences across countries. On the other hand, models that build either on marketing and information production or on the principal–agent problem between issuer and investment banker are appealing in that they afford underwriters an economically valuable role (which is totally absent in both the winner's curse and signalling models) and make what we think are realistic assumptions regarding the underlying distribution of information. The wealth of recent evidence in support of the Benveniste–Spindt model suggests that price finding and information production are among the most important functions that IPO underwriters perform.

CHAPTER 4

Institutional Explanations

Two main institutional underpricing models will be considered in this chapter. First, the litigiousness of American investors has inspired a *legal insurance hypothesis* of underpricing. The basic idea, which goes back at least to Logue (1973*b*) and Ibbotson (1975), is that companies knowingly sell their stock at a discount to insure against future lawsuits from shareholders disappointed with the performance of their shares. The notion doubtless has some superficial appeal, but for a variety of reasons it has little economic relevance in most countries, as we will argue.

Second, one of the services that underwriters provide in many countries is *price stabilization*, a marketing pledge to reduce downward price fluctuations in the after-market. They achieve stabilization via price support, which in turn can be effected in a variety of ways discussed below. One way is to place a limit order to buy shares as soon as share prices fall below the offer price. Price support is withdrawn after a certain period of time, as specified by regulators, the underwriting contract, or market conditions. In Chapter 7 we will discuss the various forms that price stabilization can take in the context of privatizations. Here, we will focus on its implications for underpricing.

The most obvious institutional explanation of underpricing, and one that we shall not pursue further here, is political interference. No doubt there are many countries, not only in the developing world, that have seen their political elites enrich themselves and their cronies via favourable allocations of deeply discounted IPOs. Similarly, some markets have imposed regulatory constraints on the price formation process which almost automatically lead to high discounts, such as the requirement that companies be floated at no higher than a particular price–earnings ratio. But meddlesome politicians and archaic valuation methods cannot explain the very existence of underpricing: something else must account for the discount at which, say, US or European companies are floated.

4.1 Legal Liability

Stringent disclosure rules in the USA expose underwriters, accountants, and issuers to considerable litigation risk: shareholders can sue them on the grounds that material facts were mis-stated or omitted from an IPO prospectus. Securities class action lawsuits are notoriously frequent in the USA: in 1986, for instance, Alex Brown & Sons and L. F. Rothschild, Unterberg, Towbin, two major-bracket investment banks, were involved in more than 130 separate IPO lawsuits between them.[1] Lowry and Shu (2000) estimate that nearly 6 per cent of companies floated in the USA between 1988 and 1995 subsequently were sued for violations relating to the IPO. Outside the USA, lawsuits are rarer but not unheard of. In May 2000, underwriters ABN Amro and Goldman Sachs were sued by the Dutch shareholder's union VEB when the market value of World Online dropped by €2 billion shortly after it transpired that Nina Brink, the founder of World Online, had herself sold shares in the company for €6.02 shortly before it went public at an issue price of €43.

Tinic (1988) and Hughes and Thakor (1992) argue that intentional underpricing may act as insurance against such securities litigation. Lawsuits are obviously costly to the defendants, not only directly— legal fees, diversion of management time, etc.—but also in terms of the potential damage to their reputation capital: litigation-prone investment banks may lose the confidence of their regular investors, while issuers may face a higher cost of capital in future capital issues. Hughes and Thakor postulate a trade-off between minimizing the

---

[1] The figures are quoted in Tinic (1988).

probability of litigation, and hence minimizing these costs, on the one hand and maximizing flotation revenue (and the underwriters' commission thereon) on the other. Crucially, they assume that the former probability increases in the offer price: the more overpriced an issue, the more likely is a future lawsuit. In addition, underpricing reduces not only (i) the probability of a lawsuit, but also (ii) the probability of an adverse ruling conditional on a lawsuit being filed, and (iii) the amount of damages awarded in the event of an adverse ruling (since actual damages in the USA are limited by the offer price). Some further testable implications regarding underwriters' reputation are listed in Table 4.1.

The tightening of disclosure and liability requirements in the 1933 Securities Act provides a convenient regime shift along which to test the hypothesis. Prior to the 1933 legislation, the principle of *caveat emptor* applied to the securities industry in an almost unfettered way, so firms and banks faced virtually no litigation risk. Since 1933, on the other hand, underpricing should have risen in line with the increased risk of future litigation. Tinic's results, reported in Table 4.1, seemingly confirm this, although the samples (70 flotations from 1923 to 1930, 134 new issues from 1966 to 1971) may be too limited and unrepresentative, given our knowledge of the immense variability in average underpricing over time. Moreover, New Zealand, which according to Vos and Cheung (1992) has a similar legal environment to the USA, saw no change in underpricing following its introduction of tough liability legislation in the 1983 Securities Regulations Act, a regime shift similar to the enactment of the 1933 Securities Act in the USA. While Tinic does find support for those conjectures that pertain to underwriter reputation, the conjectures are sufficiently general to be consistent with just about any underpricing explanation. For instance, lower underpricing among more reputable banks is equally consistent with a reduced winner's curse or superior information production during the book-building phase.

More light can be shed on the issue by investigating the effect of underpricing on the probability of litigation.[2] Early evidence on this

---

[2] Since most cases are settled out of court, settlement and legal costs are difficult to assess, and the impact of underpricing on the probability of an adverse ruling and on the amount of damages are hard to analyse in the USA.

Table 4.1. The lawsuit avoidance explanation of IPO underpricing

Result	Source	Empirical evidence	
1 In order to avoid legal liability for mis-statements in the IPO prospectus, underwriters and issuers rationally choose to underprice IPOs.	Logue (1973a) Ibbotson (1975) Tinic (1988) Hughes and Thakor (1992) Hensler (1995)	Yes: Tinic (1988) Lowry and Shu (2000) No: Drake and Vetsuypens (1993) Lee et al. (1996) Keloharju (1993b) Ljungqvist (1995a) Beller et al. (1992) Vos and Cheung (1992) Rydqvist (1994) Kunz and Aggarwal (1994) Jenkinson (1990)	[USA] [USA] [USA] [Australia] [Finland] [Germany] [Japan] [NZ] [Sweden] [Switzerland] [UK]
2 Underpricing reduces the probability of litigation.	Tinic (1988)	Yes: Lowry and Shu (2000) No: Drake and Vetsuypens (1993)	[USA] [USA]
3 Underpricing reduces the conditional probability of an adverse judgement if litigation occurs.	Tinic (1988)		
4 Underpricing reduces the amount of damages in the event of an adverse judgement.	Tinic (1988)		
5 Lawsuit avoidance should not have mattered before the 1933 Securities Act, so underpricing should be lower before 1933.	Tinic (1988)	Yes: Tinic (1988) No: Prabhala and Puri (1999) Difference in underpricing likely due to differences in risk	[USA] [USA]

Table 4.1. (*cont.*)

Result	Source	Empirical evidence	
6 Underpricing is smaller, the more experienced the underwriter is at due-diligence investigations.	Tinic (1988)	Yes: Tinic (1988)	[USA]
7 The greater is *ex ante* uncertainty, the higher is expected underpricing.	Tinic (1988) Hughes and Thakor (1992)	See Table 3.2.	
8 Underwriters with large reputation capital at stake avoid speculative small IPOs.	Tinic (1988) Hughes and Thakor (1992)	Yes: Tinic (1988)	[USA]
9 Underpricing is lower, the better the underwriter's reputation.	Hughes and Thakor (1992)	Yes: Tinic (1988) Carter and Manaster (1990)	[USA] [USA]
10 When there are unusually many speculative IPOs ('hot issue' periods), the market share of fringe underwriters should increase.	Tinic (1988)	Yes: Tinic (1988)	[USA]
11 Owing to liability being joint and several, issuers that refuse to use underpricing as legal insurance have to compensate underwriters via larger spreads.	Tinic (1988)		
12 If underwriters' compensation and the equilibrium probability of litigation increase in the IPO price, then underpricing is larger, the lower the compensation.	Hughes and Thakor (1992)		
13 On average, underpricing is higher if no underwriter is used.	Hughes and Thakor (1992)	Yes: Muscarella and Vetsuypens (1989a)	[USA]
14 After-market price support minimizes legal liability, and thus reduces the need for underpricing.	Schultz and Zaman (1994)		

was provided by Drake and Vetsuypens (1993), who claim among other things that underpricing does not reduce the probability of a lawsuit: purchasers of underpriced offerings are just as likely to sue in the USA as purchasers of overpriced ones, and firms that are sued are no more or less underpriced than comparable companies that are not sued. However, Lowry and Shu (2000) argue that such an *ex post* comparison misses the point. Theory suggests that it is litigation risk, not the actual occurrence of litigation, that is associated with higher underpricing. This is what we called, in the first edition of this monograph, the 'identification problem of not being able to rule out the existence of firms that did manage to escape lawsuits by virtue of underpricing'. Lowry and Shu's approach helps to solve the identification problem, but it does not address the question whether lawsuit avoidance is an economically significant determinant of underpricing.

Whatever the empirical success, or otherwise, of the lawsuit avoidance theory, the legal literature has voiced profound scepticism. Alexander (1993) contends that the hypothesis is based on misleading or overly simplistic assumptions about actual legal and financial liability for underwriters and issuers: (i) that underwriters do not in reality bear the costs of litigation and thus have no incentive to insure themselves; moreover, the greatest part in any settlement is paid by insurance companies under directors' and officers' liability policies and not by parties to the IPO agreement (though of course the firms bear the insurance premia); (ii) that underpricing would offer only limited protection because it is irrelevant in suits brought under the 1934 Securities Exchange Act, which in practice is virtually always invoked alongside the 1933 Securities Act; and (iii) that, since the Acts are about disclosure and not pricing, a finding of underpricing is immaterial to the outcome of litigation. She concludes that underpricing would be an inefficient and ineffective means of obtaining insurance against securities law violations.

The lawsuit idea is a good example of a US-centric model which fails in the international context: underpricing is a global phenomenon, while strict liability laws are not. The risk of being sued is not economically significant in Australia (Lee *et al.* 1996), Finland (Keloharju 1993*b*), Germany (Ljungqvist 1995*a*), Japan (Beller *et al.* 1992, Macey and Kanda 1990), Sweden (Rydqvist 1994), Switzerland (Kunz and Aggarwal 1994), or the UK (Jenkinson 1990), all of which experience underpricing. A more promising institutional approach is price support, to which we turn next.

4.2 Price Support

Given that it retards price discovery in the secondary market by obscuring the true demand and supply conditions, it may be surprising that temporary price support in IPOs is legal in many countries, including the USA (1934 Securities Act, Rule 10b-7, since replaced by Regulation M), the UK (Securities and Investments Board Rules, Chapter III, Part 10), France (Husson and Jacquillat 1989), Germany (Ljungqvist 1995*a*), Greece (Panagos and Papachristou 1993), Hong Kong (McGuinness 1993*b*) and the Netherlands (Jansen and Tourani Rad 1995).

Virtually everything we know about actual price support activities is based on evidence from the USA. We have only limited direct evidence about how extensively underwriters stabilize after-market prices because stabilizing activities are generally notifiable, if at all, only to market regulators, and not to investors at large. This means that it is virtually impossible to identify which new issues were initially supported, how the intensity of intervention varied over time, and at what time support was withdrawn. In October 1983 the US Securities and Exchange Commission ceased to require the filing of reports in respect of price support under Rule 10b-7. In a regrettable act of data destruction, the SEC subsequently destroyed almost all records of which new issues had received price support (cf. Ruud 1993). A small number of the SEC filings, on form X-17A-1, survive and are analysed in Prabhala and Puri (1999). All other empirical work is based on indirect evidence. A widely followed approach is to argue that overpriced and fully priced IPOs are more likely to have been supported than underpriced ones, especially in the face of large trading volumes. Prabhala and Puri compare this approach to X-17A-1 filings and find that the characteristics of offerings that are supported are very similar.[3]

---

[3] Aggarwal (2000*a*), on the other hand, finds that underwriters are also active after-market buyers of IPOs that open a little above their offer prices.

An alternative approach is to investigate after-market 'microstructure' data for behaviour indicative of price support, and to relate it to the underwriter's pre-market activities such as book-building. This is particularly promising on NASDAQ, where underwriters can, and usually do, become market-makers in the companies they take public. (On the New York Stock Exchange (NYSE), underwriters are rarely also 'specialists' in the stocks they take public, so price support on the NYSE is not effected via underwriters' market-making activities.) The microstructure variables of interest are the bid–ask spreads that underwriters charge (especially relative to competing market-makers who are not part of the original IPO syndicate); who provides 'price leadership' (by offering the best bid and ask prices); who trades with whom and in what trade sizes; what risks underwriters take in the after-market; and how much inventory dealers accumulate (indicating that they are net buyers). Ellis *et al.* (2000) use detailed information on underwriters' NASDAQ market-making activities to infer price support activities. This approach builds on earlier work by Schultz and Zaman (1994) and Hanley *et al.* (1993), who also investigate market microstructure data. Aggarwal (2000*a*) uses proprietary information on underwriters' short-covering transactions to identify price support. Finally, Benveniste *et al.* (1998) rely on transaction-by-transaction trading patterns to infer which IPOs were stabilized.

How widespread is price support? Asquith *et al.* (1998) infer from the distributional characteristics of initial returns that about half of all US IPOs appear to have been supported in 1982–3. For a sample of 72 large IPOs, Schultz and Zaman (1994) report that, during the first three trading days, US underwriters repurchase on average a stunning 21 per cent of the original number of shares offered. Aggarwal (2000*a*) shows that underwriters are active buyers in 81 per cent of 'weak' IPOs (those priced below the indicative filing range). Table 4.2 provides an overview of the empirical evidence regarding the existence of price support.

4.2.1 *The range of price support activities*

In general, underwriters can support prices by stimulating demand or by restricting supply in the after-market. They can stimulate demand either by posting bids at or below the offer price (stabilizing bids), or

Table 4.2. The price support explanation of IPO underpricing

	Result	Source	Empirical evidence
	Do underwriters provide price support?		
1	Initial returns are 'censored': they are non-normal and peak at zero; there is almost no negative tail.		Yes: Ruud (1991, 1993) [USA]
2	Underwriters are aggressive buyers in the after-market:		Yes: Schultz and Zaman (1994) [USA]
	• they spend more time at the highest bid for cold IPOs (IPOs trading at or below their offer price) than for hot IPOs;		
	• for cold IPOs, they spend more time at the bid than at the ask;		
	• they spend more time at the bid than at the ask compared with other market-makers, especially for cold IPOs;		
	• they quote higher bid prices than other market-makers, especially for cold IPOs.		
3	Via price support, underwriters provide other dealers with a put option; this reduces market makers' costs and thus leads to narrower spreads. Consistent with this prediction, bid–ask spreads narrow as after-market prices approach the offer price.	Hanley *et al.* (1993)	Yes: Hanley *et al.* (1993) [USA] Miller and Reilly (1987) [USA]
4	Underwriters go short in the pre-market. In underpriced IPOs, they cover the short position by exercising the over-allotment option. In overpriced IPOs, they purchase shares in the after-market, thus stabilizing prices.		Yes: Aggarwal (2000a) [USA]
5	After-market prices fail to fall below the offer price in the presence of abnormally high, sell-motivated trading volume until about 20 days after trading begins.		Yes: Benveniste *et al.* (1998) [USA]

6 Underwriters become the most active market-makers on NASDAQ and accumulate large inventories, especially in cold IPOs.		Yes: Ellis *et al.* (2000) [USA]
7 Over time, underwriters remove price support. The effects of price support are temporary, leading prices to fall as support is withdrawn.		Yes: Ruud (1991) [USA] *Prices of fully-priced or just-underpriced IPOs more likely to fall than to rise over first four trading weeks* Hanley *et al.* (1993) [USA] *Spreads widen and prices fall over time* No: Schultz and Zaman (1994) [USA] *Underwriters permanently reduce the supply of cold-IPO shares* Prabhala and Puri (1999) [USA] *Post-stabilization returns are negative but no larger than for non-stabilized offerings*
Underpricing and price support		
8 Underwriters stabilize after-market trading prices at the offer price, thus minimizing the occurrence of overpricing. This leads to censoring of the initial return distribution and the spurious impression of positive underpricing on average.	Ruud (1991, 1993)	Yes: Ruud (1991, 1993) [USA] No: Asquith *et al.* (1998) [USA] Prabhala and Puri (1999) [USA]
9 Underwriters underprice to lower the implicit strike price and thus the value of the put option to investors.	Schultz and Zaman (1994)	
10 Price support minimizes legal liability, and thus reduces the need for underpricing.	Schultz and Zaman (1994)	

Table 4.2. (cont.)

Result	Source	Empirical evidence	
11 Price support prevents informational cascades (Welch, 1992) and thus reduces the need to underprice.	Schultz and Zaman (1994)		
12 Price support is a more efficient solution to the winner's curse problem than underpricing, because it better targets uninformed investors. The main beneficiaries of price support are therefore uninformed (retail) investors.	Chowdhry and Nanda (1996)	No: Benveniste et al. (1998)	[USA]
13 Price support reduces underwriters' incentives to overprice. This improves price-finding during book-building if price support is targeted at informed investors.	Benveniste et al. (1996)	Yes: Benveniste et al. (1998)	[USA]
14 Price support provides an incentive to the underwriter to reduce pre-market informational asymmetries; this reduces required underpricing.	Prabhala and Puri (1999)	Yes: Prabhala and Puri (1999)	[USA]
Cross-sectional implications			
15 Higher-quality underwriters are more likely to engage in price support.	Ruud (1991, 1993)	Yes: Ruud (1991, 1993) Prabhala and Puri (1999)	[USA] [USA]
16 *Ceteris paribus*, the larger the syndicate, the greater its resources, the more likely it is to support prices; the larger the offering, the more likely the syndicate is to underprice instead.	Chowdhry and Nanda (1996)		
17 Price support lowers the volatility of after-market returns.	Panagos and Papachristou (1993)	No: Panagos and Papachristou (1993)	[Greece]

by actively buying back shares of weak offerings (stabilizing trades). They can also restrict supply by penalizing 'flippers' or 'stags'— investors who sell their shares when trading begins.

The theoretical literature on the costs and benefits of price support has mainly assumed that underwriters stabilize after-market prices by posting limit orders at the offer price: that is, by indicating their willingness to buy should prices fall below the offer price. On NASDAQ, such bids have to be flagged as stabilizing bids for the benefit of other market participants. According to Aggarwal (2000*a*), there is no evidence of underwriters flagging their bids in the 1990s, so it appears that price support via pure limit orders is rare on NASDAQ. This is not too surprising: under SEC regulations, stabilizing bids are permissible only until the syndicate breaks up, which it typically does before trading even starts. Thus, flagged bids would be encountered only in the unusual case that the syndicate is still in existence after trading has begun.

A more common way to stimulate demand is for underwriters to actually buy shares. Using a unique data set obtained from NASDAQ which identifies the parties to each transaction, Ellis *et al.* (2000) show that the lead underwriter always becomes the most dominant market-maker, handling more than half the trades in the first few trading days, and accumulates sizeable inventories, averaging 7.8 per cent of shares offered in the IPO after 20 trading days. Inventory positions are clearly related to how strongly an IPO performs: the lead underwriter buys back an average of only 2.5 per cent of shares offered in 'hot' offerings (those that never fell below their offer prices in the first twenty days of trading), versus 22 per cent in 'cold' offerings (those that opened below their offer prices and never recovered in the first 20 days). These inventory accumulation patterns are strong evidence of price support activities, and indicate that such activities persist for a perhaps surprising length of time.

Inventory positions of this magnitude clearly expose underwriters to considerable price risk. After all, Krigman *et al.* (1999) find that IPOs that are 'cold' on the first day continue to fall in price subsequently. However, Ellis *et al.* (2000) also show that underwriters use their short positions to manage inventory risk. As pointed out earlier, underwriters typically oversell IPOs, by allocating more than 100 per cent of shares on offer. If prices subsequently rise, they can cover their short position by exercising the over-allotment option to buy another 15 per cent of shares from the issuer; if prices fall, they leave the over-allotment option unexercised and close out their short position by open-market purchases instead.[4] Either way, they make a profit: if they exercise the over-allotment option, they earn the gross spread on the additional shares, and if they don't exercise it, they earn the difference between the offer price, at which they oversold, and the (lower) after-market trading price. So underwriters typically start their market-making activities with a considerable short position, which must be set against the long positions they subsequently acquire. *Net* inventory positions for 'cold' offerings average about 8 per cent after 20 days, much less than the 22 per cent reported previously. And even these 8 per cent might be accounted for by naked shorts, that is, by overselling beyond the extra 15 per cent covered by the over-allotment option. Aggarwal (2000*a*) provides evidence that naked shorts are ubiquitous, amounting to 2 per cent (in excess of the typical 15 per cent over-allotment) on average. In 'weak' offerings (those priced below the indicative filing range), underwriters go short by 23 per cent in the pre-market and buy back 16 per cent of the issue in the after-market.

Finally, Ellis *et al.* (2000) find that price support is not costly to underwriters. This is because, as market-makers, they earn trading commissions that are large enough to offset any losses they might suffer on their net inventory. In fact, Ellis *et al.* find no significant difference in the inventory profits of underwriters of 'hot' and 'cold' IPOs, once the initial short position is included.[5] This is of interest because most theoretical models of price support assume that it is a costly activity for which underwriters need to be compensated.

---

[4] In fact, a simple calculation shows that underwriters should exercise the over-allotment option even for some 'cold' IPOs, as long as the price decline is smaller in magnitude than the dollar gross spread they earn. For the typical US IPO, we would expect to see underwriters exercise the over-allotment option unless the trading price has fallen by more than 7% below the offer price.

[5] Occasionally, price support can be very costly indeed. Newspaper reports have suggested that underwriter ABN Amro made a 1 billion guilder ($433.8 million) loss on its after-market trading in World Online during March and April 2000. The bank denied these reports, stating only that 'results from financial transactions increased by only 6.5% [for the first half 2000 ending 30 June 2000], largely as a result of trading losses following the World Online IPO' (see press release issued on 17 August 2000).

Trading profits, on the other hand, increase in initial underpricing, which might give underwriters an unwelcome incentive to increase underpricing. (The alternative, and more innocent, interpretation is that trading volume tends to be much larger for more underpriced issues, thus driving trading profits up.)

Rather than mopping up supply via stabilizing bids or trades, IPO syndicates can attempt to prevent investors from creating selling pressure in the first place. They can either do so explicitly, by assessing 'penalty bids', or implicitly, by linking an investor's allocations in future IPOs to her flipping behaviour in past IPOs. Penalty bids work as follows in the USA. Using detailed records of individual investors' trading behaviour once the market opens, the lead manager assesses each syndicate bank's flipping record and withholds selling commissions in respect of shares flipped by the bank's clients. This creates a strong incentive for syndicate members to allocate shares only to clients who they know, or expect, will hold the shares well into the after-market. Indeed, a recent federal class-action lawsuit against leading Wall Street underwriters alleges that brokers unlawfully force retail—but not institutional—buyers to hold on to their IPO shares for as long as 90 days.[6] Using regulatory notifications in a sample of 112 US IPOs between May and July 1997, Aggarwal (2000a) shows that almost half (54) of the syndicate contracts allowed for penalty bids, but that lead managers imposed penalty bids in only half (28) of those 54 cases. (In IPOs that perform strongly in the after-market, underwriters rarely impose penalty bids.) Underwriters thus use penalty bids less often, compared with stabilizing trades via short-covering transactions.

Implicit penalties, on the other hand, may be more important economically. By their very nature, such penalties usually escape academic scrutiny. Two exceptions are the well publicized practices employed by Wit Capital and Prudential Securities. Wit Capital's web site states that clients who flip within 60 days of the IPO will be given negative points which in turn will reduce the likelihood of their obtaining shares in future IPOs. Prudential Securities operates a similar points system, aimed at its syndication partners rather than retail investors directly.[7]

---

[6] For details, see Leefeldt (2000).

[7] Boehmer and Fishe (2000) argue that, far from discouraging flipping, underwriters have an incentive to encourage it. The incentive arises because underwriters' market-making profits

4.2.2   *Price support and underpricing*

Rather than forming a symmetric distribution around some positive mean, underpricing returns typically peak sharply at zero, are highly positively skewed, and include few negative observations. Figure 4.1 illustrates this. It shows a histogram of first-day initial returns for 6,002 IPOs in the USA between January 1985 and May 2000, as well as a superimposed normal distribution with mean and variance equal to the observed distribution. The non-normality and skewness are clearly visible. Ruud (1991, 1993) takes these statistical regularities, which she calls 'censoring',[8] as her starting point to argue that underwriters do *not* underprice deliberately: rather, they price IPOs at expected market value and support those offerings whose prices fall below the offer price in after-market trading. Such behaviour would tend to eliminate the left tail of the distribution of initial returns, and thus lead to the observation of a positive average price jump. According to Ruud, what we observe is not the unconditional expectation of true initial returns—which she argues might very well be zero—but the expectation conditional upon underwriter intervention: if price support suppresses the negative tail of the initial return distribution, companies merely *appear* to be underpriced on average. Ruud (1993) estimates the unobserved unconditional mean of the return distribution in a Tobit model and claims to find first-day returns close to zero.

Asquith *et al.* (1998) investigate whether observed underpricing is the byproduct of price support, as Ruud proposes, or whether it may have independent causes. First, they note that not all IPOs will be supported, and therefore there will be two distinct distributions of initial returns: one for supported offerings and one for unsupported ones. What one observes in any sample of new issues is the mixture of these two distributions. Using statistical techniques, it is possible to disentangle the two distributions and estimate their characteristics. If Ruud is correct in saying that there is no deliberate under-

increase in the amount of after-market trading; so to generate greater after-market trading underwriters can deliberately allocate shares to investors that are likely to flip. However, this is not inconsistent with underwriters discouraging small investors from flipping while allowing larger clients to sell.

[8] In fact, the distribution is only approximately censored, since overpriced issues do occur.

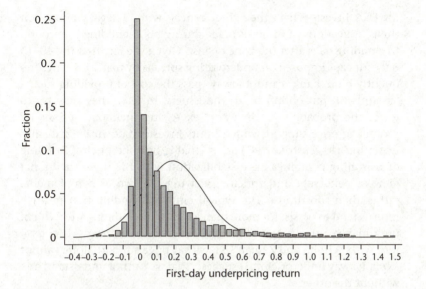

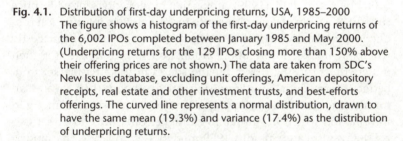

Fig. 4.1. Distribution of first-day underpricing returns, USA, 1985–2000
The figure shows a histogram of the first-day underpricing returns of
the 6,002 IPOs completed between January 1985 and May 2000.
(Underpricing returns for the 129 IPOs closing more than 150% above
their offering prices are not shown.) The data are taken from SDC's
New Issues database, excluding unit offerings, American depository
receipts, real estate and other investment trusts, and best-efforts
offerings. The curved line represents a normal distribution, drawn to
have the same mean (19.3%) and variance (17.4%) as the distribution
of underpricing returns.

pricing, then the initial return distribution of unsupported offerings
should have a mean of zero. This, however, is not what Asquith *et al.*
find. Instead, unsupported firms are underpriced by about 18 per
cent, while supported ones are not underpriced once the effects of
price support in eliminating the left tail of that distribution are taken
into account. Similarly, Prabhala and Puri (1999) calculate that 'censoring' can account for no more than 1.8 per cent of the 10.2 per cent
average underpricing in their sample.

Ruud's statistical view leaves many economic questions unan-
swered, not least why underwriters would want to provide price support. Schultz and Zaman (1994) suggest the following explanation. In

the USA, investors have the right to renege, without legal sanction, on their 'indications of interest' made during book-building for around five trading days after the issue opens.[9] Given the fact that the 10–15 per cent caps imposed on underwriting spreads by many US states frequently bind, banks cannot always pass the cost of providing such a 'cooling-off' put option on to the issuers. Instead, they may try to lower the probability of investors exercising their put options by promising price support, which limits investors' downside risk, and by setting a lower strike (IPO) price—that is, by underpricing. This line of reasoning combines price stabilization with the more traditional view of deliberate underpricing, viewing the two as complements rather than substitutes. The typical empirical finding that positive returns tend to persist for more than a month of trading—after which, presumably, price support should have been withdrawn—is consistent with Schultz and Zaman's view that price support alone cannot explain away underpricing. It suggests that we cannot understand one without the other.

Prabhala and Puri (1999) argue that underwriters provide price support as a form of commitment to more complete information production in the pre-market. Essentially, price support is most costly when pre-market information production is incomplete, for then underwriters run the risk of buying shares in the after-market from better informed traders. Promising price support then creates an incentive for the underwriter to reduce the pre-market asymmetry in information which in turn allows a higher offer price to be set (see e.g. Benveniste and Spindt's 1989 model). A corollary is that underwriters should end up supporting only offerings whose offer prices were set more accurately. Consistent with this prediction, Prabhala and Puri show on the basis of the SEC's X-17A-1 filings that underwriters are more likely to support low-risk offerings.

The innovation in Hanley *et al.*'s (1993) model is to view price support as insurance aimed primarily at rival market-makers, rather than IPO investors. As the evidence confirms, the price guarantee seems to lower market-makers' liquidity risk and accordingly leads them to charge lower bid–ask spreads, consistent with their downside risk being capped by the lead-managers' price-stabilizing limit order.

---

[9] Though whether they do is an open question: it may lead to loss of access to future IPOs.

As intervention ceases, prices for support candidates seem to fall while bid–ask spreads widen, although Schultz and Zaman (1994) show that, rather than resulting in banks trickling the acquired shares back into the market, intervention permanently reduces the supply of IPO shares—presumably because they started with a naked short position.

Benveniste *et al.* (1996) offer a different explanation of why under-writers provide price support, by formalizing Smith's (1986) informal notion of stabilization as a mechanism that 'bonds' underwriters and investors. As we discussed in the previous chapter, the fact that commission increases with gross flotation proceeds gives underwriters an incentive to set a higher offer price. Following a book-building exercise, they could for instance overstate investor interest and set an aggressive offer price. Clever IPO investors will recognize this adverse incentive and, in the absence of any counteracting force, may not cooperate in the book-building exercise in the first place. By commit-ting themselves to price support—which is costlier, the more the offer price exceeds 'true' share value—underwriters may convince investors that the issue will not be intentionally overpriced. If believed, this will allow the underwriter to reduce underpricing (cf. our discussion in Chapter 3). Of course, banks cannot be held legally to the price sup-port promises they make during the marketing phase, but perhaps the repeat nature of underwriting activities ensures that they do not renege, *ex post*, on their pledge. The lack of perfect pre-commitment, Benveniste *et al.* (1996) argue, will lead to greater deliberate under-pricing than if credible commitment were possible.

According to Benveniste *et al.*, the main beneficiaries of price support should be the institutional investors that participate in book-building.[10] Chowdhry and Nanda (1996) use the Rock (1986) frame-work discussed in Chapter 3 and predict that the main beneficiaries of price support are retail investors. Analytically, we can think of price support as a put option written by the underwriter and held by the ini-tial investors, in the sense that stabilizing activities put a floor under early after-market prices and thus act as insurance against price

---

[10] After all, if retail investors provide no pricing-relevant information in the pre-market, there is no reason to reward them by offering them price support. This is one—controversial—justification for the alleged practice of assessing penalty bids more often for retail than for insti-tutional investors; see also footnote. 6.

falls. This may reduce the winner's curse experienced by uninformed investors, which may be of particular importance in privatizations and private-sector IPOs with large retail tranches. Indeed, we may wonder why there should be any need to underprice in compensation for uninformed investors' winner's curse, as Rock argues, if investors are hedged against downside risk some or most of the time. Moreover, price support may be a more efficient way of counteracting the winner's curse than blanket underpricing, because price support is extended in the states of the world when uninformed investors suffer the most: overpriced offerings. Underpricing, on the other hand, is a blunter instrument because (absent price discrimination) it is offered to both uninformed and informed investors.

Benveniste *et al.* (1998) try to distinguish between the two predictions regarding who benefits from price support using detailed transactions data for 504 US firms floated in 1993 and 1994. They find that it is overwhelmingly large (presumably institutional) traders that execute sell orders in stabilized offerings, rather than small (presumably retail) traders. This lends support to the view that price support is offered mainly for the benefit of institutional investors, as modelled by Benveniste *et al.* (1996).

4.2.3 *Summary and conclusions*

To summarize, underwriters certainly have the opportunity, and may have a motive, to intervene in secondary market trading. There is abundant evidence that such intervention is widespread and that it has real effects on the trading behaviour of IPOs. What seems less credible is that price support alone can account for the empirical underpricing regularity, as Ruud initially postulated. More likely, stabilization is either a complement to underpricing or helps to mitigate it. The emerging consensus is that price support is best understood as one of the services underwriters sell, in a continuum of involvement spanning both the pre- and the after-market. Other services include making markets and providing liquidity, providing analyst coverage, and helping with later financing rounds. In Chapter 6 we will discuss a possible connection between price support and the long-run performance of new issues.

CHAPTER 5

Ownership and Control

Going public is, in many cases, a step towards the separation of ownership and control which is so characteristic of common law economies. The owner-manager who raises funds for investment from outside investors, the founder family that sells out to a new management team, or the firm that floats a minority stake in a subsidiary—all change the company's ownership structure in a flotation. Ownership matters for the effects it can have on the management's incentives to make optimal operating and investment decisions. In particular, where the separation of ownership and control is incomplete, an agency problem (Jensen and Meckling 1976) between non-managing and managing shareholders arises: rather than maximizing expected shareholder value, managers may maximize the expected private utility of their control benefits (say, perquisite consumption) at the expense of outsiders. The existence of such agency costs has long been recognized. However, they would appear to be particularly pertinent to small firms going public and raising large amounts of money, as opposed to the more usual scenario of rights issues by large already-listed companies whose managers hold only tiny equity stakes.

Two principal models have sought to rationalize the underpricing phenomenon within the bounds of an agency cost approach. Their predictions are diametrically opposed: while Brennan and Franks (1997) view underpricing as a means to entrench managerial control and the attendant agency costs by *avoiding* monitoring by a large outside shareholder, Stoughton and Zechner's (1998) analysis instead suggests that underpricing may be used to minimize agency costs by *encouraging* monitoring.

In this chapter, we will develop these two models in greater detail. In our view, this literature is interesting for the different interpretation it offers of underpricing. Similar to the undoing of Modigliani and Miller's (1958) famous capital structure irrelevance proposition, the choice of a particular level of underpricing will here affect the future cash flows of the firm and thus its value, implying that underpricing *per se* is not a valid measure of the efficiency of the flotation process.

5.1 Underpricing as a Means to Retain Control

Brennan and Franks (1997) develop a model in which underpricing gives managers the opportunity to protect their private control benefits by allocating shares strategically when taking their company public. Managers would wish to avoid a single investor assembling a large stake for fear that their non-value-maximizing behaviour would receive unwelcome scrutiny. By deliberately underpricing the flotation, they can ensure that the offer is over-subscribed and that investors will therefore need to be rationed in their allocations. Rationing, in turn, allows managers to discriminate between applicants of different sizes and so to reduce the block size of new shareholdings. With smaller new stakes there will be less monitoring, owing to two free-rider problems. First, because it is a public good, shareholders will invest in a sub-optimally low level of monitoring (Shleifer and Vishny 1986). Second, greater ownership dispersion similarly implies that incumbent managers benefit from a reduced threat of being ousted in a hostile takeover (Grossman and Hart 1980), giving them an added incentive to engineer a diffuse shareholder structure. We might expect that vigilant non-managing shareholders or outside directors could constrain managerial discretion when the offer price is set, but at least in the USA IPO firms have proportionately fewer outside directors than listed companies, while a majority (55 per cent) of the equity is held by management prior to going public (cf. Beatty and Zajac's 1995 survey of the 1984 IPO cohort). In Japan too, IPO firms are tightly controlled by directors, with unusually low institutional shareholdings (cf. Cai and Wei 1997).

5.1.1 *Testable implications and evidence*

The two principal testable implications to emerge from the Brennan–Franks model concern the relationship between underpricing on the one hand and the initial size and subsequent secondary market evolution of equity blocks on the other (cf. Table 5.1). Using detailed proprietary data on individual applications and allocations in 13 UK flotations, Brennan and Franks confirm that large applications are discriminated against in favour of small ones, an effect that is stronger the more an issue is underpriced and oversubscribed.[1] The US Securities and Exchange Commission, in its 1971 *Institutional Investor Study Report*, similarly reported that underwriters typically divide over-subscribed issues into very small allocations.

The obvious objection to Brennan and Franks's reasoning is that the effect of discriminatory allocations could easily be undone: shareholders receiving smaller-than-desired allocations could simply re-adjust their stakes in the secondary market. Brennan and Franks counter this objection by asserting that such open-market purchases may not be profitable. If the market anticipates the gains that would accrue if management were monitored by a sufficiently large outside shareholder, prices will rise in response to large-scale buying. This will tend to make it unprofitable to assemble a large block of shares in the after-market, the more so the more diffuse the ownership structure is to start with. In other words, the marginal cost of assembling large stakes in the secondary market must increase in the initial ownership dispersion at flotation for underpricing to be useful in entrenching management. If this is true, one would expect smaller blocks to be assembled after IPOs with greater underpricing. Using a larger sample of 43 new issues, Brennan and Franks confirm this prediction.

A somewhat unintuitive corollary of Brennan and Franks's model is the assumption that, for purely exogenous reasons, the non-managing shareholders (the 'non-directors') are keen to liquidate part of their

---

[1] The need for detailed data unfortunately limits Brennan and Franks's sample size: post-flotation ownership information is available for 43 firms, pre-IPO ownership data for 28, and allocation data for 13. The 69 IPOs that Brennan and Franks identify overall for 1986–9 represent less than 14% of all firms coming to market in that period, which raises some doubt as to the representativeness of the results.

Table 5.1. Ownership and control explanations of IPO underpricing

	Result	Source	Empirical evidence	
1	IPOs are deliberately underpriced to create, via oversubscription and rationing, a more *dispersed* ownership structure; this . . .	Brennan and Franks (1997)		
1a	. . . creates a free-rider problem which will minimize the possibility of challenges to the manager-shareholders' ('directors') control of the firm and thus will protect the private benefits they enjoy at the expense of non-directors			
1b	. . . provides a more liquid secondary market for the shares	Booth and Chua (1996)		
1c	. . . creates a free-rider problem which helps controlling owners to extract more surplus from a potential after-market buyer of the rest of the firm.	Zingales (1995)		
2	In order to protect their private benefits, directors use underpricing and the consequent over-subscription to discriminate against large applications and in favour of small ones.	Brennan and Franks (1997)	Yes: Brennan and Franks (1997) [UK] SEC (1971) [USA] No: Habib and Ljungqvist (2001) [USA]	
3	If rationing implies more diffuse shareholdings post-IPO, then it is more costly to assemble large stakes in the after-market; therefore, the higher underpricing, the smaller the blocks assembled after the IPO.	Brennan and Franks (1997)	Yes: Brennan and Franks (1997) [UK]	

4	Directors should not sell many shares, so their share of underpricing costs should be lower than non-directors'.	Brennan and Franks (1997)
5	The lower the fraction of underpricing costs borne by directors, the greater their incentives to use underpricing to protect their private benefits, so the greater is underpricing.	Brennan and Franks (1997) Yes: Brennan and Franks (1997) [UK]
6	IPOs are deliberately underpriced to create a more *concentrated* ownership structure; this ensures that managerial discretion is mitigated by monitoring through a large external shareholder.	Stoughton and Zechner (1998)

stakes. This ensures that the flotation can go ahead in the first place: otherwise non-directors' rational response to managers' flotation plans would be to avoid selling underpriced shares at the IPO by selling out in the after-market instead. The exogenous liquidity constraint that Brennan and Franks impose amounts to non-directors being held hostage by managers: either they surrender the pricing decision to the managers, or the company won't go public. Whether this is a reasonable assumption is best judged against the empirical evidence. Brennan and Franks show that non-directors sell as little as possible at the IPO (subject to the constraint of floating at least 25 per cent as required by the London Stock Exchange), while directors sell only a tiny fraction of their stakes at flotation. Moreover, over the following seven years, non-directors' holdings are almost entirely eliminated, while directors sell very little. This is consistent with non-directors evidently wanting to sell out but minimizing the underpricing cost.

The Brennan–Franks model predicts that underpricing is greater, the lower the fraction of underpricing costs borne by directors, since this increases their incentives to use underpricing to protect their private benefits. The evidence here is more mixed. It is true that directors, as predicted, sell fewer shares than non-directors and thus empirically suffer only half the underpricing costs that non-directors bear. But this may simply be due to managers owning smaller stakes —and thus having fewer shares to sell—than non-managing shareholders before flotation.

Finally, the Brennan–Franks model implies that managers, to ensure a wide distribution of stock, will deliberately underprice beyond what would be optimal in the absence of control considerations. Habib and Ljungqvist (2001 define optimal underpricing as that level which minimizes wealth losses when any action that might reduce underpricing further is costly. Wealth losses in their model are purely monetary and do not include non-monetary considerations such as private benefits of control. Their empirical findings, discussed in Chapter 3, suggest that US issuers do indeed choose underpricing so as to minimize their monetary-only wealth losses. In other words, they do *not* underprice beyond what would be optimal, and in particular, that they do not use underpricing to entrench their private benefits of control.

5.1.2 Why do firms go public?

By and large, the UK evidence reported in Brennan and Franks (1997) is consistent with their model. However, intent is very difficult to infer from any of it: directors may sell few shares at flotation, hold on to most of their holdings in the following few years, and be content with large applications being discriminated against, for reasons other than entrenchment. In particular, two rival models offer quite different interpretations of the value of greater ownership dispersion. Booth and Chua (1996) argue that owners do underprice, as in Brennan–Franks, in order to achieve a more dispersed ownership structure via over-subscription and rationing. But their motive for doing so is, innocently enough, to provide a more liquid secondary market for their shares. Zingales (1995), on the other hand, argues that firms seek a diffuse ownership structure in the IPO only in order to extract more surplus from a potential after-market buyer of the shares. Greater dispersion creates a free-rider effect not dissimilar to the one preventing outside shareholders from profitably assembling large after-market stakes in Brennan–Franks. Mello and Parsons (1998) use a model similar to Zingales's and find that an IPO aimed at dispersed shareholders generates valuation and demand information which the issuer can use in subsequent negotiations with potential buyers of controlling blocks.

Zingales, and Mello and Parsons, assume that an IPO is frequently only the first stage in a multi-period sell-out strategy which will culminate in the complete transfer of ownership and control from the original founders to new owners. Brennan and Franks, on the other hand, assume that the IPO is designed to *prevent* a transfer of control in spite of the partial transfer of ownership. Who is right? The empirical evidence is more nearly consistent with the staged-sale notion. Pagano *et al.* (1998) document that most Italian flotations are followed by private sales of controlling blocks to large outside investors. Indeed, control turnover is twice as common in newly listed firms as in the universe of unlisted companies. Högholm and Rydqvist (1997) report that over the first five years of listing control changes hands in 36 per cent of Swedish and 34 per cent of British IPO firms. In the USA, control turnover in the first five years is 29 per cent in IPO firms with at least five years of trading history prior to flotation and 13 per cent for younger companies (Mikkelson 1997). Similarly, officers and directors in US flotations on average own 66 per cent of equity before the IPO and 44 per cent immediately afterwards, which is reduced to 29 per cent over the subsequent five years, and to 18 per cent ten years later (Mikkelson *et al.* 1997).

Since these models go well beyond trying to explain why we observe underpricing, the key to distinguishing them is not to do with underpricing, but with the more fundamental question of why firms go public in the first place. In the Brennan–Franks' model firms are floated for exogenous reasons (non-managers wish to liquidate their stakes), while Booth and Chua, Zingales, and Mellow and Parsons base the going-public rationale on the potential benefits of a public listing (greater trading liquidity or efficient transfers of control).

Roëll's (1996) survey highlights three key reasons why companies go public: (i) to obtain liquidity for the company's shares which can increase the effectiveness of employee incentive schemes; (ii) to convey information, via the share price (and press coverage) about a company's prospects to customers, suppliers, employees, and potential providers of finance; and (iii) to access outside capital on more competitive terms. Pagano *et al.* (1998) find that Italian firms go public not to raise funds for further investments, but to consolidate their balance sheets in the wake of large-scale investment programmes. Following their listings, these companies also enjoy lower costs of credit.

5.1.3 *Discussion*

Whatever the empirical success of the Brennan–Franks model, there are at least two good reasons to doubt its practical relevance. First, if owner–managers are so worried about greater scrutiny, why don't they put in place takeover defences or simply issue non-voting stock? Field and Karpoff (2000) show that the majority of US firms deploy at least one takeover defence just before going public, especially when private benefits of control appear large and internal monitoring mechanisms look weak—that is, when managers' compensation packages are unusually generous, their own stakes are small, and non-directors play a smaller role in corporate governance. Note that these firms are still underpriced—though we do not know whether they are *less* underpriced than firms that choose to entrench their managers via the Brennan–Franks mechanism—so the protection of private benefits cannot be the only explanation of underpricing in the USA.

The UK is somewhat less lenient when it comes to allowing take-over defences, though companies have the option to issue non-voting shares.[2] This would guarantee that managers could retain control of the company and all attendant private benefits. Whether it dominates the Brennan–Franks underpricing mechanism is an empirical matter. Non-voting shares tend to trade at lower multiples than voting shares. This voting discount could be smaller or larger than the money left on the table via underpricing. Smart and Zutter (2000) find that US companies that issue non-voting stock in their IPOs are less underpriced and have higher institutional ownership after the IPO. This is consistent with the notion that non-voting stock can substitute for the Brennan–Franks mechanism. At the same time, Smart and Zutter find that non-voting IPO stock trades at lower multiples, though they do not investigate how these compare with the benefit of lower underpricing. Internationally, Brennan and Franks would predict no underpricing in countries where non-voting stock is regularly issued, as the control retention argument fails. However, many German and Swedish companies have floated only non-voting shares but have been underpriced, on average, by just as much as firms selling voting equity—which indicates that underpricing has causes independent of mere control considerations.

Moreover, if discriminating against potential monitors is so important in the UK, why not move to a system that optimizes discrimination? Book-building gives issuers wide-ranging discretion to discriminate against any investors on the basis of their identity. This is a much more refined way of fine-tuning the post-flotation ownership structure than the crude rationing strategy based on application size. As we have noted earlier, book-building is certainly quickly becoming the offering method of choice in continental Europe, and has been used in recent privatization offerings and other large

---

[2] It is often said that the London Stock Exchange (LSE) prohibits the issuance of non-voting shares. This is incorrect. It is true, however, that the LSE does not look favourably on companies issuing such shares.

international flotations in the UK (Wellcome's being a good example). But, far from eliminating the need to underprice, book-built IPOs still appear to be floated at the typical 10–20 per cent IPO discount!

5.2   Underpricing as a Means to Reduce Agency Costs

At the heart of the Brennan–Franks approach is the assertion that, in the wake of the separation of ownership and control, managers try to maximize their expected private utility by entrenching their control benefits. However, there is a hidden assumption underlying this belief which deserves discussion. Granting that managers' incentives are likely not to be perfectly aligned with owners' interests in many firms on the threshold of a public listing, managers may actually wish to allocate the issue in a way that minimizes, rather than maximizes, their scope for discretion. Why? Agency costs are ultimately borne by the owners of a company, in the form of a lower flotation and subsequent market value for their shares. To the extent that managers are part-owners, they bear some of the costs of their own non-profit-maximizing behaviour. If their stakes are large enough that the agency costs they bear outweigh the private benefits they enjoy, it will be in their interest to reduce, not entrench, their discretion. The post-flotation ownership structure may therefore increase firm value by affecting the efficiency of corporate governance.[3] Brennan and Franks must implicitly assume that this trade-off is, in practice, decided in favour of entrenchment.

Based on this intuition, Stoughton and Zechner (1998) observe that, in contrast to Brennan and Franks, it may be value-enhancing to allocate shares to a large outside investor who is able to monitor managerial actions. Monitoring, as we have already noted, is a public good. Since any large shareholder will monitor only in so far as this is privately optimal (which is a function of the size of her stake), there will be underinvestment in monitoring from the point of view of both shareholders and incumbent managers. To encourage better

---

[3] Cf. Burkart *et al.* (1997) for a formal analysis of the trade-off between too little monitoring (managerial discretion) and too much monitoring (intrusive interference in managerial initiatives).

monitoring, managers may try to allocate a particularly large stake to an investor. However, if the allocation is sub-optimally large from the investor's point of view, an added incentive may be offered in the form of underpricing. Such underpricing may not even represent an opportunity cost: in the absence of monitoring, the firm would have had to be floated at a lower price anyway, owing to outside shareholders anticipating the extent of managerial agency costs.

A closer look at Stoughton and Zechner's model is constructive. The selling mechanism is modelled as a two-stage process akin to book-building. In the first stage, issuers extract the demand schedule from a likely monitor and set the offer price such that this investor optimally chooses a large enough number of shares to engage subsequently in effective monitoring. In the second stage, small investors are allocated shares at the same price (unless price discrimination is possible, which in practice it rarely is). Rationing is observed at this stage, as small investors would like to buy further shares at the low offer price. The setup is reminiscent of Benveniste and Spindt's (1989), but here underpricing is not a measure of the efficiency of the selling mechanism. The Benveniste–Spindt argument turns on the value of the information that can be extracted from regular investors during the marketing phase and which allows firms to obtain a keener price in a two-stage sale than they would in an auction. In Stoughton and Zechner's model, on the other hand, underpricing is higher in a two-stage sale than in a Walrasian auction (where it would be zero), but that is beside the point: the auction would not allow the issuer to treat large investors favourably and thus reap the value-enhancing benefit of monitoring—which more than offsets the underpricing cost.[4]

As in the book-building literature reviewed in Chapter 3, owners would prefer a discriminatory allocation and pricing regime which would allow them to favour a potential monitor without extending the underpricing discount to small investors. Consequently, allocational freedom would lead to the optimal level of underpricing.

---

[4] Like Zingales (1995) and Mello and Parsons (1998), Stoughton and Zechner model a two-stage sale, but there is an important difference. Zingales, and Mello and Parsons, show that it is generally best first to distribute a fraction of the firm publicly in an IPO, and later to sell control to a blockholder. In contrast, Stoughton and Zechner (1998) argue that it is optimal first to satisfy the demand of the blockholder and then to allocate the remainder to small shareholders.

Empirically, we would expect that countries which prohibit price and/or quantity discrimination should experience higher underpricing, on average, than countries with lightly regulated offering mechanisms. This prediction is the same as Benveniste and Wilhelm's (1990) (cf. Chapter 3), but again the international evidence, reported in Loughran *et al.* (1994), is inconclusive: there is no clear empirical relationship between a country's offering mechanism and the level of underpricing it experiences.

5.3   Discussion

Why are the predictions of Brennan and Franks and Stoughton and Zechner so different? There are at least two reasons. The first is the different institutional environments in which the models are placed. Brennan and Franks effectively model a fixed-price, pro rata allocation open-offer regime, while Stoughton and Zechner model a fixed-price, discretionary allocation book-building regime. In a pro rata regime Stoughton and Zechner would have difficulty allocating enough stock to the large shareholder to ensure effective monitoring. In a book-building regime, Brennan and Franks would not need to underprice to discriminate against large investors. This illustrates the importance of the institutional assumptions made in IPO modelling.

Second, Stoughton and Zechner work on the assumption that managers internalize the agency costs they impose on outside investors, via the lower price that investors are willing to pay for the stock. This internalization is absent from the Brennan–Franks model.

The ownership and control dimension is a promising though as yet nascent field in the study of initial public offerings. Much more empirical evidence is needed before we can assess the validity of the theoretical contributions and before we can say whether control considerations are of first or second order when offer prices are set.

This concludes our overview of underpricing theories and evidence. We will return to these matters in Chapter 8, where we will offer our assessment of the theoretical literature as well as some suggestions on optimal pricing. In the meantime, we will turn our attention to theoretical explanations for the long-run underperformance phenomenon.

CHAPTER 6

Long-Run Performance

The most recently discovered stylized fact—the tendency of new issues to underperform in the long run—is the least well understood regularity in the IPO literature. Is it an equilibrium phenomenon that arises from some asymmetry in information endowments or from institutional peculiarities? Or are we faced with evidence of irrational behaviour by the investing public? Or is it instead simply a figment of our imagination, the result of our inability to measure long-run performance precisely, to control for risk correctly, or to devise statistical significance tests properly? The three sections of this chapter will explore these questions in turn, reviewing the existing conjectures, contributing new hypotheses, and assessing the available evidence.

At this point, a definitive answer still eludes us. The explanations that have been offered remain speculative in nature, owing to the relative lack of structured tests designed not merely to produce results consistent with some theory or other, but to falsify their testable predictions. However, recent methodological innovations indicate that there may not actually be any long-run underperformance requiring an explanation.

The first section concentrates on the question of whether long-run underperformance has any place in the underpricing models discussed in the preceding three chapters. Few studies have attempted to explain both underpricing and long-term underperformance in a unified framework. In some cases long-run performance results can shed light on the plausibility of an explanation for underpricing, as in the signalling approach whose long-term predictions meet with little empirical support. While the literature has barely begun to

explore the links between the two phenomena, at least one promising avenue for future research emerges here in the guise of price
support. The second section is devoted to expectations-based and
behavioural explanations of long-run underperformance, while the
final section addresses the problems of return and risk measurement
over extended event windows.

6.1   Long-Run Underperformance in Theories of Underpricing

6.1.1   *Signalling*

Of the asymmetric-information-based underpricing models surveyed
in Chapter 3, only the signalling and book-building theories have
anything to say about long-run performance. Rather than predicting
that newly floated companies will underperform in the long run, signalling theories seem to require *positive* after-market returns, given
that firms underprice in order subsequently to be able to sell further
shares at a higher price than in the absence of the signal. A falling
share price would hardly be consistent with the strategy of multiple-
stage sales assumed in the signalling approach: why delay divestment
if IPO firms on average perform poorly? Hence a rather obvious
empirical corollary is that only firms experiencing positive share
price performance should return to the equity market within a short
period of time.[1] This indeed seems to be the case in the USA, the UK,
and Germany.

Of course, long-run performance studies typically measure performance relative to some benchmark. Thus, the poor abnormal returns
we documented in Chapter 2 do not necessarily rule out that absolute
share prices at the time of subsequent equity sales are higher than
initial trading prices. However, it is easy to control for this, simply by
looking at both raw and excess returns. The average German IPO
firm, for instance, traded below its first-day price after three years

---

[1] This is assuming that the sole reason why firms sell seasoned equity is because they
planned to do so when they devised their signalling strategy for flotation. Of course, there are
plenty of other reasons for equity issues which will add noise to empirical testing.

(after adjusting for stock splits, etc.) and managed a *positive* raw three-year return (of 5 per cent) only as a result of dividend payments (cf. Ljungqvist 1997).

For the average IPO firm, therefore, signalling seems to make no sense. However, what is true on average may not be true across the quality distribution of issuers. In particular, if firms underprice to signal their quality, and if a separating equilibrium obtains in this game, high-quality firms should—perhaps by virtue of this signal—perform better than low-quality ones. A number of testable implications emerge. Assuming that companies do follow the underprice-to-signal strategy, (i) firms issuing seasoned equity should be high-quality (this is implied by successful separation); (ii) they should hence outperform non-reissuing firms, in terms of both share price performance (as discussed above) and operating performance; (iii) firms that underprice should exhibit superior post-listing performance relative to those that do not; (iv) in order to reap the benefits from signalling, any seasoned equity issue should be undertaken as soon as is possible lest the signal is dissipated; and (v) firms that float smaller equity stakes (in anticipation of later seasoned offers), which on the reckoning of the signalling models means high-quality firms, should outperform those retaining relatively small stakes.

The first prediction is hard to test, as any definition of what constitutes a high-quality issuer is inherently subjective. We are not aware of any direct attempts at making such a definition operational. The second prediction finds support at least as far as share price performance is concerned (cf. Table 6.1), although operating performance—as yet unstudied in the present context—would probably make for a more clear-cut test. Prediction (iii) is soundly rejected in every country in which it has been studied: greater underpricing and better long-run performance—be it share price (cf. Ritter 1991) or operating performance (cf. Jain and Kini 1994)—do not go hand-in-hand. The evidence we discussed in Chapter 3 does not indicate that firms return to the market sufficiently quickly for the underpricing signal not to be dominated by other information, violating prediction (iv). Finally, while the last prediction does receive some support in Singapore, it is contradicted by the German evidence.

In our view, the poor empirical performance of these predictions provides the final nail in the coffin of the signalling models. In

Table 6.1. Equilibrium explanations of IPO long-run performance.

	Hypothesis	Source	Empirical evidence
	Signalling		
1	Firms raising further equity financing after their IPO are high-value and hence outperform non-issuing firms.	–	Yes: Levis (1993b) [UK] Michaely and Shaw (1994) [USA] Ljungqvist (1996) [Germany]
2	Firms that underprice exhibit superior post-listing returns relative to those that do not.	–	No: Jain and Kini (1994) [USA] Ritter (1991) [USA] Ljungqvist (1996) [Germany] Cai and Wei (1997) [Japan]
3	The greater their quality, the more capital firms retain initially and the better they perform; thus, expected long-run returns increase in the retention rate.	–	Yes: Koh et al. (1992) [Singapore] No: Ljungqvist (1996) [Germany]
	Marketing		
4	Companies priced at the upper end of the initial price range should perform better than those priced at the lower end.	Hanley (1993)	No: Hanley (1993) [USA]
	Legal Liability		
5	The finding of underperformance is due to failure to include value of legal damages in performance evaluation.	Hughes and Thakor (1992)	No: Alexander (1993) [USA]

Price Support

6 The long-term underperformance finding may be due to price support; if so, firms whose shares were initially supported should underperform if measured from the first trading day, . . .	Ljungqvist (1995a)	Yes: Ljungqvist (1995a) [Germany]
7 . . . but should perform neutrally if measured from the date when support is withdrawn.	Ljungqvist (1995a)	Yes: Ljungqvist (1995a) [Germany]
8 *Corollary*: Firms not receiving price support should perform neutrally when measured from the first trading day.	Ljungqvist (1995a)	No: Ljungqvist (1995a) [Germany]

Agency costs

9 The less managers' equity stakes are reduced at flotation, the better the long-run operating performance.	–	Yes: Mikkelson *et al.* (1997) [USA]
10 The greater managerial equity stakes post-flotation, the better the long-run operating performance.	–	Yes: Jain and Kini (1994) [USA] No: Mikkelson *et al.* (1997) [USA] Cai and Wei (1997) [Japan]

Chapter 3 we discussed a number of reasons why we doubt their practical relevance, notably the fact that the underpricing signal may well be dominated, in cost-effectiveness terms, by the certification role performed by reputable investment bankers and other professionals. Here, we have argued that the long-run performance results are inconsistent with what are, in our opinion, logical implications of signalling, leading us to conclude that signalling retains little credibility as an explanation of underpricing.

6.1.2   *Theories of book-building*

Benveniste and Spindt (1989) model underpricing as a reward to better informed investors for truthfully revealing their information during the book-building phase. A noisy signal of the information these investors reveal is the direction and extent of the revision in the offer price relative to the initial price range: issues for which more positive information is revealed to the underwriter will see their offer prices revised upwards. However, as we explained in Chapter 3, the price revision will not be complete, as some money must be left on the table to reward investors for their truthful disclosure. Given this noisy signal, one might conjecture that subsequent performance will correlate positively with the initial price revision. This provides a cross-sectional implication, which is easily testable in the USA and other countries that use marketing mechanisms similar to book-building. Furthermore, it may even explain the existence of underperformance: if there are more cases of negative information than of positive information, long-run performance may well be negative on average. However, the only available evidence to date is unsupportive: firms priced above the initial range in Hanley's (1993) US sample did not fare any better than those priced below it. Perhaps this is not too surprising: given that the price revision is known at the issue time, it should have little long-term predictive power in an efficient market.

6.1.3   *Legal liability*

Hughes and Thakor (1992) argue that their legal insurance model of underpricing is consistent with long-run underperformance if, along with the underwriter, the issuer also is liable for damages. They interpret damages as extra 'dividends' paid out by the firm to its shareholders. IPO investors are effectively buying a package consisting of a share and a 'litigation put' which enables them to recover part of any subsequent losses from the issuer. Failing to include the monetary value of these 'litigation dividends' in calculations of long-run returns, the authors argue, will result in an understatement of true economic returns and may lead to the observation of spurious underperformance.

However, we do not concur with this view, partly for the reasons noted in Chapter 4, and partly because, as legal scholars such as Alexander (1993) have pointed out, in practice, 'litigation dividends' would not be available during the first three or five years of trading, the period over which underperformance is usually observed. Moreover, even before any 'litigation dividends' are actually paid, share prices should have adjusted to incorporate the expected value of such payments. Therefore, the share prices used to compute long-run performance should not understate true economic returns, unless the market is informationally inefficient or systematically underestimates the value of litigation payouts. Finally, the fact that litigation risk is not economically significant in many countries, such as most European and many Asian markets, which nevertheless experience underperformance, leads us to conclude that legal reasons can probably not explain the poor after-market returns earned by IPO firms.

6.1.4 *Price support*

In the first edition, we suggested that the practice of price support may well be consistent with both underpricing and poor long-term returns. The reason is that, if first-day trading prices are kept artificially high by supportive underwriters, they are the wrong starting point for a long-run performance evaluation. Once support is withdrawn, prices will adjust downwards to the true market equilibrium. Starting the clock on the first trading day thus wrongly leads to an observation of negative returns. If many IPOs receive such price support, it is conceivable that the resulting estimation bias is sufficiently large to lead to a spurious finding of abnormal underperformance.

We conjectured three testable implications: (i) offerings whose initial prices were supported should have poor long-run abnormal returns if measured from the start of trading, but (ii) not compared with the end of the support period; (iii) conversely, issues not initially supported should perform neutrally on average.

The principal difficulty in testing these predictions is one of identification: which new issues were initially supported, and at what time was support withdrawn? In the absence of such information, any test must rely on—invariably inferior—proxies. One approach is to argue that overpriced and fully priced IPOs are more likely to have been supported than underpriced ones, and to compare the long-run performance of overpriced issues with that of the cohort of *ex post* underpriced offerings. However, Ritter (1991) found a weak tendency for highly-underpriced IPOs to underperform more in his sample.[2] The more recent identification procedures which we discussed in Chapter 4 may hold more promise. Ellis *et al.* (2000) use detailed information on underwriters' subsequent market-making behaviour on NASDAQ to infer price support activities. Aggarwal (2000*a*) uses proprietary information on underwriters' short-covering transactions to identify price support. Benveniste *et al.* (1998) rely on transaction-by-transaction trading patterns to infer which IPOs were stabilized. And finally, Asquith *et al.* (1998) use a mixture-of-distributions procedure to investigate the effects of price support on underpricing. Using any or all of these identification procedures may help shed light on the interaction between price support and long-run performance.

6.1.5   *Agency costs: separation of ownership and control*

The operating performance literature has proposed an explanation for poor long-term performance based on Jensen and Meckling's (1976) conflict of interest between managers and shareholders. With the reduction in managerial ownership as a firm sells shares to a wide(r) circle of investors may come an increase in agency costs: managers' incentives to maximize firm value rather than private benefits (say,

---

[2] However, as Jay Ritter has pointed out to us, this may be due to the effects of stock price manipulation on IPOs with offer prices below $5, a segment of the market that has largely disappeared owing to tighter NASDAQ listing requirements.

perquisite consumption) decrease in the fraction of equity capital held by outside shareholders. Consequently, firm performance will suffer post-flotation—unless the relative size of the managers' stakes is unaffected by the transition to public ownership, as would be the case if the firm sold only either the non-managerial portion of a capital increase or secondary shares held by non-managing shareholders.

This idea can easily be put to a test. If issues in which the relative size of managers' equity stakes remains unaltered at flotation do not experience poor long-run operating performance, while firms whose managers' equity stakes are reduced at flotation do, agency costs may well explain declining operating performance. In addition to this change effect, there may be a levels effect: the greater are managerial equity stakes post-flotation, the better will a company perform in the long run. We will discuss the evidence in a moment. We note first, however, that Jensen and Meckling's divergence-of-interests hypothesis has been challenged outside the IPO literature. DeAngelo and Rice (1983) and Stulz (1988) argue that high levels of managerial ownership concentration may preclude the possibility of hostile takeover and thus limit the effectiveness of the market for corporate control in disciplining non-profit-maximizing managers. This entrenchment effect may lead managers to pursue private benefits at the expense of outside minority shareholders. Whether the entrenchment or divergence-of-interests effect dominates depends on the level of managerial ownership, a prediction supported empirically in Mørck et al. (1988) and McConnell and Servaes (1990).

At first glance, the IPO evidence seems mildly supportive of the existence of a divergence of interests. Mikkelson et al. (1997) find a positive relationship between operating performance and the change in the fraction of equity capital held by officers and directors in the USA: the more managers' stakes decline at flotation, the worse is post-listing operating performance. Curiously, while the authors concede that this correlation is consistent with the Jensen–Meckling explanation, they are reluctant to attribute it to it. As to the levels effect, the evidence is more mixed. Jain and Kini (1994), who do not discriminate between managers' and non-managers' relative participation in the public offering, find a positive relationship between post-flotation operating performance and overall retention rates, as predicted in the presence of Jensen–Meckling agency costs. Using a more comprehensive sample which partly overlaps with Jain and Kini's data, however, Mikkelson *et al.* instead find a negative relationship between the same variables. For Japanese issuers, Cai and Wei (1997) find no relationship between changes in profitability and managerial ownership.

Moreover, Loughran and Ritter's (1997) study of seasoned equity offerings casts doubt on divergence of interests as the primary determinant of poor operating performance: many already-listed firms are widely held when seasoned equity issues are initiated, but they experience the same pattern of anomalous declines in operating performance post-issue as do IPO firms. Given that a seasoned equity issue should not change the agency-cost status quo much, this would argue against a conflict-of-interest explanation.

However applicable the agency cost argument may be to the observed decline in operating performance following equity issues, it is a questionable explanation of long-run share-price underperformance. Rational IPO investors should take changes in managers' incentives into account when valuing newly listed firms. In other words, worsening agency problems should not come as a surprise and thus should not be reflected in poor returns. Hence increased agency costs cannot explain, in a semi-strongly efficient market, what happens to share prices.

6.1.6 *Discussion*

No underpricing theory predicted, before Ritter's seminal (1991) paper, that IPOs would underperform in the first few years after flotation. *Ex post* attempts at arguing that long-run underperformance is in fact consistent with this or that underpricing model have not, as we have argued, proved particularly fruitful. The one approach that we believe holds promise is price support. However, much more—and better!—evidence is needed before the practical merits of this idea become clear. In the meantime, we turn next to behavioural explanations of anomalous long-run performance.

6.2   Behavioural Explanations of Long-Run Underperformance

6.2.1   *Heterogeneous expectations*

E. M. Miller (1977) explores the effect on asset pricing of relaxing the usual assumption of homogeneous expectations. Allowing investors to have different opinions about the future cash flows and growth potential of an enterprise introduces an element of realism which perhaps can help explain long-run underperformance. A crucial feature of the model is that, given the small size of the typical flota-tion, a small number of investors is usually sufficient to absorb the firm's entire 'free float'. If there is divergence of opinion, this minor-ity will consist of those investors who are most optimistic about the company in question. Rather than reflecting the unbiased evaluation of all publicly available information, as the efficient-markets hypoth-esis would require, the market-clearing share price under heteroge-neous expectations will be set by the marginal investor who is just optimistic enough about the prospects of a company to buy its shares. This may account for the initial price jump: first-day buyers are particularly optimistic about the firm, and will buy even though it is widely known that no further underpricing gains can be hoped for beyond the opening trade. The very fact that there are investors who are willing to buy from staggers during the first few days, and thus hand these investors tidy underpricing profits, suggests there must be a fair amount of optimism around.

As the divergence in opinion becomes smaller, the marginal investor's evaluation and hence the trading price are lowered. If—as seems likely— heterogeneity is greatest at flotation but declines over time with the arrival of more information, the fact that a handful of once-optimistic investors adjust their beliefs about the value of the company will drive the price down, even though the *average* belief might never have changed. It is worth pointing out that the new information need not even be particularly negative: any piece of information that decreases the spread of opinion about a firm will lead to a lower price.

Applying Miller's model to long-run performance, two empirical implications arise. First, long-run performance should be negatively related to the initial extent of divergence of opinion. Second, it should also be negatively related to the speed with which hetero-geneity is reduced by new information: that is, long-run returns decline sooner, the faster expectations converge. The first prediction requires a measure of divergence of opinion. The recent literature has explored three possible proxies. Krigman *et al.* (1999) propose the ratio of sell-initiated large-block trading volume to total volume traded on the first day, which they call the 'flipping ratio', as a measure of the sentiment of institutions. Using US data, they find that IPOs that are flipped more on the first day underperform low-flipping IPOs over the next 12 months. Aggarwal and Conroy (2000) investigate the time-to-first-trade in the context of underpricing. Delaying the first trade may enable the underwriter better to gauge market demand and could thus be an indication of greater initial divergence of opinion. Aggarwal and Conroy document that under-pricing increases in time-to-first-trade. Houge *et al.* (2000) further show that late-opening IPOs significantly underperform over the sub-sequent three years. They analyse the relationship between long-run performance and the size of the bid–ask spread set by market-makers when the IPO opens. The bid–ask spread should at least in part reflect the market-maker's uncertainty regarding the company's value. Consistent with this interpretation, Houge *et al.* find that subsequent abnormal performance decreases in the opening spread. All three proxies support the first testable implication of Miller's model.

A test of the second implication requires a proxy for the speed of adjustment, or convergence, in beliefs. We are aware of no empirical work pertaining to this question.

One possible theoretical objection to Miller's model is that, logi-cally, there should be one pessimistic investor for every optimistic one, who via short-selling would put downward pressure on share prices such that firms are priced at (roughly) expected value. More precisely, since a market with many over-optimistic investors but a small number of arbitrageurs and a fully rational, homogeneous market are observationally equivalent (in the absence of market imperfections such as trading costs), there must be some structural or institutional reason why arbitrageurs cannot take advantage of the predictable trading patterns of Miller's model. The obvious such reason is the practical difficulty of implementing an IPO shorting strategy: casual empiricism, reported in Loughran and Ritter (1995), suggests that shorting new issues is hard even in a well-developed market such as the American one, at least in the first few months of trading. Houge *et al.* (2000) discuss some of the reasons why this may be. First, brokers can allow clients to short-sell only if delivery of the borrowed shares can be guaranteed, which effectively rules out short sales in the first few days, as share allocations are not distributed immediately. Second, short sellers face difficulty borrowing stock, as regulations and market practices restrict the potential supply of stock. Stock could in principle be borrowed from corporate insiders, syndicate banks, or investors holding shares in the after-market. However, insiders in most US IPOs (and increasingly in non-US IPOs as well) are 'locked-up' for some period of time following the IPO, usually 180 days, which prevents them from selling or lending their shares. Banks in the IPO syndicate are prohibited by the SEC from lending shares in the first 30 days of trading. And most IPOs involve such a small part of the equity that the 'free float' in public hands tends to be very small.

More seriously, perhaps, the accumulated evidence of poor IPO performance should sooner or later put pressure on the divergence of opinion—surely, even optimistic investors must eventually draw the conclusion that new issues are not worthy of such high expectations. Whether this learning process will, in the future, lead to the disappearance of the long-run performance anomaly remains to be seen. Meanwhile, Miller's model can potentially explain both initial underpricing and subsequent underperformance.

6.2.2 Fads, timing, and learning

It is only a small step from Miller's model to the claim that primary-market investors behave irrationally. Aggarwal and Rivoli (1990), for instance, argue that there are fads in the IPO market, with investors initially being over-optimistic about the prospects of newly listed companies and bidding up initial trading prices beyond fair value. This assertion goes to the heart of traditional underpricing models, which assume that the immediate after-market values a flotation efficiently. According to Aggarwal and Rivoli, one cannot rule out the possibility that it is the—lower—long run rather than the initial trading price that reflects a firm's true value. This would imply that the notion of IPO underpricing is a misnomer: the first-day price jump is due not to the offer price having been set too low, but rather to faddish investors overvaluing a firm when trading starts. However, this raises two questions: (i) why don't investors learn from past mistakes? and (ii) why don't issuers take full advantage of investors' overoptimism by raising offer prices until there is no longer a price jump?

There is some evidence that may indicate that investors indeed consistently overestimate the future prospects of firms coming to market. Mikkelson *et al.* (1997) show that long-run share price performance and the change in operating performance from before to after flotation are negatively related: when operating performance fails to sustain pre-listing levels of profitability, share prices fall, indicating that investors were surprised by the change in operating performance. Brav and Gompers (1997) show that returns of IPO firms are highly correlated in calendar time even if firms go public in different years, pointing to common factors affecting IPOs at certain times. As further evidence consistent with investor sentiment, Brav and Gompers document that underperformance is concentrated among small, non-venture-backed companies. These are the sorts of companies whose stock is more likely to be owned by individuals, who in turn *may* be more easily influenced by fads or lack of complete information. Jain and Kini (1994) document that at flotation investors value IPO companies at unusually high price–earnings and market–book ratios (compared with matched non-issuers), but that these decline significantly over time in line with the fall in operating performance. What this proves is unclear, however. Given recent evidence on the cross-section of expected returns (cf. Fama and French 1992), we note that the market–book ratio may be a proxy for non-beta risk factors as well as for investors' expectations of future earnings growth.

Loughran *et al.* (1994) go one step further than Aggarwal and Rivoli. Noting a curious coincidence of years in which many firms go public and the buoyancy of the equity market, they assert that companies may be able to predict when over-optimism is most likely to occur. If so, firms will time their flotations to coincide with these windows of opportunity during which particularly favourable offer prices can be obtained. As more information becomes available, investors correct their initial overvaluation, leading to poor long-run returns.

This, of course, is a much stronger claim than the mere existence of fads. Loughran *et al.*'s explanation rests on the—perhaps tenuous—assumption that companies are somehow able to distinguish between a temporary fad, which will soon revert to normality, and a sustainable rise in valuations. Even if it is true that investors consistently and mistakenly extrapolate past earnings growth when valuing newly listed firms (and as a result overpay), the claim that companies can predict time variations in investor sentiment is certainly contentious.

The empirical evidence, listed in Table 6.2, is mixed. Consistent with the existence and exploitation of windows of opportunity, Loughran and Ritter (1995) note that subsequent stock price performance is significantly lower for companies going public in 'hot' markets. Helwege and Liang (1996*b*) investigate this claim further, by examining the quality of firms coming to market in hot and cold markets. IPO signalling models suggest that hot markets draw in higher-quality issuers, whereas the over-optimism hypothesis links hot markets to managerial opportunism and investor irrationality. Interestingly, the authors find no difference in operating performance (their measure of issuer quality) between hot-market and cold-market issuers, though they do corroborate Loughran and Ritter's (1995) claim that hot-market issuers have worse stock-price returns. Ali (1995) investigates whether the market's estimates of the prospects of IPO firms are optimistically biased. Comparing the 'optimistic bias' in analysts' consensus earnings forecasts for issuers and matched non-issuers, he finds that, while analysts tend to be unduly optimistic in general, they are more over-optimistic about issuers than about non-issuers. Moreover, this bias is greatest for smaller issuers, which Ritter (1991) and Loughran and Ritter (1995) show underperformed particularly badly. Rajan and Servaes (1997) also look at analysts following after the IPO and find that, not only are analysts over-optimistic about earnings and long-term growth prospects, but issuers may take advantage of windows of opportunity: more US companies went public when analysts were particularly over-confident about recent IPOs in the same industry. Interestingly, IPOs with low forecast growth rates subsequently outperform IPOs with high forecast growth rates, by a margin of more than 100 per

Table 6.2. Behavioural explanations of IPO long-run performance

	Result	Source	Empirical evidence	
	Heterogeneous expectations			
1	Share prices are set by the marginal, most optimistic investor; as information flows increase with seasoning, divergence of expectations decreases and thus prices are adjusted downwards; long-run performance is negatively related to the initial extent of divergence of opinion.	Miller (1977)	Yes: Houge et al. (2000) Krigman et al. (1999) Aggarwal and Conroy (2000)	[USA] [USA] [USA]
2	Long-run returns decline sooner, the faster expectations converge.	Ljungqvist (1995a)		
	Fads and timing			
3	Firms go public when investors are over-optimistic about the growth prospects of IPO companies; investors overpay initially but mark prices down as more information becomes available; expected long-run returns therefore decrease in initial investor sentiment.	Loughran et al. (1994) Loughran and Ritter (1995) Ritter (1991) Rajan and Servaes (1994)	Yes: Rajan and Servaes (1994) Rajan and Servaes (1997) Lerner (1994) Helwege and Liang (1996b) Loughran and Ritter (1995) Jain and Kini (1994) Teoh et al. (1998b) Mikkelson et al. (1997) Ali (1995) Cheng (1996) *seasoned issues*	[USA] [USA] [USA] [USA] [USA] [USA] [USA] [USA] [USA] [USA]

	No:	Högholm and Rydqvist (1995) [Sweden]
		Ljungqvist (1996) [Germany]
		Leleux (1992) [USA]
		Lee (1997) *seasoned issues* [USA]
		Bossaerts and Hillion (1998) [USA]

4 The greater the fraction of equity capital initial owners retain at flotation, the lower their incentive to take advantage of over-optimistic investors, since the value of their retained shares would fall as and when the new investors become less optimistic; therefore, expected long-run returns increase in the retention rate.

Ljungqvist (1996)

Yes: Koh *et al.* (1992) [Singapore]

No: Ljungqvist (1996) [Germany]

cent over five years. Lerner (1994) finds that venture-backed biotech-nology firms appear to have timed their IPOs to coincide with peaks in stock market valuations, and choose private venture capital financ-ing when public-market valuations are low. Cheng (1996) shows that US companies which are expected not to use the proceeds of sea-soned equity issues for investment purposes underperform more than investing firms, a finding that is consistent with the non-investing firms selling equity because they are overvalued (cf. Myers and Majluf 1984). The fact that both types of issuer significantly underperform the market is troubling, though: granted that the non-investing firms underperform solely because they 'timed' their issue, why do the investing firms also underperform?

On the other hand, Leleux (1992) finds a negative relationship in the USA between the extent of initial underpricing and the time to dis-tressed delisting, which he argues is inconsistent with investor over-reaction: if investors did initially overpay as a result of over-optimism, underpricing should be unrelated to fundamental firm value, and therefore should not affect attrition rates. The fact that firms that are relatively more underpriced are delisted sooner than less underpriced ones instead suggests that underpricing leaves firms undercapitalized.[3] For seasoned offerings, managers have no incentive to 'market time' in countries with pre-emptive rights, as no wealth transfers from new to existing shareholders are involved. Nevertheless, South Africa—where this is the case—has a similar degree of long-run underperformance to that of the USA (see Affleck-Graves and Page 1995). Looking at the effect of various proxies for investor sentiment on long-run perfor-mance, Ljungqvist (1996) fails to find any evidence of companies' supposed timing ability in Germany. And finally, I. Lee (1997) shows that directors' and other insiders' trading in the USA is unrelated to performance subsequent to seasoned equity issues, which strongly suggests that, despite their presumably superior information, man-agers share the market's mistaken expectations of future cash flows.

In an innovative paper, Bossaerts and Hillion (1998) question whether IPO underperformance violates investor rationality and

---

[3] Incidentally, Leleux's results throw yet more doubt on signalling explanations of under-pricing: to the extent that it is high-value firms that signal, they should survive for longer, which is not the case empirically.

informational market efficiency. They argue that it is unrealistic to demand of the market to have correct beliefs, at the time of each IPO, about all return-relevant future events. Therefore, *ex post* IPOs can very well be subject to a degree and time profile of 'failure' that was not foreseen at the time of flotation, thus generating negative abnormal returns on average. Moreover, efficient pricing and investor rationality does not require the market to have unbiased beliefs at the time of each IPO—so overly optimistic IPO investors are not inconsistent with rational pricing, as we know from Miller's (1977) model with restrictions on short sales. What rationality does require is that investors 'learn', meaning that they update their prior beliefs as new information arrives using Bayes's Rule. This implies that investors should not hold on to beliefs proven false by subsequent events. Using this logic, Bossaerts and Hillion test whether the long-run underperformance in Ritter's (1991) data reflects overly optimistic beliefs at the IPO date, or subsequent failure to 'learn'. Overall, they find little evidence that changes in the market's beliefs were irrational, but beliefs held on the first day were over-optimistic in the sense of underestimating the subsequent failure rate of the IPOs. This implies that new information is incorporated efficiently into prices, satisfying the standard definition of market efficiency. This result holds in the sample as a whole. Interestingly, it does not hold among IPOs with low offer prices: here, the authors do find evidence of over-reaction to subsequent news pertaining to the likelihood of failure. Since low-priced offerings also tend to be smaller, and smaller offers are more likely to be aimed at retail investors, it is possible that retail investors' learning behaviour is systematically different from that of institutional investors. If so, it would be interesting, in time, to apply the Bossaerts–Hillion test to the internet IPOs of 1998 and 1999.

6.2.3 *Window-dressing*

A final link in the behavioural chain is firms' incentives actively to encourage optimistic views of future performance. The US literature has shown that companies typically go public after what appears to be particularly strong operating performance, but then fail to sustain the growth rates achieved in the year or two before flotation. While it is possible that the original owners float their companies after periods of genuinely strong performance, which they—unlike investors— know cannot be sustained in future, it is equally likely that pre-issue performance has been deliberately overstated.

DeGeorge and Zeckhauser (1993) point out that managers have extraordinary incentives to make their firms 'shine' before flotation. To use their example, consider a manager who owns 10 per cent of a firm that normally earns US$1 million and that will sell at eight times earnings when it goes public. Every US$1,000 increase in pre-flotation earnings means another US$800 for the manager. Compare this with typical performance-related pay sensitivities—Jensen and Murphy (1990) report that a US$1,000 increase in firm value raises median CEO remuneration by a mere US$26—and it is not surprising that managers endeavour to present the best possible figures in their prospectuses.

There are several ways in which managers can engage in 'window-dressing'. First, they can 'borrow' earnings from other periods. To borrow from the future, simply lower prices temporarily to boost sales now, or defer any spending (R&D, staff training) whose returns will occur only in the longer term. Similarly, past performance can be borrowed by slowing down earnings growth in the year before the flotation year. The effect will be stellar performance just before the IPO, with a later decline in operating performance. Of course, investors will expect this and will therefore downgrade the multiple they are willing to pay. Earnings manipulation and the subsequent post-IPO operating performance downturn should not come as a surprise and so should have no share price effect. This is, of course, not true empirically of IPOs.[4] Second, US generally accepted accounting principles (GAAP) give IPO firms great freedom to massage their earnings before initial or seasoned equity issues, including the authority to restate *retroactively* all financial information presented in prospectuses, mainly through the use of accruals. There is evidence, reported

---

[4] However, DeGeorge and Zeckhauser find it to be true for US leveraged buy-outs (LBOs) that are subsequently refloated: they have the same operating performance pattern as IPOs but perform neutrally compared with matched firms in terms of share price. Reverse LBOs are different from IPOs in that, having been traded before, more information is available about them at re-flotation. They are also similar to large IPOs in terms of size, which Ritter (1991) shows are less likely to underperform in the long run. Thus, the neutral performance of reverse LBOs does not necessarily contradict the evidence of IPO long-run underperformance.

in Teoh *et al.* (1993), that IPO firms make extensive use of this free-dom. Finally, managers could fraudulently overstate their earnings performance, an option that may seem a distinct possibility in some less regulated markets around the world, but which empirically plays only a minor role in the USA (cf. Teoh *et al.* 1998*b*).

While earnings management may explain the poor post-issue oper-ating performance, rational investors should not be fooled, and con-sequently the share price performance should be unaffected by discretionary accounting practices. However, we know this is not the case. In fact, Teoh *et al.* (1998*a*, *b*) and Rangan (1998) show that earn-ings management and long-run excess returns are significantly nega-tively related in initial and seasoned offerings. This may suggest that investors are fooled by such discretionary accruals adjustments and initially fail to fully discount them. Having overestimated future cash flows at flotation, investors mark down share prices when the expected high level of profitability fails to materialize. Mikkelson *et al.* (1997) findings, discussed earlier, paint a similar picture.

Finally, there is now evidence that IPO firms strategically 'purchase' after-market research coverage when choosing their underwriters, and that underwriters issue positively biased research recommendations in the first year after the IPO. Krigman *et al.* (2001) survey 572 US firms that completed seasoned equity offerings within three years of their IPOs. Those that switched to a different underwriter appear to have done so either to 'trade up' to a bank with more prestigious research analysts or to increase the amount of coverage they receive. Why do issuers care about research coverage? Partly because they hope for increases in share prices following from greater investor interest; but perhaps also partly because there is an implicit under-standing that underwriters will put out *positive* recommendations. Michaely and Womack (1999) present evidence that lead underwriter-affiliated analysts are more likely to issue buy recommendations after an IPO than are independent analysts, and that they do so after share price declines. An efficient market should see through the conflicts of interest and should discount affiliated buy recommendations relative to independent ones. Indeed, this appears to be the case—the market reaction to the former is less positive than to the latter—but not suffi-ciently so: IPOs recommended by their own underwriters underper-form IPOs recommended by independent brokers by more than 50 per cent over two years. Investors thus appear to be fooled by the systematic bias in underwriters' 'buy' recommendations.[5] While Rajan and Servaes's (1997) results of analyst behaviour can be read as evidence of 'innocent' over-optimism, Michaely and Womack's results hint at deliberate biases in analyst reports.[6] To distinguish between these alternative motivations, one might investigate whether investment banks' reputation capital suffers from promoting IPOs that subsequently underperform. While no study we know of addresses this question directly, Nanda *et al.* (1995) document that underwriters lose IPO market share following poor long-run performance—but not if they are highly ranked, established underwriters. This is partly because IPOs underwritten by highly ranked banks perform better in the long run (Carter *et al.* 1998). But it may also imply that the market sees no duplicity in the poor realized performance of their IPOs. It would be interesting to study the connection between underwriters' loss of market share and their research coverage, for a given level of reputation. One might expect that the market penalizes banks that promote recent IPOs in an 'excessively' biased fashion.

In summary, the empirical patterns are consistent with managers playing to investors' over-optimism by 'massaging' accounting ratios to create the impression of superior pre-flotation performance ('window-dressing') and hiring investment banks at least partly to get favourable research coverage, and investors failing to figure such behaviour into prices. Again, however, the crucial question arises: why don't investors learn? Until a convincing structural or institutional answer is forthcoming, we find it hard to believe that behavioural explanations can solve the new issues puzzle.

---

[5] In an unpublished but interesting paper, Dunbar *et al.* (1997) take issue with Michaely and Womack's (1999) analysis. They point out that first (as opposed to later) buy recommendations by affiliated analysts are uninformative, since, by underwriting the IPO, the lead manager has implicitly rated the stock a 'buy'; reiterating this 'buy' recommendation shortly after the IPO adds no further information. Dunbar *et al.* argue further that the post-recommendation long-run underperformance in Michaely and Womack (1999) is due to a subset of firms for which affiliated analysts reverse their initial 'buy' recommendation.

[6] With the virtual disappearance of 'sell' or even 'hold' recommendations in the USA, the bias may well have increased in recent years.

6.3   Measurement Problems

Underperformance could have a more trivial cause: it might simply be due to bad luck. Welch (1996) points out that the companies driving Ritter's (1991) results were small, infrequently traded, and bunched in certain specific industries (most notably, oil and gas exploration in 1980) that subsequently experienced industry-specific exogenous shocks (for instance, the oil price collapse in the early 1980s). Can we therefore rule out the alternative explanation that long-run underperformance is merely due to bad luck? Perhaps not, but the overwhelming evidence from around the world suggests that IPOs are indeed poor long-term bets in need of an explanation.

A growing literature questions the methodology used in many of the early empirical long-horizon studies. The three main methodological building blocks in such studies are the choice of benchmark defining the 'normal' or 'expected' return, the measurement of investor returns over long horizons, and the test statistic used to accept or reject neutral performance. Fama (1998) calls benchmark-related issues the 'bad-model problem'. Any test of long-run performance is a joint test of the validity of the chosen benchmark and of sample performance relative to that benchmark. Since there is no benchmark model that correctly prices all securities all of the time (see e.g. Fama and French's 1992 critique of the Capital Asset Pricing Model), the 'bad-model problem' is unavoidable. Few long-run performance studies have acknowledged this problem explicitly.

The early studies of American IPOs, and most studies of IPOs outside the USA, compared IPO returns to returns on market-wide stock indices. This implies the—unstated—assumption that all IPO companies have average systematic risk, or that their betas are equal to one. Clearly, this can seriously bias long-run performance estimates if betas are in fact not equal to one. If, as seems likely, IPOs typically have greater-than-average market risk, then wrongly imposing unit betas will lead to a spurious finding of underperformance when the market index falls over the holding period. Of course, the converse is also true: falsely imposing unit betas in a rising market will impart an upward bias in performance estimates if true betas are greater than one. Which way the bias will go in practice depends on the empirical question of whether IPOs trade mostly in rising or declining markets. Moreover, studies that use index-adjusted returns implicitly assume that systematic risk is constant over time. However, investors' required risk premia could well change over time. Clarkson and Thompson (1990), for instance, document non-stationary betas for IPO firms in the USA, with betas declining from their initial high levels. However, this alone does not appear sufficient to remove the underperformance result: those authors (listed in Table 6.3) who have tried to adjust for time-varying beta risk still find that newly listed firms underperform.

Beginning with Ritter (1991), long-run studies of US IPOs have generated abnormal return estimates by matching issuing and non-issuing firms on the basis of criteria observed at the time of the IPO. Ritter, for instance, matches on firm size and industry. This procedure is in logic similar to a two-factor arbitrage pricing theory (APT) model where the required risk premia relate to size and industry affiliation and—because firms are not rematched—remain constant over time. Later studies (notably Loughran and Ritter 1995; Brav and Gompers 1997) match on size and book-to-market ratio instead of size and industry. Interestingly, long-run underperformance tends to disappear when book-to-market effects are controlled for or when penny stocks (with offer prices below $5) are excluded. But since many financial economists have difficulty providing an economic intuition for this factor, it is unclear why the performance of IPO firms should track that of non-IPO firms with similar book-to-market profiles.

As an alternative to matching firm by firm, some studies use the Fama–French (1992) three-factor model estimated over portfolios of issuing and non-issuing firms. This implies an asset pricing model that is effectively an APT model with a market (beta) factor, as well as size and book-to-market effects. In an attempt to better understand the underlying economic rationale for the book-to-market effect, Eckbo and Norli (2000) add two further factors to this: namely, leverage and liquidity. They document that IPO firms in the USA have systematically lower financial leverage than matching firms (which is logical given their young age, clustering in 'new' industries, and the equity infusion of the IPO itself) and are therefore less sensitive to interest rate and inflation shocks than are matching firms. Similarly, IPO firms appear to be more liquid and thus to require lower liquidity-risk premia. The upshot is that the required returns of IPO firms

Table 6.3. Mis-measurement explanations of IPO long-run performance

Result	Source	Empirical evidence
Mis-measurement of risk		
1 Studies of long-run performance suffer from the 'bad-model problem': they are joint tests of the validity of the return-generating benchmark and the presence of anomalous returns. Results are sensitive to small changes to the benchmark.	Fama (1998)	Yes: Brav and Gompers (1997) [USA] Brav et al. (2000) [USA] *Negative abnormal returns disappear if value-weight or match on book-to-market*
2 The market risk of IPOs is time-varying.		Yes: Clarkson and Thompson (1990) [USA]
2' Failing to account for this can induce spurious long-run underperformance.		No: Ritter (1991) [USA] Keloharju (1993b) [Finland] Ljungqvist (1995a) [Germany]
Mis-measurement of long-run returns		
3 Published studies of long-run performance suffer from the following biases: (i) rebalancing bias; (ii) skewness bias; (iii) new listing bias; and (iv) pre-event survivor bias.	Barber and Lyon (1997) Kothari and Warner (1997)	
Mis-measurement of significance		
4 Significance tests in published studies of long-run performance suffer from failure of cross-sectional independence.	Brav (2000) Mitchell and Stafford (2000)	

are in fact lower than those of matching firms. Failure to control for this will tend to lead to spurious estimates of IPO underperformance.

In addition to questions about the correct asset pricing model to be used, questions have been raised about the statistical properties of long-run performance measurement. Barber and Lyon (1997) show that long-horizon studies are subject to three biases. (i) *Rebalancing bias* arises where studies use an equally weighted reference portfolio (such as a stock index) as benchmark. The compound returns on the reference portfolio are typically calculated assuming periodic (generally monthly) rebalancing, while the returns of sample firms are compounded without rebalancing. This results in an inflated return on the reference portfolio, since the rebalancing removes recent 'losers' and promotes recent 'winners'. The abnormal returns of sample firms are therefore negatively biased. (ii) *Skewness bias* arises when long-run abnormal returns are computed relative to an index. Since indices are suitably weighted averages of many companies, index returns are much less likely to be very large in absolute magnitude than are the returns on individual sample firms. Very large abnormal returns, defined as the difference between sample and index returns, are therefore overrepresented in the sample compared with a normal distribution. Even a small amount of positive or negative skewness can result in observed average abnormal returns that seem very large in absolute magnitude. In the IPO context, a handful of particularly bad performers might be enough to generate a highly negative average abnormal return. At the same time, skewness bias reduces statistical power, since the extreme abnormal returns not only affect the average but also increase the standard deviation of the abnormal returns. (Barber *et al.* 1999 propose test statistics that adjust for skewness.) (iii) *New listing bias*, finally, arises because newly listed firms are usually not represented equally in the sample and the index. For instance, in studies of the long-run performance following seasoned equity offerings, the index is likely to contain more newly listed firms than is the SEO sample. Abnormal returns will then be negatively biased if newly listed firms have a tendency to underperform. However, this to us appears to be a non-sequitur: Barber and Lyon's new listing bias accepts the stylized fact that IPOs underperform, when it is equally possible that the appearance of IPO underperformance is due to the rebalancing and skewness biases. The more general point, crystallized by Kothari and Warner (1997) and Fama (1998), is that particular firm character-istics may not be represented equally in the sample and the bench-mark: sample firms may be smaller than benchmark firms, may have lower book-to-market ratios, higher beta risk, and so on.

Based on their analysis, Barber and Lyon (1997) propose that sample firms be matched to control firms on the basis of company characteristics (book-to-market and size), where eligible control firms have been purged of recent IPOs to avoid the new listing bias. Kothari and Warner (1997), however, note that this may lead to another bias. Requiring that control firms have been listed for (say) five years induces pre-event survivor bias: IPOs firms would be matched with firms that have performed well enough to have survived for at least five years. This causes standard parametric test statistics to violate the usual zero-mean and unit-normality assumptions and therefore to be mis-specified. There is thus a trade-off between Barber and Lyon's new listing bias and Kothari and Warner's pre-event survivor bias. Kothari and Warner's preferred solution is to ensure that control firms and sample firms are subject to similar biases.

Loughran and Ritter (1995), Kothari and Warner (1997), Brav (2000), and Mitchell and Stafford (2000) argue that test statistics suffer from failure of independence of observations. The long-run performance of different firms may in fact be correlated in calendar time. This would be the case, for instance, where internet companies go public in a cluster and subsequently perform alike in the wake of 'internet euphoria' or 'disillusion'. This will tend to reduce the cross-sectional variance in abnormal returns and thus to overstate their significance. As a remedy, these authors propose to use 'bootstrapping', a technique based on a simulated return distribution. Fama (1998) proposes an alternative used by Jaffe (1974) and Mandelker (1974) in the 1970s. The essence of the Jaffe–Mandelker approach is to treat the internet companies in the previous example as a single observation, recognizing that they will behave alike.

Where does this leave us? Fama (1998) concludes that 'the apparent [long-run performance] anomalies are methodological illusions' (p. 285). He argues that even small changes to the methodology can change the empirical results. Loughran and Ritter (2000), on the other hand, argue that abnormal performance *should* be sensitive to methodology because different methodologies have different power.

Loughran and Ritter (1995) find that IPOs underperform size-matched control firms in their 1970–90 sample period. However, Fama and French (1993) have shown that average returns during that period were subject to book-to-market effects, in the sense that small growth stocks performed poorly. Not controlling for this effect among IPOs—many of which are small growth stocks—might therefore bias the results. Consistent with this prediction, Brav and Gompers (1997) document that Loughran and Ritter's IPO underperformance anomaly disappears entirely when control firms are selected on the basis of book-to-market in addition to size. Brav *et al.* (2000) document the same effect with respect to the apparent long-run underperformance following SEOs. This indicates that there is no 'new issues puzzle' (the title of the Loughran–Ritter 1995 paper). Instead, the puzzle may be why small growth stocks in the 1970s and 1980s performed so poorly. Maybe—but outside the USA—a new issues puzzle may survive: Kang *et al.* (1999) find that Japanese SEOs are followed by significant underperformance even when controlling for size and book-to-market as in Brav and Gompers (1997) and Brav *et al.* (2000). And some of the more recent long-run IPO studies summarized in Table 2.2 above employ similarly sophisticated methodology and yet find abnormally poor performance. This underscores one of the themes of this book: the importance of investigating IPO phenomena from an international perspective rather than a US-centric one.

Part III

POLICY IMPLICATIONS

CHAPTER 7

Privatization

Privatizations constitute a particular class of initial public offerings, where the vendor is not an entrepreneur (or private investor) but rather the government. In practice, therefore, the main beneficiary of a privatization is usually the Treasury, rather than the company itself, although privatizations are often accompanied by financial restructurings of the companies concerned. In part as a result of the sheer scale of many privatizations, a number of governments have looked seriously at the alternative ways of structuring the IPO, and have, in some cases, been quite innovative in their approach. We identify some of these innovations in this chapter. Governments were among the first to include foreign investment banks in IPO syndicates, to use book-building techniques for pricing and allocation, to introduce multi-tranche IPOs with blocks of shares reserved for particular groups of investors (such as small investors, or overseas investors), to attempt to limit the downside risks faced by investors, and to negotiate (down) the fees paid to investment banks. Some of these innovations are now commonplace, and arguably the worldwide privatization movement was a major catalyst for the changes that have been observed in private sector IPOs.

In terms of revenue raised by IPOs, privatizations have dominated the new issue market in many countries in recent years. Megginson and Netter (2000) report that the cumulative proceeds raised by privatizing governments worldwide exceeded US$1 trillion by the end of 1999. Annual worldwide proceeds grew steadily over the 1990s, peaking in 1997 at over $160 billion per annum, since which time annual worldwide proceeds have been around $140 billion per annum.

Megginson and Netter also report that, as of the end of 1999, 12 of the 15 largest IPOs ever conducted (worldwide) were privatizations.

Many governments have multiple objectives when conducting a programme of privatization. For example, the objective of extending private share ownership can result in the government actually aiming to underprice the shares in privatized companies, viewing the forgone revenue as the price of achieving such objectives. We look critically at such arguments in the next section. In Section 7.2 we consider the various techniques available to governments conducting a privatization programme. In the final section of this chapter we show how the various objectives and available techniques interact, illustrating the discussion with reference to the extensive UK privatization programme.

7.1   Privatization Objectives

There are some important ways in which privatization IPOs may differ from those conducted by private-sector companies. Governments often use privatizations to achieve multiple, and frequently conflicting, objectives, some of which are concerned with broad public policy issues that are of no interest to private-sector firms going public. We explore below the impact of these various objectives on the way privatization IPOs have been structured. It should be noted that, although in this chapter we concentrate on the issues relevant to the way privatization transactions are conducted, the most important objective that most governments aim to achieve through privatization is simply to promote the efficiency of the companies concerned.

7.1.1   *Objective 1: revenue raising*

Revenue raising is the most obvious objective of many privatizations. Governments are able to use privatization proceeds to reduce public borrowing: governments essentially undertake a debt–equity swap, raising money from the sale of the equity to private investors to reduce the accumulated debt of the public sector. This may result in reduced taxation in the future. However, it should be noted that governments also lose a claim on the net cash flow generated by the companies sold, and so taxes will be lower in the future only if the sale proceeds exceed the net present value of the future earnings that would have been earned under public ownership.

In practice, it is difficult to know whether this condition is satisfied, although in many cases the net cash raised for the public purse from privatization (taking account of balance sheet restructurings before the sale) has been quite limited. Clearly, the sale value of any firm will reflect investors' expectations of *future* profitability, taking account of any anticipated efficiency savings resulting from the transfer into private ownership. What is noticeable in the case of many privatizations is that, unlike private-sector IPOs, the longer-term performance of the companies has often been extremely strong, suggesting that at the time of the IPO investors were not aware of the extent of the inefficiencies existing under public ownership. This suggests that, quite apart from the more technical considerations about how privatization IPOs should be conducted, government should attempt to rationalize and improve efficiency as much as possible before the sale of the company, in order to appropriate as many of the gains as possible for taxpayers rather than the shareholders. A further implication may be that some form of 'claw-back' of unanticipated profits should be considered, although such provisions will inevitably depress the initial sale price. (However, this effect will be outweighed in the event of such unanticipated profits materializing). An alternative approach, which we consider more fully below, is the use of staged sales, so that the government retains an equity interest in the future performance of the company.

As has been argued earlier in this book, discounts on IPOs are essentially transfers between the original owners of the company and those that are allocated shares at the IPO. In the case of a privatized company the initial owner is the government, and the wealth transfer that takes place in the event of the IPO being discounted is between taxpayers in general and the initial shareholders. These wealth transfers will often be *ad hoc*, depending on who participates in the privatization IPO and who is allocated shares in the event of over-subscription, and will frequently be regressive, with wealthier members of society participating to a greater extent than those with few financial resources to invest in the IPO. As a consequence, one aim of governments should be to maximize the proceeds of the flotation, although governments differ considerably in the vigour with which they pursue this objective.

An alternative model, which has been used in Eastern Europe and elsewhere, is simply to give the company away to all citizens in the form of free shares. In this way equality of treatment is assured, although the government raises no funds as a result of the transfer into private ownership. Severe doubts have also been raised about the effectiveness of corporate governance—and the incentives to improve efficiency—in the case of voucher privatizations.

7.1.2   *Objective 2: wide share ownership*

Privatization programmes have been used by many governments to encourage participation in the stock market by individual investors. For example, the UK government stated explicitly that 'the promotion of wider and deeper share ownership—both among employees and the general public—is part of the Government's policy of extending the ownership of wealth more widely in the economy, giving people a direct stake in the success of British industry, and removing the old distinctions between "owners" and "workers"' (HM Treasury 1995). However, the promotion of stock market participation by encouraging individual investors to subscribe to privatization IPOs is not without its problems. First, a highly dispersed shareholder base could result in principal–agent problems, with little effective control being exercised by the dispersed owners over the managers. We consider this issue more fully later. Second, some have argued (see e.g. Jenkinson and Mayer 1988) that if wide share ownership is a public policy aim it could be achieved more efficiently via the provision of tax breaks to equity ownership; for example, a certain amount of dividend income and capital gain arising from equity investment each year could be tax-free.

Evidence from the UK suggests that, even after a lengthy privatization programme, share ownership, while wider, is not deeper, and that few additional investors have regularly bought non-privatization shares. The number of small shareholders in 1979 numbered around 3 million, rising to around 11 million in 1991 before falling back to just over 9 million in 1993. However, according to the partly government-funded Pro-Share, which tracks share ownership, 72 per cent of all retail investors hold shares in only one or two companies. The clear evidence is that many of the early privatizations, which were discounted very heavily, simply induced stagging by retail investors. For example, the British Aerospace privatization in 1981 attracted 26,000 retail investors, although soon after the sale the number of small investors had fallen to just 3,000. More recently, the privatization of the 12 regional electricity companies in 1991 resulted in 35 per cent of retail investors selling their shares within the first month of trading. Therefore, if the objective is to encourage longer term, broadly based, participation in the stock market, providing up-front incentives to participants in IPOs may be a relatively expensive and ineffective approach. Longer-term incentives to encourage equity ownership—such as annual tax breaks on dividend income—may be much more effective.

The objective of encouraging workers to have a stake in their companies clearly has much more substance, and may contribute significantly to increased efficiency. However, it is worth noting that standard portfolio theory would suggest that such individuals, who already have significant amounts of human capital invested in the company they work for, should actually diversify their equity portfolios to include companies other than the one they work for in order to reduce risk. While the encouragement of employee share ownership may have excellent incentive effects, it may none the less encourage an inefficient allocation of investment funds.

Moreover, from a theoretical perspective the objective of wide share ownership can create problems. Many of those potential investors who are the target of government attempts to broaden the shareholder base will often be relatively uninformed, certainly in comparison with institutional investors. The existence of investors with diverse information will inevitably result in winner's curse problems, with the result that discounts will have to increase in order that uninformed investors earn a reasonable rate of return. Hence attempts to broaden share ownership potentially conflict with the realization of proceeds that are close to asset valuations. It is possible that some of these problems can be avoided, or at least reduced, by giving preferential allocations to individual investors in the event of excess demand for the privatization shares. Many recent privatizations have used multi-part offerings with a designated tranche allocated to small investors. Governments often employ a 'claw-back' technique whereby if the public offer is over-subscribed less stock is allocated to institutional investors. This biasing of allocations in the event of excess demand should certainly help to increase the expected returns to the relatively uninformed investors, and reduce the winner's curse. On the other hand, claw-backs also reduce the underwriters' ability to reward informed investors for revealing their information about an issue's value, which in turn could lead to less accurate pricing.

7.1.3   *Objective 3: government credibility*

Whatever the weight given to the various objectives of government in privatizing—and these vary greatly across countries—there is a fundamental difference between privatizations and IPOs conducted by private-sector companies. Unlike private companies, for whom an IPO is a one-off event, governments typically own a whole range of assets which can be sold off sequentially as part of a privatization *programme*. As a result, individual privatizations cannot be viewed in isolation: a government may, quite rationally, want to invest in a reputation (for instance, for selling companies at fair prices) during the early phases of a privatization programme, to encourage investor participation in later stages. There have been many examples of government privatization programmes being set back significantly by an overpriced issue, or by a company that performs poorly in the after-market.

For example, the Spanish privatization programme started running into difficulties in 1995 following the poor performance of previous privatization offerings. (For example, Argentaria's share price had fallen by around 35 per cent since its sale in November 1993.) In order to reverse negative investor sentiment, it was necessary for the Spanish government to re-stimulate interest in the privatization programme. It chose, in addition to discounting the shares in the next sale—Repsol—to offer investors a one-year money-back guarantee, which would compensate investors for any losses up to 10 per cent. (We discuss such schemes more fully below.) The important lesson is that investors can quickly become disillusioned with privatizations and that the cost to a government, especially one in the early stages of an extensive privatization programme, of losing credibility may be considerable, and difficult to reverse. Consequently, governments rightly place importance on privatizations being viewed as a 'success', although, as will be discussed more fully later in this chapter, there are various ways of promoting the participation of investors that are more sophisticated than simply underpricing the shares by an enormous amount.

The importance of government reputation may also influence the *structure* of privatizations. As Guney and Perroti (1993) point out, even after a firm is privatized, it may be vulnerable to changes in government policy. The most obvious examples of these problems relate to industries that are still regulated by government after privatization, such as many utility industries. In these cases there may be advantages to the use of staged sales, whereby the government retains a stake in the company for some period of time. The retention of an equity interest should reduce the temptation to change policy in a way that would reduce the value of the firm, and should therefore increase the confidence of potential investors in the credibility of government policy.

7.1.4   *Objective 4: effective control*

One of the main arguments for privatization is that control is shifted from the public sector to private capital markets. Companies are required to report in a standard format to investors on a regular basis and are subject to the analysis and criticism of investors and analysts. However, there are two concerns that arise regarding the effectiveness of the corporate control mechanism for privatized companies.

First, wide share ownership may have detrimental control implications. A large number of very small shareholders may provide little effective monitoring of management, principally because of free-rider and coordination problems. However, in practice, once secondary trading begins, institutional investors soon accumulate significant stakes in privatized companies. This is especially so if the privatized company becomes a constituent of the leading benchmark stock market indices of the country, as is often the case. Hence, although the initial dispersal of ownership and control may be a problem in certain privatizations, the importance of this argument should not be overstated.

Second, in many cases governments retain a special share in the company that bestows certain control rights. Examples include the 'golden shares' existing in many UK privatized companies, and the *noyeaux durs*—or 'hard core'—owned by the French government. These special shares are put in place for various reasons—for example to protect certain industries deemed to be of strategic importance from foreign takeover—but their effect is inevitably to weaken the corporate control exercised by the capital market. In many cases such shares may remove entirely the threat of a hostile takeover, which in some countries is likely to be far more potent as a threat than the direct intervention of investors. However, some special shares are of limited time duration, and in some cases governments have waived their control rights when a change in corporate control has been proposed (for example in the case of Ford's takeover of privatized Jaguar).

Governments clearly differ in their weighting of these various privatization objectives, and in the trade-offs that are chosen when, as is frequently the case, the objectives conflict. In the next section we consider the various options available to governments during the IPO and how these interact with the privatization objectives.

7.2   Privatization Techniques

7.2.1   *Structuring the sale*

Governments often have strong preferences about the desired final allocation of shares in privatization IPOs. In particular, the objective of encouraging small investors to participate is often paramount. However, there are various ways to achieve this objective, and the techniques employed by governments have changed considerably in recent years.

In some early privatizations, the entire IPO was sold via a public offer of the shares at a fixed price. Early UK privatizations—during the mid-1980s—were conducted in this way, with the price of the issue being set by the government, in conjunction with its advisers, on the basis of very little information as to the likely demand for the shares. It is difficult to know precisely how the issue price was determined in these early cases; certainly no book-building exercise was undertaken. What is more certain is that these early privatizations resulted in some of the most spectacular examples of underpricing. While such underpricing certainly caught the attention of the public, who subscribed with growing enthusiasm to these early issues, the immediate large gains also resulted in considerable stagging, and criticism from various commentators and, in particular, by the National Audit Office in their reports on the sales.

The problem of achieving the dual aims of relatively accurate pricing and the participation of small investors in privatizations has tended to be addressed by the use of multi-tranche offerings, where the issue is divided into institutional and retail tranches. In some cases these tranches are further split into those targeted at domestic and overseas investors. For the institutional tranches, book-building techniques have increasingly been used; indeed, privatizations were among the first issues outside of the USA to use book-building. As discussed in earlier chapters, book-building allows the investment bank some discretion over the allocation of the issue, which may be important in inducing informed investors to reveal valuable information regarding the value of the company. The price determined via the book-building—participation in which is limited to institutional investors—can then be used to set the price in the retail tranche. Many governments have pre-announced a discount on this retail tranche, whereby the price paid by retail investors is set at a fixed discount to the price that is arrived at as a result of the book-building, although other forms of incentives, such as bonus shares or reductions on bills, may also be offered to retail investors. In this way, discounts can be accurately targeted on small investors, and preferential allocation can in principle be targeted at specific investors who reveal particularly valuable information during the book-building. There is a cost, however, in the sense that a pre-commitment to meeting retail demand decreases the underwriter's allocation discretion and so may reduce its ability to induce truthful information revelation.

While the clear trend has been towards the use of book-building for the institutional tranche of privatizations, there have been some cases (for example in France and the UK) where pricing and allocation have been conducted by means of a tender. An early example of a procedure that was extremely efficient in maximizing proceeds, and eliciting investors' valuations, was the tender component of the 1987 privatization of the British Airports Authority (BAA). The IPO was split into two tranches: (i) a public offer at a fixed price (for 75 per cent of the equity) aimed at individual shareholders, and (ii) a tender offer (for the remaining 25 per cent) aimed at institutional shareholders (although retail investors were not excluded). In the tender offer investors were invited to submit price/quantity bids. The interesting aspect of the tender was that those bids that were successful paid the price *bid*, rather than a common *strike price*. While discriminatory price auctions have been used in a number of other markets (in particular auctions of Treasuries), such techniques are rarely used in the case of IPOs. One interesting aspect in this privatization was that the price for the offer for sale tranche was fixed before the outcome of the tender was known. In the event, while the fixed-price offer was discounted by some 16 per cent, the average price paid under the tender offer was actually slightly higher than the trading price at the end of the first week.

This example illustrates a general point: in the early days of the privatization process, certain governments experimented with various techniques designed to achieve the various objectives they set for the privatization process. In fact, the UK government used no further discriminatory price auctions, and moved over time instead to using book-building in the institutional tranche of multi-tranche offerings, with the price in the retail tranche being set as a fixed discount on the institutional tranche. However, it is worth stressing an important point regarding the use of book-building for privatization IPOs: after having gone through the extensive marketing and information-gathering stages, governments frequently choose an issue price that generates considerable initial returns. Thus, the politics of privatization often conflicts with one of the main potential benefits of book-building, namely pricing IPOs more accurately.

7.2.2   *Price stabilization*

Price support   Price support, via intervention in the market immediately after the IPO, has been common for many years in the USA. In Europe, before the advent of book-building, price support practices were relatively opaque, taking the form of supply-reducing trading by the underwriter in the after-market. More recently, the use of over-allotment options has become popular. As discussed in Chapter 4, over-allotment options allow the investment bank initially to go short on the IPO and then, in the event of weak demand, to cover the short position by open-market purchases. As explained in the first chapter, these over-allotment options tend to be of a relatively short duration, and normally expire after around a month.

In privatizations the form that stabilization takes varies widely, ranging from intervention in the secondary market by the sponsor in the days or weeks immediately following the IPO to outright price guarantees by the government. In all cases, the main motivation is usually to attempt to reduce short-term share price volatility, and in particular to reduce downside risk for investors.

Among the recent privatizations that have used over-allotment options are the second and third tranches of British Telecommunications (BT2 and BT3), and the second tranche of the UK electricity generators PowerGen and National Power (GenCo2). Probably the most interesting case is that of GenCo2. There was very strong demand for the issue, which was split between an offer for sale to the public and an international institutional offer conducted by book-building, with the public offer being twice subscribed. The coordinators of the sale (Barclays de Zoete Wedd and Kleinwort Benson) took on a covered short position by selling 37 million additional shares in National Power and 24 million additional shares in PowerGen. Soon after the shares started trading, the UK electricity regulator announced that he was going to reopen a review of the prices that could be charged by electricity distribution companies. This announcement resulted in sharp falls in the shares of all companies in the electricity sector, even though the implications for the electricity generators were far from apparent. The GenCo shares rapidly fell to below their issue price, and the coordinators intervened in the market, reducing excess supply and supporting the price. By the end of the 30-day option period, the coordinators were left with a short position totalling only 15.3 million shares, implying that they had repurchased 45.7 million shares in the market. In this case the volatility in the shares was genuinely short-lived, as investors realized the limited impact the regulator's announcement would have on electricity generators, and the shares rapidly regained the initial losses and rose above the issue price.

One interesting aspect of this exercise is that it demonstrates how valuable the over-allotment option can be to the syndicate of investment banks selling the issue. Since the banks will buy back the shares in the market only if the price is below the issue price, in closing (partially or in full) their short position they make profits. These profits accrue to the syndicate itself, as the holder of the option, rather than to the government (or other vendors). Since such profits in many cases will be genuine windfalls, there is a strong case for writing contingencies into the underwriting contract to adjust the total remuneration of the syndicate in the event of profitable price support. There are clearly many ways in which this could be done, ranging from an almost completely fixed-fee contract (where the total remuneration of the syndicate as a whole is fixed) to a system of claw-back of a proportion of any excess remuneration accruing from price support. In the case of recent UK privatizations, the government has fixed a target income for the global coordinators and one-third of any excess income is clawed back. This preserves the incentives of the syndicate to intervene to support the price. It could be argued, however, that, given the low cost of actually performing the price support, the claw-back of this potential source of income for the syndicate should be much greater, or even complete. There seems little justification for the syndicate gaining once through additional selling commissions and then again through entirely risk-free repurchases at a lower price.

This episode illustrates some of the benefits to the vendor of granting over-allotment options, particularly in cases where there is short-run pressure on the share price. One minor disadvantage is that granting such an option results in uncertainty as to the total proceeds raised by the issue.

Price guarantees Price support, backed up by an over-allotment option, can certainly help in limiting short-run downward movements in share prices, and the provision of such (relatively limited) insurance should be valuable to risk-averse investors. However, in some recent privatizations price stabilization has been extended to such lengths that some governments have actually started offering money-back guarantees within a given period. One recent example is Repsol, the Spanish oil group, which announced that, if its share price were to fall below the issue price in the year following the sale, it would compensate investors in cash for losses up to 10 per cent; any fall in excess of 10 per cent would be borne by the investors.

While on first sight this approach seems a rather extreme form of insurance, from the perspective of the issuer it is similar to offering investors a one-for-ten bonus share issue, except that the bonus is not paid at all if the shares remain above the issue price, and will be paid only partially in the event of a fall of less than 10 per cent. Such bonus issues have been used extensively in privatizations in various countries, although in most cases the only contingency has been that the original investor has to retain ownership of the shares for some length of time, rather than being related to share price performance. The obvious advantage of the price guarantee variant of the scheme is that it will be a much cheaper way of providing insurance to risk-averse retail investors than a simple bonus share scheme, as well as being more obviously risk-reducing to unsophisticated investors.

In the case of Repsol, a large tranche of shares were sold at a time (April 1995) when retail investors had suffered losses on the stock market, both in general and in particular on previous privatization issues. For example, shares in Endesa, privatized less than a year previously, had fallen by around 20 per cent, and shares in Argentaria, whose second—heavily over-subscribed—tranche had been issued just 16 months previously, had fallen by 35 per cent. The price guarantee certainly seemed to be effective, as the Repsol offer was heavily over-subscribed in both its domestic and international tranches. Most significant was the retail offer, which was over twice subscribed.

The Spanish government seems to have used this issue to kick-start its remaining privatization programme by recreating confidence— both among small shareholders and foreign investors—in the performance of privatization IPOs. Interestingly, the subsequent sale of part of the telecommunications group Telefonica by the Spanish government reverted to more traditional incentives—a discount to the institutional price for retail investors and a one-for-twenty bonus issue for those shareholders who retained their shares for one year.

Hedging via the use of derivatives The desire of governments to promote wide share ownership, combined with the risk-averse attitudes of many investors (especially following previous privatizations whose performance has been disappointing), has inevitably resulted in some intermediaries attempting to design schemes that hedge the downside risk. This is especially important in the case of employees of a privatizing company, as investing financial capital in addition to human capital in the same company can result in a very undiversified portfolio of assets. A downturn in the fortunes of the company could result in an increased chance of workers losing their jobs as well as a reduction in the value of their investments in the company. Since governments frequently seek to encourage employees to participate in a privatization, the attractions of offering a hedge—perhaps paid for in part by a less significant discount—can be considerable.

An example of the type of scheme that has been offered is that devised by Bankers Trust for the French government, which had been frustrated in its aim of encouraging more extensive employee participation in early privatizations. The scheme involved the government using part of the discount it would have offered to members of the employee share ownership plan (ESOP) to buy a hedge against price falls, with the risk being taken on by Bankers Trust. The floor that was placed under the share price meant, in turn, that the shares could be used as collateral against a loan, which could be used to buy additional shares. For each share bought with their own money, investors could buy an additional nine with money borrowed from a bank, with Bankers Trust guaranteeing that the value of the shares would be sufficient to repay the loan. The cost to the members of the ESOP was that they received any share price appreciation on only six out of the ten shares, with the remainder going to Bankers Trust. However, the leveraged nature of the investment meant that potential returns were very high with no downside risk at all.

It should be clear that, although such schemes were first employed in privatization issues, the same techniques could be used in a private-sector IPO, where a financial intermediary, rather than the government, is providing the price guarantee. Although the idea of using derivatives to protect initial investors in an IPO is certainly relatively novel, such schemes may be a cheaper and more effective way of encouraging individual investors to participate in new issues, and it is possible that in the future initial underpricing may to some extent be replaced by such hedging, paid for in part by the company and in part by investors.

7.2.3 *Part payment*

A technique that has frequently been used in privatizations is that of selling shares on a partly paid basis. By allowing investors to pay only a proportion of the purchase price at the time of issue, the government essentially provides investors with free leverage to their holding. Put another way, the government provides investors with an interest-free loan for the period between the first instalment and the final instalment. Although the shares are traded on a partly paid basis, their volatility is far in excess of a fully paid equivalent, as is consistent with standard asset pricing models. For example, compare the behaviour of a fully paid share valued at 100p and a partly paid share in the same company with only half currently paid. Good results which increase the fully paid share price by 5 per cent to 105p will add the same absolute increase to the partly paid share price, which should rise from 50p to 55p, producing a 10 per cent return on the investment.

The advantage of employing such schemes from a government's perspective is that even relatively modest premia on privatization IPOs can become very impressive first-day returns when the shares are issued on a partly paid basis. Part-paid investors are also typically eligible to receive the full dividend, which can increase the yield on the partly paid shares dramatically. For investors wary of the stock market, governments often use such techniques to produce impressive initial returns, although more sophisticated investors should realize that they will subsequently have to pay the remaining instalments upon which there will be zero initial premium. None the less, the implicit interest-free loan is certainly an added inducement to invest, and the cost of providing such financing should essentially be viewed as additional implicit underpricing of the IPO.

However, there are possible disadvantages from using part-payment schemes. Most significant is that it can encourage stagging, with investors able to reap impressive initial returns on the leveraged investment. Certainly, if the intention is to encourage retail investors to participate in the stock market in a long-term and responsible manner (rather than viewing new issues as a source of guaranteed profits), then part-payment schemes appear much less appropriate than long-term incentive schemes. There are many variants of the latter, including bonus share schemes for retail investors who hold on to their initial holding for a set period of time, or discount schemes whereby investors receive discounts off their bills (often used in the case of utility privatizations). In some recent privatizations governments have adopted a belt-and-braces approach, offering both part-payment and long-term incentives to retail investors. It remains to be seen if such schemes represent money well spent by government, which, as argued above, might be better advised to use such resources to encourage equity investment more generally.

Finally, it should be noted that in some recent privatizations governments have been prepared to price the subsequent instalments of the shares to reflect the benefits (in terms of leverage and yield) that investors receive from a part payment scheme. For example, in the sale of the second tranche of the UK electricity generators in 1995, the government issued the shares on a partly paid basis but set the subsequent instalments such that the fully paid price was around 6 per cent *above* the trading price of the existing fully paid equivalent shares. Individual investors were given a discount on the initial instalment in addition to bonus shares or additional discounts for those investors who had registered at 'Share Shops' by a particular date. This reflects a general trend observed in the later stages of the UK privatization programme towards using incentives tied to establishing broker–investor relationships. By promoting such relationships the UK government sought to encourage investors to participate in equity investment more generally, rather than concentrating their attention on privatizations.

7.2.4   *Staged sales*

Given the problems that many governments have experienced in setting the correct price for privatizations, one obvious response is to conduct the sale in stages. A market price can be established on an initial tranche and subsequent tranches can be sold at more accurate prices later. Numerous governments have adopted the staged sale technique, although it is not always clear that the maximization of proceeds is the prime justification.

One potential attraction of staged sales is that wide share ownership can thereby be encouraged. Clearly, if individual investors are given significant incentives to apply for shares at each stage, this should increase their participation in the market. This will be particularly effective if the privatized company has performed strongly since privatization.

An alternative reason why staged sales may be employed for privatizations is to increase confidence in the minds of investors that the government will not change policy or intervene in ways that would harm the company and reduce shareholders' returns. Although in principle privatization should mean the company being freed from government control, in practice many companies are still highly vulnerable to government policies. The most obvious example of such issues would be in the case of privatized utility industries, where governments typically establish regulatory agencies to control—at least—the natural monopoly activities of the privatized company. Although such regulators frequently have the appearance of being autonomous, governments are often able to influence decisions that directly impact on the profitability of the company in numerous ways. By retaining an equity stake in the company, which will subsequently be sold, the government has a direct interest in maintaining the value of the company, at least for some time.

While there are various potential advantages in using staged sales, there is also one disadvantage. When privatizations are conducted in stages, with the government attempting to encourage wide share ownership at each stage, a logical problem arises. Given that each tranche will be sold at a discount, with second and further tranches being sold at a discount to the market price, investors should sell their initial holding just before a further tranche is issued, as they can sell at the market price and then buy back at a discount to the market price. But this logic suggests that investors should, where possible, go further and short the issue (sell more shares than they own), covering the short position by purchases in the next stage of the sale. There is evidence of this occurring in the USA (cf. Safieddine and Wilhelm 1996).

However, such behaviour by investors will tend to drive down the market price, which will reduce the proceeds accruing to government from the sale of the remaining shares (which are offered at a discount to the market price). Indeed, this problem may be particularly acute during a book-building exercise, as it is in the interest of investors to drive the issue price down towards the bottom of the indicative range, only for the price to jump back up following the sale. There have been numerous examples of such problems in both private-sector secondary offerings and staged sale privatizations, including allegations of short-selling in the run up to the Eurotunnel and Wellcome secondary offerings in the UK.

There was also much concern at the time of the sale of the third tranche of British Telecommunications by the UK government in 1993, which illustrates graphically the potential problems posed by shorting. S. G. Warburg, the global coordinator of the book-building exercise, went to elaborate lengths to ensure that investors who shorted the shares before the offer were denied the opportunity to cover their positions by being allocated shares. Obviously, it is necessary either to have detailed information about share transactions around the time of the offering or to structure the rules regarding trading such that short sales are made less profitable. Both routes were attempted by the coordinators, which caused considerable friction with institutional investors. A report by the UK National Audit Office on the sale refers to the remarkable fact that the Treasury asked financial regulators to give it information on the identity of those selling BT shares just before the issue, so that they could be denied allocations. However, lawyers advised that this would clearly be illegal, and so other less direct methods were employed. The London Stock Exchange undertook to monitor large transactions in BT shares just before the issue, and international investors were not told until the last minute how many shares they could buy (this being conditional upon domestic demand), thus making shorting more difficult. Warburg also asked the Stock Exchange to impose immediate cash settlement on BT shares in an attempt to reduce short sales, although the Stock Exchange decided against such a move.

In the event, the problems posed by short sales in this case seem not to have materialized, with the BT share price holding its value relative to the market between the date the sale was announced and the ultimate sale. However, governments considering staged sales should take such potential problems seriously. Various options, in addition to those employed above, exist to reduce such problems. For example, regulators could require the immediate publication of short sales in the period before a secondary sale, which would provide the coordinators with the required information to discriminate against those with short positions. Less extreme would be publication of the aggregate short position existing in the market as a whole, which could help the coordinators judge how much the current market price was being artificially depressed by such actions, and price the secondary offering accordingly. A final option might be to regulate short sales in some way, such as the US 'up-tick' rule, whereby short sales are allowed only when the last movement in the price was upwards. The problem, in any case, is likely to be less pronounced in markets where settlement occurs rapidly.

7.3   Case study: The UK Privatization Programme

The previous two sections have discussed the main objectives of privatization, and the techniques that have been employed by many governments in achieving these various objectives. In this section we use the extensive privatization programme undertaken in the UK to show the development of the various techniques, and to illustrate the problems of achieving the multiple, often conflicting, objectives in practice.

As can be seen from Figure 7.1, the UK privatization programme started modestly, in terms of proceeds raised, but gathered momentum in the mid-1980s as the key utility industries were successively privatized. Table 7.1 provides details of the individual privatizations, including the method used in the IPO, the proportion sold at the IPO, the techniques used in secondary sales, whether an over-allotment option was granted, and whether the government retains a special share in the company.

As noted earlier in this chapter, many of the early privatizations in the UK adopted a very simple approach. Public offers at a fixed price were employed on all the main IPOs with the exception of two oil companies—Britoil and Enterprise Oil—which were sold by tender. Some of the initial returns recorded on these early offers for sale were spectacular. The British Telecom IPO, for example, was underpriced by some 33 per cent on a *fully paid basis*. Given that investors were also given the advantage of part payment, the short-term returns available to those stagging the issue were as impressive as the proceeds forgone by government.

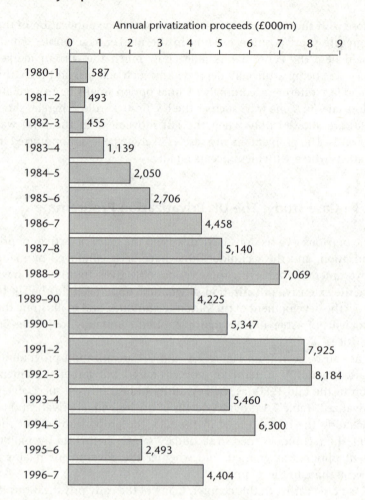

Annual privatization proceeds (£000m)

Year	Proceeds
1980–1	587
1981–2	493
1982–3	455
1983–4	1,139
1984–5	2,050
1985–6	2,706
1986–7	4,458
1987–8	5,140
1988–9	7,069
1989–90	4,225
1990–1	5,347
1991–2	7,925
1992–3	8,184
1993–4	5,460
1994–5	6,300
1995–6	2,493
1996–7	4,404

Fig. 7.1. Proceeds from UK privatizations, 1981/1–1996/7
Source: HM Treasury (1995) and Treasury website at www.hm-treasury.gov.uk.

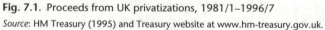

It is interesting, however, that even quite early in the programme the government was experimenting with alternative methods of sale. The first attempt at tendering resulted in the Britoil issue being only 0.3 times subscribed, and the trading price for the shares falling to 20 per cent below the issue price. A tender of Enterprise Oil in 1984 was

Table 7.1. The UK privatization programme

Company	Date of IPO	Proceeds[a] (£m)	Technique	Proportion retained at IPO (%)	Staged sales 2nd tranche	Staged sales 3rd tranche	Special shares[d]
British Petroleum	11/79	284	OFS	51.0	9/81 T	10/87 OFS & T	
British Aerospace	2/81	43	OFS	48.4	5/85 OFS		yes
Cable and Wireless	10/81	181	OFS	50.6	12/83 T	12/85 OFS	yes
Amersham International	2/82	64	OFS	nil			
Britoil	10/82	334	T	49.0	8/95 OFS		
Associated British Ports	2/83	46	OFS	48.5	4/84 T		
Enterprise Oil	6/84	384	T	nil			
Jaguar[b]	7/84	297	OFS	nil			
British Telecom	11/84	3,685	OFS	49.8	12/91 OFS & BB; OAO	7/93 OFS & BB; OAO	yes
British Gas	12/86	3,691	OFS	3.3	7/90		yes
British Airways	2/87	858	OFS	2.5			yes
Rolls Royce	5/87	1,032	OFS	0.4			yes
British Airports Authority	7/87	1,223	OFS & T	4.4			yes
British Steel	12/88	2,425	OFS	0.1			
10 water companies	12/89	3,395	OFS	1.6			
12 regional electricity companies	12/90	3,395	OFS	1.5			
National Power	3/91	1,341	OFS & T[c]	40.0	3/95 OFS & BB; OAO		yes
PowerGen	3/91	822	OFS & T[c]	40.0	3/95 OFS & BB; OAO		yes
Scottish Hydro-Electric	6/91	920	OFS & T[c]	3.5			yes
Scottish Power	6/91	1,955	OFS & T[c]	3.5			yes
Northern Ireland Electricity	6/93	684	OFS	3.3			yes
Railtrack	3/96	1,900	OFS & BB	nil			yes

[a] The 'Proceeds' figures include the value of the sale of ordinary shares at the IPO but not the value of any debt or preference shares created in the company that are repayable to the government, or the proceeds from the second and third tranches of staged sales.

[b] In the case of Jaguar, the proceeds of the sale were retained by its parent company (British Leyland).

[c] In these cases the tenders were 'back-end' tenders.

[d] Only special shares that are still in place are noted here. Some special shares were created that expired at certain dates (e.g. for the water companies and the regional electricity companies); others (e.g. in the case of Jaguar) were redeemed at the time of a takeover.

Abbreviations: OFS: offer for sale at a fixed price; T: tender; BB: book-building; OAO: over-allotment option granted.

Source: HM Treasury (1995) and Treasury website at www.hm-treasury.gov.uk

similarly under-subscribed—this time by only 0.4 times—although the shares actually traded at a 2 per cent premium to the issue price by the end of the first week. At the time of these early privatization tenders, it was quite common for private-sector companies to go public via a tender in the UK. However, the use of tenders for both private-sector IPOs and privatizations essentially stopped around this time. The only other privatization that included a tender element was the sale of the British Airports Authority in 1987, which we discussed earlier. Despite the apparent success of this issue, with the average tender price being almost exactly the resulting market price, the UK government chose not to use this technique again.

Indeed, the subsequent sales of British Steel, the ten water companies, and the 12 regional electricity companies all resorted to public offers at a fixed price. While the former was priced relatively accurately, the latter two issues were significantly underpriced, with end-of-first-week share price rises of 22 and 21 per cent respectively, again on a fully paid basis. The loss of potential proceeds in these two cases was made worse by the fact that not only were the sales not staged, but the performance of the companies over the next few years was exceptionally strong. In cases where information regarding the true value of the company is sparse, there are very strong arguments in favour of staged sales.

A major criticism we would make of the UK privatization programme is that the relative neglect of the benefits of staged sales was a costly mistake, and one that was repeated in the 1996 sale of Railtrack, the UK rail network operator. Political considerations may well have dominated economic argument in this respect, with the government keen to sell its entire stake in order that any future government of a different complexion would find it more difficult to reverse the privatization or seize effective control by re-establishing majority control.

Around 1991 the UK government started to use book-building techniques, which it has employed in the secondary offerings of BT, PowerGen, and National Power. It has also used book-building for the Railtrack offering. The approach has been to segment the offer into a public offer (aimed at small investors), an international tender offer (conducted by book-building and involving only institutional investors), and, in some of the more recent offers, a retail tender, aimed at relatively sophisticated individual investors which want to increase their allocation over and above what they might receive through the public offer. The public offer price has been set at a fixed discount to the price established through the book-building exercise. This approach seems much more sensible than the earlier public offers at a fixed price, where the government, in its desire to encourage wide share ownership, discounted the shares to both individuals and institutions alike.

Special shares have been widely employed in UK privatizations, as can be seen in the final column of Table 7.1. This shows the special shares that are currently in existence; in fact, a number of the other companies—such as the water companies and regional electricity companies—also had special shares in place that have since expired. In practice, the UK government has on a number of occasions waived its control rights, and allowed several mergers and acquisitions to occur. It did, however, use its veto in 1996 to block the attempt by a US electricity utility to take over National Power, the largest UK generating company.

Price stabilization has taken place only in a few recent sales, and has taken the form of the granting of over-allotment options. The benefits to the government, or investors, of the existence of these options seem rather marginal, although it could be argued that they contribute to price stability in the initial trading period. Price guarantees, which have been used in other European countries, have not been used in the UK, where bonus share allocations and other incentives—such as reduced bills—have been the main form of long-term incentive. However, as argued above, there are good arguments for partial price guarantees which may be a more effective and cheaper way of encouraging wide share ownership.

In conclusion, this chapter has discussed the various objectives of privatization programmes and the techniques available to government to achieve these objectives. While many of the issues we discussed in this chapter are similar to those facing a private-sector company conducting an IPO, there are significant differences. In particular, governments generally undertake privatization *programmes*—selling many companies over a period of time—and so return to the market on numerous occasions; the success of the programme depends in large part upon gaining investor confidence during the early stages. In contrast, a private-sector company goes public only once, and so relies more on the reputation of the investment banks, or other advisers, than on its own reputation. In addition, governments frequently place considerable emphasis on using privatization programmes to promote wide share ownership for more general (and, we would argue, not entirely convincing) public policy reasons. Achieving high levels of participation by small investors has been a challenge for many governments, although more recent moves towards the use of multi-tranche offerings—with book-building being used to set the issue price in the institutional tranche, and a fixed discount on this price being offered to small investors—is certainly a major improvement on earlier (generally fixed price) techniques. Indeed, in recent years a number of big private-sector IPOs have sought to encourage retail participation in their IPO and have also employed the multi-tranche approach.

CHAPTER 8

Conclusions and Future Developments

Whenever economists find an empirical anomaly, a sizeable theoretical literature usually develops. In the case of initial public offerings, two apparent anomalies have been suggested: initial underpricing, and long-run underperformance. It is not surprising, therefore, that the resultant theoretical and empirical literature is so extensive. However, at present the bulk of the theoretical explanations have been associated with underpricing. In part this is simply because underpricing is such a long established international stylized fact; papers on long-run underperformance only (re)appeared in journals around 1991.[1] However, it is also true that the empirical support for long-run underperformance is not nearly as clear-cut. As we predicted in the first edition of this volume, written in 1995–6, the proliferating research in this area has since undermined the validity of the claim that IPOs underperform the relevant benchmark in the long run.

One of the principal aims of this book has been to provide a critical assessment of the plausibility of the alternative theories that attempt to explain these phenomena, drawing in particular upon international evidence. The international perspective is especially valuable in that it allows explanations based upon particular institutional, legal, or regulatory arrangements to be tested. Initial underpricing is truly an international stylized fact, but the financial systems in which

---

[1] As in many other areas of economics, an earlier literature existed on long-run underperformance; see e.g. Stoll and Curley (1970). However, the recent resurgence in research activity in this area really dates from the 1990s.

it is observed differ greatly. While in many papers evidence has been presented for particular countries (especially the USA) that is claimed to be 'consistent' with particular theories, it is clear from Part II of this book that few theories could claim to provide a convincing international explanation of underpricing. As a result, any theory whose conclusions are dependent on a restrictive set of assumptions about financial institutions or company law is likely to lack general validity or plausibility.

In this final chapter we first review the state of the theoretical debate in this spirit, suggesting which classes of theory provide the most insights. We finish by speculating on some possible future developments in the way firms go public, and on the roles of the intermediaries involved in the IPO process.

8.1   An Assessment of the Theoretical Literature

We split the discussion of the theoretical explanations of underpricing into three main groups: models based upon asymmetric information, models that focus on institutional factors, and models that relate underpricing to ownership and control considerations. In general, we find those based upon the assumption of information asymmetries most convincing. However, this is not to say that all of the theories in this relatively large class are equally compelling. In particular, while we believe that principal–agent and information revelation explanations have quite general plausibility, we are much less convinced of the general relevance of winner's curse explanations. We are less convinced still of signalling explanations. Among models that are not based upon asymmetric information, we find price support explanations to be most interesting. Models of underpricing based upon ownership and control considerations are an interesting current area of research, but as yet the empirical analysis has not convincingly discriminated between the competing (and opposing) models. We now briefly discuss the reasons for these views.

Companies go public once only, and for this reason there is obviously a role for intermediaries who repeatedly sponsor new companies, who have reputations to preserve, and who have established clienteles for the shares of new companies. The typical issuing company is likely to be better informed about its own business and prospects, but in other respects is likely to be at an informational disadvantage relative to the investment bank, particularly regarding likely investor demand. There are, as a result, numerous ways in which the interests of intermediaries and companies may not always be perfectly aligned, resulting in potential principal–agent problems.

Most obviously, in cases where the issue is underwritten by an investment bank, the latter will have an incentive to reduce its underwriting risk by increasing the extent of (expected) underpricing. Similarly, it becomes easier to sell future issues to repeat investors if previous issues have been underpriced. While such explanations lack the complexity of other principal–agent models, we believe they should not be discarded lightly. However, there are other more sophisticated principal–agent explanations, for example where underpricing emerges as a second-best incentive-compatible contract between the issuer and bank.

One general issue we have highlighted throughout this book is the problem of how to induce those with information about the valuation of the firm going public to reveal that information truthfully. Information production is costly, and any investor who bears the cost of becoming informed will require an incentive to reveal the information to anyone else. The investment banks running an IPO would like to set the issue price conditional upon the honest views of informed investors, but they need to be able to reward such investors for their information production. In our view, many of the most interesting papers that have been produced in recent years consider the underpricing issue from this perspective, and pay close attention to the important role played by the investment bank and the discretion enjoyed by the investment bank in pricing and allocation decisions.

Many of these theoretical models are constructed with the bookbuilding approach in mind. Until the early 1990s, book-building methods were more or less confined to the USA. However, the last few years have witnessed the widespread adoption of book-building techniques outside the USA, making this literature of particular relevance. The various theoretical models, building on the original Benveniste–Spindt analysis, now constitute a coherent and important research programme. This research is important not least because it provides regulators and policy-makers with a theoretical lens through which the IPO process can be analysed. This lens provides some key insights, such as the possible drawbacks of 'equal treatment' rules regarding the allocation of shares in an IPO. It also suggests that allowing intermediaries to price-discriminate might improve the IPO process, a point to which we return below in the context of possible future developments. And finally, it suggests that price stabilization, a matter being discussed actively in a number of countries, may have a role if price discrimination is not allowed.

On the other hand, to test many of these theories—which often make predictions about the way the investment bank should use its discretion—requires detailed knowledge of the bids received during the book-building process, and the actions taken by the investment bank. Unfortunately, empirical analysis has, with a couple of notable exceptions, been frustrated by the unwillingness of investment banks to reveal such detailed information. While we understand this unwillingness, we believe that greater openness about the book-building process would not only contribute to academic research and understanding, but would also enable an informed analysis of the role played by investment banks to be undertaken. Indeed, given the relatively concentrated market for book-building services in many countries, and recurring doubts about the size of fees charged, it may be only a matter of time before the financial or competition regulators of some country require such disclosure.[2] Needless to say, if any bank would like to make such information available, please contact us!

Turning to other theoretical explanations, probably the most widely cited theory of IPO underpricing is that of the winner's curse. This is also an asymmetric information theory, although the nature of the information asymmetry is of a very different nature. Some investors are assumed to be relatively more informed than others, but both the issuing firm and its investment bank are assumed to be equally uninformed. There are, as a result, no principal–agent problems in the winner's curse theory, and, indeed, the investment bank plays no particular role. We do not find these assumptions regarding

---

[2] Indeed, as this book was going to press, investigations started in the USA into the conduct of certain investment banks during IPOs.

the nature of the asymmetric information problem very convincing, but even if they are accepted, a major problem with winner's curse explanations is that it is unclear why companies *need* to attract these persistently 'uninformed' investors. In some countries small shareholders (who are likely to be relatively uninformed on average) have never participated to any great extent in IPOs, and even in countries with active retail sectors many companies completely ignore them (for example through private placements). We still observe underpricing in these situations. The winner's curse model relies upon an assumption that without the uninformed investors' participation there would be insufficient demand for the shares; in an increasingly global capital market, we find this hard to believe. Of course, it may be that the original owners *want* to encourage wide share ownership, for some reason. If this is the case, the winner's curse is likely to be relevant, although there are more sophisticated ways of addressing this issue (such as multi-tranche offerings at differential prices) than high levels of underpricing for all investors.

Among the explanations that are not based upon asymmetric information, we find those associated with price support most relevant. In fact, as noted in Chapter 3, price support is not entirely divorced from asymmetric information explanations of underpricing, as the promise to offer price support—particularly if this can be targeted at those who provide valuable information—may be a second-best way of rewarding information revelation by investors. However, a rather different observation is that the quite widespread use of various techniques to limit price falls in the after-market, at least for a short period of time, may well help to explain the observed extent of underpricing. Since initial underpricing is typically measured over a short period—such as the first trading week—during which intermediaries may be intervening in the market to bolster demand, there may be a sense in which such initial trading prices do not accurately reflect underlying market prices. This is likely to be most important for those issues whose initial trading prices are close to, or below, the issue price, since intervention will be heaviest in these cases. The effect of such price support may be to produce a distribution of initial discounts that is artificially truncated on one side—with fewer overpriced issues than would be observed in the absence of such intervention. As a result, estimates of average initial underpricing may be somewhat misleading. Our reading of the existing evidence is that, while relevant, on its own, price support explains only a relatively small fraction of observed underpricing in most countries.

We turn now to the theories that we view as less convincing. Despite the proliferation of models suggesting a signalling explanation for IPO underpricing, we find these an implausible set of theories. There is clearly something in the argument that companies do not want to overprice their IPOs, as investors may remember and subsequently not subscribe to secondary equity offerings. Indeed, more generally, companies may want to avoid the 'bad publicity' of an overpriced issue, although to a great extent the blame ought to attach to the investment bank conducting the sale. However, this does not imply that initial underpricing is the most likely way for companies to signal their quality. Indeed, even the previous argument is questionable: since bygones should be bygones for investors, it is not clear why it is rational to boycott a secondary offering if the primary offering was overpriced. While there is some evidence from the USA that is 'consistent' with the models, in many other countries the institutional arrangements are such as to make the models completely irrelevant—notably those countries where investors enjoy pre-emption rights. In any case, the models are often based upon very questionable assumptions, for example that companies require equity, rather than other forms of finance, to get going in the first place.

Similarly, we find little general relevance in the theories that stress the role of underpricing in reducing the threat of legal action. While such theories may have some relevance to the USA, we have argued that the far greater protection afforded to intermediaries and issuing companies in most other countries renders such explanations of very limited relevance.

Finally, a relatively new set of explanations points to the possible links between initial underpricing and ownership and control. The models that have been proposed suggest that the principal–agent problem is between managers and shareholders. However, the relationship between underpricing and such agency costs is currently the subject of much unresolved debate. One theory suggests that underpricing, via the attendant over-subscription and the power to ration bids, results in dispersed shareholdings and the entrenchment of management control. An alternative theory suggests quite the opposite: that underpricing may be used to minimize agency costs by encouraging monitoring. At present this literature is relatively speculative and in need of more powerful empirical tests to discriminate between these opposing hypotheses.

8.2   Possible Future Developments

As we noted at the start of this book, the last few years have witnessed a number of important developments in primary equity markets. To a considerable extent, these changes have resulted from the increasingly global nature of capital markets. The leading investment banks that conduct IPOs are now, in many countries, big international organizations. A large proportion of IPOs now target investors outside the country of origin of the company going public. Even the choice of exchange(s) on which to list an IPO is increasingly an important choice variable. This increasing irrelevance of national boundaries is having some profound effects. As noted earlier, since the first edition of this book was published we have seen the widespread adoption of book-building techniques outside the USA, and numerous attempts by stock exchanges—particularly those in Europe —to merge or form alliances with other exchanges. At present, the future 'industrial organization' of stock exchanges is unclear, although the competitive pressure on national exchanges from various quarters is unlikely to abate.

In part, this globalization of capital markets has been linked to technological developments. The enormous reduction in the cost, and increase in the speed, of information flows between investors, intermediaries, and markets makes physical location increasingly an irrelevance. Such developments clearly started with the implementation of private networks by investment banks and large investors, but have spread through to the retail investor via the growth of the internet. The ultimate impact of the internet on the IPO market could be considerable. For example, many companies are attempting to develop the 'internet IPO' business model. There are various permutations on this model, although the key features are usually

(i) making the entire IPO transaction electronic (from the publication of the prospectus through to delivery of shares) and (ii) actively promoting the involvement of retail investors in IPOs. Indeed, the way many of these companies explain their business model is in terms of 'democratizing the IPO market', and enabling retail investors to participate on an equal footing with institutional investors.

What impact might such developments have? We think there are, broadly, two possible outcomes. First, these new ventures may cooperate with existing investment banks. They would offer a useful, low-cost distribution channel for involving retail investors in IPOs, but investment banks would retain most of their existing functions (in terms of information production, marketing, pricing/allocation, and distribution). Essentially, the internet-based intermediary would simply be another member of the selling syndicate with a particular role in retail marketing and distribution. It might well provide services to the syndicate in terms of monitoring flipping by its clients, and might, over time, develop ways to reward those who not only invested regularly but did not flip (for example by allocating each client a 'flipping score'). This cooperation is already being seen in many countries, and the main question is not *whether* such developments will occur, but *which* company will ultimately emerge as the leading internet-based intermediary.

While an important development, the emergence of new internet-based retail brokers would have a relatively modest impact on the IPO process. However, there is a second possible outcome: that the IPO pricing and allocation mechanisms are *disintermediated* via the internet. As previous chapters have stressed, investment banks perform a number of tasks in taking a company public. They perform the due diligence and produce the prospectus for the issue. They then coordinate the marketing effort. Next, they determine the price and allocation of the shares (often using a book-building approach). Finally, they may provide certain other services, such as short-term price support or longer-term analyst coverage. At present, the whole pricing and allocation process is, to a considerable extent, shrouded in mystery. Investment banks are usually loathe to reveal the bids they received, how the price was set, or how allocation was determined. In large part this is probably driven not only by a fear that exposing such information to public scrutiny would make relationships with their investor networks more difficult, but also for fear of legal action (particularly in the case of IPOs where the shares subsequently flop). However, concerns about the discriminatory nature of the allocation decision, possible conflicts of interest, and lingering doubts about the competitive structure of the investment banking market remain. These concerns have led some to champion the idea of taking the investment bank largely out of the pricing and allocation process.

On one level, this is not such a radical suggestion. Perhaps the most obvious way to determine the price of an object, particularly one that is quite difficult to value, is to gather together as many buyers as possible and ask them to value it via an auction mechanism. Indeed, at various times in various countries auctions have been used for IPOs, although it is interesting that, on closer inspection, many of these auction mechanisms allow for the intervention of an intermediary (often the investment bank) to either set the final price or disregard certain bids. Hence, they are not fully disintermediated processes. Clearly, one of the most striking developments resulting from the widespread use of the internet has been the growing use of auctions for all sorts of goods and services, not only at the business–consumer level, but also at the business–business level and the consumer–consumer level. There seems little reason why IPOs should not similarly be priced and allocated via formal auctions, and a number of new ventures have already been established with this goal, although the number of deals completed to date is very limited.

However, as the analysis in Part II of this book should make clear, there are clear challenges to be faced in designing appropriate auction mechanisms for IPOs. For example, given that gathering information and conducting research on an IPO is costly, ways have to be found to reward those investors who undertake such activities, and thus enable the issue price more accurately to reflect the market value. Some existing IPO methods, with discretionary allocation mechanisms, allow this. A fully disintermediated pricing and allocation mechanism would have the auction rules fully defined *ex ante*, and could be operated by a computer rather than an investment banker. One big challenge would be to design the auction such that information production was encouraged, perhaps by giving preferential allocations or prices to those who provided early information.

Auction theory, and practical applications of such theories (for example in auctions of spectrum for mobile phone use), demonstrates how important it is to design the auction appropriately. There is the generic problem of the winner's curse (similar to that discussed in Chapter 3), and it is not necessarily the case that the standard auction methods—such as open uniform price auctions—would encourage information production. Indeed, while the theory of single unit auctions is well developed, the same is not true of the multi-unit settings, except in the case where bidders demand only a single unit each (see Klemperer 1999). In the case of IPOs the multi-unit setting is clearly applicable, with bidders submitting a variety of—and possibly multiple—quantity/price bids. The theoretical analysis of multi-unit auctions is currently a major area of research, and such research will be directly relevant to using auction methods to run the pricing and allocation of IPOs. However, it may well be that experiments by companies running IPO auctions actually proceed ahead of theory, and it will be interesting to see how such auctions are designed to promote information production and overcome strategic behaviour by large investors. As noted by Klemperer (1999), the main message of much of the current research on multi-unit auctions is that it is very hard to achieve efficient outcomes.

This more radical possibility would, therefore, result in a refocusing of the role of the investment bank. The company conducting an IPO would still require the services of an investment bank—or some such institution—to play a role in due diligence and production of the initial prospectus. However, the middle stages of the IPO process might well be radically changed. The marketing of the issue might well be achieved, in the main, electronically. The days of the personal telephone call to institutional investors may be limited, as may be the time-consuming and expensive road-shows around the world. Analysis and prospectuses will increasingly be made available in electronic format, and there is no reason why presentations by, and interviews with, the main operating officers of companies conducting IPOs should not similarly be available via the internet. The fact that financial services regulators are increasingly concerned that all relevant information should be made available to all potential investors may be a further factor that curtails the use of such one-to-one or selected audience marketing. Once information on an IPO is made available electronically, there seem few reasons why retail investors cannot be included in offerings alongside institutional investors on an equal footing. As discussed in the previous paragraph, it may also be possible to use formal auction mechanisms to determine the pricing and allocation of an IPO. This would be a key development, as it would, at a stroke, remove many of the concerns regarding conflict of interest between the investment bank and the issuing company, most of which involve the discretion enjoyed by the investment bank in allocating IPO shares. The final stage of the IPO process—providing short-term price support and longer-term analysis—would still remain a function that would involve a traditional investment bank. Indeed, if the role of the investment bank were to be refocused in this way, it would be interesting to see how the charges associated with the remaining tasks compared with the current 'full service' charges observed at present.

It should be stressed that these possible future developments regarding the role of intermediaries in the IPO process are speculative, based upon an interpretation of developments in the theoretical literature, technological change, and the ways in which the market is evolving. But it should be stressed that developments may be driven as much by regulation as by technology. As noted earlier, the investment banking industry will almost certainly be subject to continued scrutiny by competition and financial services regulators, and such attention is more, rather than less, likely as new companies attempt to enter various parts of the IPO process.

Turning to the IPO transaction itself, there are a number of possible developments. The previous brief summary of the theoretical literature showed that underpricing may, to some extent, be the result of incomplete contracts between the various parties to the transaction. The company going public may typically want to be sold at a modest discount to the resulting trading price in order to avoid both the bad publicity and the initial disgruntled set of shareholders that might result from an overpriced issue. At the same time, the company may want to give strong incentives to its investment bank to market the issue vigorously, achieve a high sale price, and avoid excessive underpricing. Investors, some of whom may be the least informed parties to the transaction, may value some implicit or explicit insurance against possible price falls.

There are also various ways to align the incentives of the issuing company and the investment bank. For example, a relatively simple innovation (that we have never heard of in practice) would be to make the investment banks' fees contingent on underpricing not being 'excessive'. Investors require encouragement to participate in the IPO rather than invest in the after-market, and so a company might have a target level of underpricing of, say, 0–5 per cent. Underpricing in excess of this could result in a reduction in the fees paid to the investment bank on a sliding scale basis. In principle, a highly underpriced issue could result in the investment bank actually paying money to the company, rather than vice versa. In this way, the investment bank would share in the 'success' of the issue, where success is as defined by the company, rather than by the intermediaries—who traditionally herald a hugely over-subscribed and underpriced issue as a success. However, as discussed earlier, the feasibility, or desirability, of such arrangements might be contingent on the ability of the investment bank to discriminate, either by price or allocation, in favour of investors who revealed valuable information to the investment bank.

Of course, as investment banks are the repeat players, one might expect that, in a competitive market, previous history on underpricing would be taken into account when deciding which underwriter/manager to choose. Intermediaries that had been associated historically with highly underpriced issues would be avoided by companies; those that had overpriced previous issues would be avoided by investors. Consequently, a rational strategy for an investment bank might be to aim to be *average*—at least in terms of underpricing—and various investment banks have actually suggested to us that this is indeed their aim. However, while reputations based upon past performance are clearly important, they are not the same as proper financial instruments or contracts.

Turning to the relationship between the investors and the company, there might in the future be significant innovations in the way IPOs are sold, making more extensive use of derivatives contracts. We have already seen such innovations in the case of privatizations, with options being used to provide downside insurance and/or leverage potential gains. There is no reason why such contracts could not be written for private-sector IPOs. For example, an intermediary might guarantee that the share price would not fall below a specified level over a particular period, as we have seen in the case of some French privatizations. Risk-averse, and possibly informationally disadvantaged, investors might be especially attracted to such schemes, and companies might find them a cheaper and more effective way of attracting investors, thus lowering the cost of equity capital. Interestingly, we know of one recent example of such insurance: the IPO of Shuttlesoft AG in Germany in July 1999. In the case of company insolvency during the first five years of trading, investors will be repaid 50 per cent of the IPO price. This is guaranteed by the venture capital subsidiary of Deutsche Ausgleichsbank, a state-owned bank.

Indeed, the use of such instruments may provide a quick way for new entry to occur by intermediaries who lack established reputations for sponsoring IPOs, as investors care less about reputations when they are offered explicit financial deals (as witnessed by the growth of various forms of guaranteed income bonds with upside potential engineered by using derivatives). What would still matter, of course, was that the financial instruments backing up the package were adequately secured, although in practice positions would probably be substantially hedged.

In principle, it is even possible for the company itself, or more accurately the initial owners of the company, to offer price guarantees. There have been examples in the USA of the use of 'puttable stock' whereby investors are sold a unit comprising a share of common stock and an option provided by the issuing company (see the examples cited in Chen and Kensinger 1988). The option gives the unit-holder the right at a predetermined time to claim more stock (or, possibly, cash or other securities) if the market price has fallen below a specified level. If the market value of the shares rises above this level, the option becomes worthless and is not exercised. If the share price has fallen below the guaranteed level at the relevant date, the original investors (whose shares were not sold in the IPO) will see the value of their shares fall as the IPO shareholders are compensated. Clearly, if the company experienced really hard times, complete dilution of the original investors' stakes might be insufficient to cover the cost of the guarantee, which necessitates a supplementary mechanism for entering bankruptcy.

There are close analogies between puttable stock and convertible bonds, as both types of security allow investors to share in the upside gains while downside risk is limited. This is another example of dis-intermediation. Although, clearly, intermediaries may be involved in the initial design of such schemes, they do not bear the risk or neces-sarily put their reputation on the line.

In conclusion, there are many ways in which the IPO market may develop in the future. Probably the greatest uncertainty involves the impact of technological change on the IPO process, and in particular the role of investment banks in the future. As we have stressed throughout this book, much of the theoretical and empirical work has involved analysing the role that intermediaries play in the IPO process; and yet, predicting the future industrial organization of the investment banking industry requires a liberal use of the crystal ball. Since the first edition of this book was published there have been a number of major developments. Many countries have witnessed an unprecedented boom in the number of companies going public, in part linked to innovations introduced by stock markets to encour-age more IPOs. There has also been an extraordinary hot issue period, with remarkable levels of underpricing observed in many countries through 1999 and much of 2000. In addition, the techniques used for taking companies public have changed in many countries, with the widespread adoption of US-style book-building techniques. These developments have only served to increase the attention of researchers. Indeed, our firmest prediction is that initial public offer-ings will continue to be the subject of intense academic debate. As we have noted, more recent research has cast considerable doubt on the evidence that IPOs underperform in the long run, and we no longer consider that the balance of evidence supports the existence of a 'long-run underperfomance' anomaly. Whether future research activity produces more convincing—and internationally relevant—explanations for the remaining anomaly of initial underpricing remains to be seen.

References

Affleck-Graves, J. and M. J. Page, 1995, 'The Timing and Subsequent Performance of Seasoned Offerings: The Case of Rights Issues', mimeo, University of Notre Dame.

—— and D. K. Spiess, 1995, 'Underperformance in Long-Run Stock Returns Following Seasoned Equity Offerings', *Journal of Financial Economics* 38, 243–267.

Aggarwal, R., 2000a, 'Stabilization Activities by Underwriters after IPOs', *Journal of Finance* 55, 1075–1103.

—— 2000b, 'Allocation of Initial Public Offerings and Flipping Activity', mimeo, Georgetown University.

—— and P. Conroy, 2000, 'Price Discovery in Initial Public Offerings and the Role of the Lead Underwriter', *Journal of Finance* 55, 2903–2922.

—— and P. Rivoli, 1990, 'Fads in the Initial Public Offering Market?', *Financial Management* 19, 45–57.

—— R. Leal, and L. Hernandez, 1993, 'The After-market Performance of Initial Public Offerings in Latin America', *Financial Management* 22, 42–53.

Akerlof, G., 1970, 'The Market for "Lemons": Quality Uncertainty and the Market Mechanism', *Quarterly Journal of Economics* 84, 488–500.

Alderson, M. J. and B. L. Betker, 1997, 'The Long-run Performance of Companies that Withdraw Seasoned Equity Offerings', mimeo, Saint Louis University.

Alexander, J. C., 1993, 'The Lawsuit Avoidance Theory of Why Initial Public Offerings Are Underpriced', *UCLA Law Review* 17, 17–73.

Ali, A., 1995, 'Bias in Analysts' Earnings Forecasts as an Explanation for the Long-Run Underperformance of Stocks Following Equity Offerings', mimeo, University of Arizona.

Allen, F. and G. R. Faulhaber, 1989, 'Signaling by Underpricing in the IPO Market', *Journal of Financial Economics* 23, 303–323.

Alphao, R. M., 1989, 'Initial Public Offerings on the Lisbon Stock Exchange', mimeo, Faculdade de Economia, Universidade Nova de Lisboa.

Asquith, D., J. D. Jones, and R. Kieschnick, 1998, 'Evidence on Price Stabilisation and Underpricing in Early IPO Returns', *Journal of Finance* 53, 1759–1773.

Aussenegg, W., 1999, 'Short and Long-Run Performance of Initial Public Offerings in the Austrian Stock Market', mimeo, Vienna University of Technology.

Aussenegg, W., 2000, 'Privatisation versus Private-Sector Initial Public Offerings in Poland', mimeo, Vienna University of Technology.

Balvers, R. J., B. McDonald, and R. E. Miller, 1988, 'Underpricing of New Issues and the Choice of Auditor as a Signal of Investment Banker Reputation', *Accounting Review* 63, 605–622.

Barber, B. M. and J. D. Lyon, 1997, 'Detecting Long-Run Abnormal Stock Returns: The Empirical Power and Specification of Test Statistics', *Journal of Financial Economics* 43, 341–373.

—— —— and C. Tsai, 1999, 'Improved Methods for Tests of Long-run Abnormal Returns', *Journal of Finance* 54, 165–201.

Baron, D. P., 1982, 'A Model of the Demand for Investment Banking Advising and Distribution Services for New Issues', *Journal of Finance* 37, 955–976.

—— and B. Holmström, 1980, 'The Investment Banking Contract for New Issues under Asymmetric Information: Delegation and the Incentive Problem', *Journal of Finance* 35, 1115–1138.

Barry, C. B., C. J. Muscarella, J. W. Peavy, and M. R. Vetsuypens, 1990, 'The Role of Venture Capital in the Creation of Public Companies: Evidence from the Going-Public Process', *Journal of Financial Economics* 27, 447–471.

Beatty, R. P., 1989, 'Auditor Reputation and the Pricing of Initial Public Offerings', *Accounting Review* 64, 693–709.

—— and J. R. Ritter, 1986, 'Investment Banking, Reputation, and the Underpricing of Initial Public Offerings', *Journal of Financial Economics* 15, 213–232.

—— and I. Welch, 1996, 'Issuer Expenses and Legal Liability in Initial Public Offerings', *Journal of Law and Economics* 39, 545–602.

—— and E. J. Zajac, 1995, 'Managerial Incentives, Monitoring and Risk Bearing in Initial Public Offering Firms', *Journal of Applied Corporate Finance* 8, 87–96.

Beller, A. L., T. Terai, and R. M. Levine, 1992, 'Looks Can Be Deceiving: A Comparison of Initial Public Offering Procedures under Japanese and US Securities Laws', *Law and Contemporary Problems* 55, 77–118.

Benveniste, L. M. and W. Y. Busaba, 1997, 'Book-building versus Fixed Price: An Analysis of Competing Strategies for Marketing IPOs', *Journal of Financial and Quantitative Analysis* 32, 383–403.

—— and P. A. Spindt, 1989, 'How Investment Bankers Determine the Offer Price and Allocation of New Issues', *Journal of Financial Economics* 24, 343–361.

—— and W. J. Wilhelm, Jr., 1990, 'A Comparative Analysis of IPO Proceeds under Alternative Regulatory Environments', *Journal of Financial Economics* 28, 173–207.

—— W. Y. Busaba, and W. J. Wilhelm, Jr., 1996, 'Price Stabilization as a Bonding Mechanism in New Equity Issues', *Journal of Financial Economics* 42, 223–255.

—— S. M. Erdal, and W. J. Wilhelm, Jr., 1998, 'Who Benefits from Secondary Market Stablization of IPOs?', *Journal of Banking and Finance* 22, 741–767.

—— W. Y. Busaba, and R.-J. Guo, 2001, 'The Option to Withdraw IPOs During the Premarket', *Journal of Financial Economics* 60, 73–102.

—— —— and W. J. Wilhelm, Jr., 2000, 'Information Externalities and the Role of Underwriters in Primary Equity Markets', forthcoming in *Journal of Financial Intermediation*.

—— W. J. Wilhelm, Jr., and X. Yu, 2000, 'Evidence of Information Spillovers in the Production of Investment Banking Services', mimeo, Boston College.

Biais, B. and A. M. Faugeron-Crouzet, 1998, 'IPO Auctions,', mimeo, Université de Toulouse.

Bloch, E., 1989, *Inside Investment Banking*, 2nd edn. New York: Irwin.

Boehmer, E. and R. P. H. Fishe, 2000, 'Do Underwriters Encourage Stock Flipping? A New Explanation for the Underpricing of IPOs', mimeo, US Securities and Exchange Commission.

Booth, J. R. and L. Chua, 1996, 'Ownership Dispersion, Costly Information and IPO Underpricing', *Journal of Financial Economics* 41, 291–310.

—— and R. Smith, 1986, 'Capital Raising, Underwriting and the Certification Hypothesis', *Journal of Financial Economics* 15, 261–281.

Bossaerts, P. and P. Hillion, 1998, 'IPO Post-issue Markets: Questionable Predilections but Diligent Learners?', Social Science Working Paper no. 1014, California Institute of Technology.

Brav, A., 2000, 'Inference in Long-Horizon Event Studies: A Bayesian Approach with Application to Initial Public Offerings', *Journal of Finance* 55, 1979–2016.

—— and P. Gompers, 1997, 'Myth or Reality? The Long-Run Underperformance of Initial Public Offerings: Evidence from Venture and Non-Venture Capital-Backed Companies', *Journal of Finance* 52, 1791–1821.

—— C. Geczy, and P. Gompers, 2000, 'Is the Abnormal Return Following Equity Issuances Anomalous?', *Journal of Financial Economics* 56, 209–249.

Brealey, R. A. and S. C. Myers, 1991, *Principles of Corporate Finance*, 4th edn. New York: McGraw-Hill.

Brennan, M. J. and J. Franks, 1997, 'Underpricing, Ownership and Control in Initial Public Offerings of Equity Securities in the UK', *Journal of Financial Economics* 45, 391–413.

—— and P. J. Hughes, 1991, 'Stock Prices and the Supply of Information', *Journal of Finance* 46, 1665–1692.

Buijs, A. and H. G. Eijgenhuijsen, 1993, 'Initial Public Offerings in the Netherlands 1982–1991: An Analysis of Initial Returns and Long-Run Performance', mimeo, Free University of Amsterdam.

Burkart, M., D. Gromb, and F. Panunzi, 1997, 'Large Shareholders, Monitoring and the Value of the Firm', *Quarterly Journal of Economics* 112, 693–728.

Cai, J. and K. C. J. Wei, 1997, 'The Investment and Operating Performance of Japanese Initial Public Offerings', *Pacific-Basin Finance Journal* 5, 389–417.

Carter, R. B. and S. Manaster, 1990, 'Initial Public Offerings and Underwriter Reputation', *Journal of Finance* 45, 1045–1067.

—— F. Dark, and A. Singh, 1998, 'Underwriter Reputation, Initial Returns, and the Long-Run Performance of IPO Stocks', *Journal of Finance* 53, 285–311.

Chemmanur, T. J., 1993, 'The Pricing of Initial Public Offerings: A Dynamic Model with Information Production', *Journal of Finance* 48, 285–304.

—— and P. Fulghieri, 1999, 'A Theory of the Going Public Decision', *Review of Financial Studies* 12, 249–279.

Chen, A. H. and J. W. Kensinger, 1988, 'Puttable Stock: A New Innovation in Equity Financing', *Financial Management* 17, 27–37.

Chen, H. L., 1992, 'The Price Behaviour of IPOs in Taiwan', mimeo, University of Illinois.

Chen, H.-C., and J. R. Ritter, 2000, 'The Seven Percent Solution', *Journal of Finance* 55, 1105–1131.

Cheng, L.-L., 1996, 'Equity Issue Under-Performance and the Timing of Security Issues', mimeo, National Economic Research Associates, White Plains, NY.

Cherubini, U. and M. Ratti, 1992, 'Underpricing of Initial Public Offerings in the Milan Stock Exchange, 1985–91', mimeo, Banca Commerciale Italiana.

Cheung, Y.-L., S. L. Cheung, and R. Y.-K. Ho, 1993, 'Listing Requirements, Uncertainty, and Underpricing of IPOs', mimeo, City Polytechnic of Hong Kong.

Chowdhry, B. and V. Nanda, 1996, 'Stabilisation, Syndication, and Pricing of IPOs', *Journal of Financial and Quantitative Analysis* 31, 25–42.

Clarkson, P. M. and J. Merkley, 1994, '*Ex Ante* Uncertainty and the Under-pricing of Initial Public Offerings: Further Canadian Evidence', *Canadian Journal of Administrative Sciences* 11, 54–67.

—— and R. Thompson, 1990, 'Empirical Estimates of Beta When Investors Face Estimation Risk', *Journal of Finance* 45, 431–453.

Cornelli, F. and D. Goldreich, 1999, 'Book-building and Strategic Allocation', mimeo, London Business School.

—— —— 2000, 'Book-building: How Informative is the Order Book?', mimeo, London Business School.

Cusatis, P. J., J. A. Miles, and J. R. Woolridge, 1993, 'Restructuring through Spin-offs: The Stock Market Evidence', *Journal of Financial Economics* 33, 293–311.

Davis, E. W. and K. A. Yeomans, 1976, 'Market Discount on New Issues of Equity: The Influence of Firm Size, Method of Issue and Market Volatility', *Journal of Business Finance and Accounting* 3, 27–42.

Dawson, S. M., 1987, 'Secondary Stock Market Performance of Initial Public Offers, Hong Kong, Singapore and Malaysia: 1978–84', *Journal of Business Finance and Accounting* 14, 65–76.

DeAngelo, H. and E. Rice, 1983, 'Anti-Takeover Charter Amendments and Stockholder Wealth', *Journal of Financial Economics* 11, 329–360.

DeGeorge, F. and R. Zeckhauser, 1993, 'The Reverse LBO Decision and Firm Performance: Theory and Evidence', *Journal of Finance* 48, 1323–1348.

Dhatt, M. S., Y. H. Kim, and U. Lim, 1993, 'The Short-Run and Long-Run Performance of Korean IPOs: 1980–90', mimeo, University of Cincinnati.

Drake, P. D. and M. R. Vetsuypens, 1993, 'IPO Underpricing and Insurance against Legal Liability', *Financial Management* 22, 64–73.

Dunbar, C. G., 1995, 'The Use of Warrants as Underwriter Compensation in Initial Public Offerings', *Journal of Financial Economics* 38, 59–78.

—— 2000, 'Factors Affecting Investment Bank Initial Public Offering Market Share', *Journal of Financial Economics* 55, 3–41.

—— C.-Y. Hwang, and K. Shastri, 1997, 'Underwriter Analyst Recommendations: Conflict of Interest or Rush to Judgment?', mimeo, University of Western Ontario.

Eckbo, B. E. and Ø. Norli, 2000, 'Leverage, Liquidity and Long-run IPO Returns', mimeo, Dartmouth College.

Ellis, K., R. Michaely, and M. O'Hara, 2000, 'When the Underwriter is the Market Maker: An Examination of Trading in the IPO After-market', *Journal of Finance* 55, 1039–1074.

Emilsen, N. H., K. Pedersen, and F. Saettem, 1997, 'Børsintroduksjoner', *BETA Tidsskrift for Bedriftsøkonomi* 11, 1–13.

Fama, E. F., 1998, 'Market Efficiency, Long-term Returns, and Behavioral Finance', *Journal of Financial Economics* 49, 283–307.

—— and K. R. French, 1992, 'The Cross-Section of Expected Stock Returns', *Journal of Finance* 47, 427–465.

—— —— 1993, 'Common Risk Factors in the Returns on Stocks and Bonds', *Journal of Financial Economics* 33, 3–56.

Fernandez, P., E. Martinez-Abascal, and A. Rahnema, 1992, 'Initial Public Offerings: The Spanish Experience', mimeo, IESE.

Field, L. C., 1995, 'Is Institutional Investment in Initial Public Offerings Related to Long-Run Performance of These Firms?', mimeo, University of California, Los Angeles.

—— 1998, 'The IPO as the First Stage in the Sale of the Firm', mimeo, Pennsylvania State University.

—— and J. M. Karpoff, 2000, 'Takeover Defences at IPO Firms', mimeo, Pennsylvania State University.

Finn, F. J. and R. Higham, 1988, 'The Performance of Unseasoned New Equity Issues-cum-Stock Exchange Listings in Australia', *Journal of Banking and Finance* 12, 333–351.

Firth, M., 1997, 'An Analysis of the Stock Market Performance of New Issues in New Zealand', *Pacific-Basin Finance Journal* 5, 63–85.

—— and C. K. Liau-Tan, 1997, 'Signalling Models and the Valuation of New Issues: An Examination of IPOs in Singapore', *Pacific-Basin Finance Journal* 5, 511–526.

Gande, A., M. Puri, and A. Saunders, 1999, 'Bank Entry, Competition, and the Market for Corporate Securities Underwriting', *Journal of Financial Economics* 54, 133–164.

Garfinkel, J. A., 1993, 'IPO Underpricing, Insider Selling and Subsequent Equity Offerings: Is Underpricing a Signal of Quality?', *Financial Management* 22, 74–83.

Giudici, G. and S. Paleari, 1999, 'Underpricing, Price Stabilization and Long-Run Performance in Initial Public Offerings: A Study on the Italian Stock Market between 1985 and 1998', mimeo, Politecnico di Milano.

Gompers, P. A. and J. Lerner, 1997, 'Venture Capital and the Creation of Public Companies: Do Venture Capitalists Really Bring More than Money?', *Journal of Private Equity* 1, 15–32.

Göppl, H. and A. Sauer, 1990, 'Die Bewertung von Börsenneulingen am deutschen Aktienmarkt: Eine empirische Notiz', in W. R. Heilmann *et al.* (eds.), *Geld, Banken und Versicherungen*, vol. 1. Karlsruhe: VVW.

Grinblatt, M. and C. Y. Hwang, 1989, 'Signalling and the Pricing of New Issues', *Journal of Finance* 44, 393–420.

Grossman, S. and O. Hart, 1980, 'Takeover Bids, the Free-Rider Problem and the Theory of the Corporation', *Bell Journal of Economics* 11, 42–64.

Guney, S. E. and E. C. Perotti, 1993, 'The Structure of Privatisation Plans', *Financial Management* 22, 84–98.

Habib, M. A. and A. P. Ljungqvist, 1998, 'Underpricing and IPO proceeds: A Note', *Economics Letters* 61, 381–383.

—— —— 2001, 'Underpricing and Entrepreneurial Wealth Losses in IPOs: Theory and Evidence', *Review of Financial Studies* 14, 433–458.

Hamao, Y., F. Packer, and J. R. Ritter, 2000, 'Institutional Affiliation and the Role of Venture Capital: Evidence from Initial Public Offerings in Japan', *Pacific-Basin Finance Journal* 8, 529–558.

Hanley, K., 1993, 'The Underpricing of Initial Public Offerings and the Partial Adjustment Phenomenon', *Journal of Financial Economics* 34, 231–250.

—— and J. R. Ritter, 1992, 'Going Public', in J. Eatwell, M. Milgate, and P. Newman (eds.), *The New Palgrave Dictionary of Money and Finance*. London: Macmillan.

—— and W. J. Wilhelm, 1995, 'Evidence on the Strategic Allocation of Initial Public Offerings', *Journal of Financial Economics* 37, 239–257.

—— A. A. Kumar, and P. J. Seguin, 1993, 'Price Stabilisation in the Market for New Issues', *Journal of Financial Economics* 34, 177–197.

Hansen, R. S., 2001, 'Do Investment Banks Compete in IPOs? The Advent of the "7 per cent Plus Contract"', *Journal of Financial Economics* 59, 313–346.

Helwege, J. and N. Liang, 1996a, 'Is There a Pecking Order? Evidence from a Panel of IPO Firms', *Journal of Financial Economics* 40, 429–458.

—— —— 1996b, 'Initial Public Offerings in Hot and Cold Markets', Discussion Paper 96/34, Board of Governors of the Federal Reserve System.

Hensler, D. A., 1995, 'Litigation Costs and the Underpricing of Initial Public Offerings', *Managerial and Decision Economics* 16, 111–128.

Hertzel, M., M. Lemmon, J. S. Linck, and L Rees, 1999, 'Long-Run Performance following Private Placements of Equity', mimeo, University of Rochester.

H. M. Treasury, 1995, *Her Majesty's Treasury Guide to the UK Privatisation Programme*. London: HMSO.

Högholm, K. and K. Rydqvist, 1995, 'Going Public in the 1980s: Evidence from Sweden', *European Financial Management* 1, 287–315.

Houge, T., T. Loughran, G. Suchanek, and X. Yan, 2000, 'Divergence of Opinion in IPOs', mimeo, University of Iowa.

Hughes, P. J., 1986, 'Signalling by Direct Disclosure under Asymmetric Information', *Journal of Accounting and Economics* 8, 119–142.

—— and A. V. Thakor, 1992, 'Litigation Risk, Intermediation, and the Underpricing of Initial Public Offerings', *Review of Financial Studies* 5, 709–742.

Husson, B. and B. Jacquillat, 1989, 'French New Issues, Underpricing and Alternative Methods of Distribution', in R. M. C. Guimaraes, B. G. Kingsman, and S. J. Taylor (eds.), *A Reappraisal of the Efficiency of Financial Markets*. Berlin, Heidelberg: Springer-Verlag.

Ibbotson, R. G., 1975, 'Price Performance of Common Stock New Issues', *Journal of Financial Economics* 2, 235–272.

—— and J. F. Jaffe, 1975, '"Hot Issue" Markets', *Journal of Finance* 30, 1027–1042.

—— J. R. Ritter, and J. L. Sindelar, 1994, 'The Market's Problems with the Pricing of Initial Public Offerings', *Journal of Applied Corporate Finance* 7, 66–74.

Ikenberry, D., J. Lakonishok, and T. Vermaelen, 1995, 'Market Underreaction to Open Market Share Repurchases', *Journal of Financial Economics* 39, 181–208.

Ikoku, A. E., 1995, 'The Pricing of New Issues of Equity in the Emerging Capital Markets of Africa', unpublished Ph.D. dissertation, University of Southern California.

Jacquillat, B. C., 1986, 'French Auctions of Common Stock: Methods and Techniques of New Issues, 1966–86', in *Going Public: An International Overview*, Euromobilaire Occasional Paper 2.

Jaffe, J., 1974, 'Special Information and Insider Trading', *Journal of Business* 47, 410–428.

Jain, B. A. and O. Kini, 1994, 'The Post-Issue Operating Performance of IPO Firms', *Journal of Finance* 49, 1699–1726.

James, C., 1992, 'Relationship-Specific Assets and the Pricing of Underwriter Services', *Journal of Finance* 47, 1865–1885.

—— and P. Wier, 1990, 'Borrowing Relationships, Intermediation and the Cost of Issuing Public Securities', *Journal of Financial Economics* 28, 149–171.

Jansen, B. and A. Tourani Rad, 1995, 'IPOs and the Morning After: Underwriter Price Support in the Netherlands', mimeo, University of Limburg.

Jegadeesh, N., M. Weinstein, and I. Welch, 1993, 'An Empirical Investigation of IPO Returns and Subsequent Equity Offerings', *Journal of Financial Economics* 34, 153–175.

Jenkinson, T. J., 1990, 'Initial Public Offerings in the United Kingdom, the United States, and Japan', *Journal of the Japanese and International Economies* 4, 428–449.

—— and C. P. Mayer, 1988, 'The Privatisation Process in France and the UK', *European Economic Review* 32, 482–490.

—— and J. M. Trundle, 1990, 'New Equity Issues in the United Kingdom', *Bank of England Quarterly Bulletin*, May: 243–252.

Jensen, M. and W. Meckling, 1976, 'Theory of the Firm: Managerial Behaviour, Agency Costs and Ownership Structure', *Journal of Financial Economics* 3, 306–360.

—— and K. Murphy, 1990, 'Performance Pay and Top Management Incentives', *Journal of Political Economy* 98, 225–264.

Jog, V. M. and A. K. Srivastava, 1996, 'The Canadian Environment for Initial Public Offerings: Underpricing, Long-Term Performance and the Process of Going Public', mimeo, Carleton University, Ottawa.

Johnson, J. M. and R. E. Miller, 1988, 'Investment Banker Prestige and the Underpricing of Initial Public Offerings', *Financial Management* 17, 19–29.

Kandel, S., O. Sarig, and A. Wohl, 1999, 'The Demand for Stocks: An Analysis of IPO Auctions', *Review of Financial Studies* 12, 227–247.

Kaneko, T. and R. H. Pettway, 1994, 'The Effects of Removing Price Limits and Introducing Auctions upon Short-Term IPO Returns: The Case of Japanese IPOs', Working Paper no. 52794, Financial Research Institute, University of Missouri.

Kang, J.-K., Y.-C. Kim, and R. M. Stulz, 1999, 'The Underreaction Hypothesis and the New Issue Puzzle: Evidence from Japan', *Review of Financial Studies* 12, 519–534.

Kazantzis, C. and D. Thomas, 1996, 'The IPO Puzzle and Institutional Constraints: Evidence from the Athens Stock Market', in M. Levis (ed.), *Empirical Issues in Raising Equity Capital*. Amsterdam: North-Holland.

Keloharju, M., 1993a, 'Initial IPO Returns and the Characteristics of Post-IPO Financing in Finland', mimeo, Helsinki School of Economics and Business Administration.

—— 1993b, 'The Winner's Curse, Legal Liability, and the Long-Run Price Performance of Initial Public Offerings in Finland', *Journal of Financial Economics* 34, 251–277.

—— 1996, 'The Anatomy of Finnish IPO Investors', mimeo, Helsinki School of Economics and Business Administration.

Kim, J. B., I. Krinsky, and J. Lee, 1993, 'Motives for Going Public and Underpricing: New Findings from Korea', *Journal of Business Finance and Accounting* 20, 195–211.

—— —— —— 1995, 'The After-market Performance of Initial Public Offerings in Korea', *Pacific-Basin Finance Journal* 3, 429–448.

Kiymaz, H., 1998, 'Turkish IPO Pricing in the Short and Long-Run', mimeo, Bilkent University, Turkey.

Klemperer, P., 1999, 'Auction Theory: A Guide to the Literature', *Journal of Economic Surveys* 13, 227–286.

Koh, F. and T. Walter, 1989, 'A Direct Test of Rock's Model of the Pricing of Unseasoned Issues', *Journal of Financial Economics* 23, 251–272.

—— J. Lim, and N. Chin, 1992, 'The Signalling Process in Initial Public Offerings', *Asia Pacific Journal of Management* 9, 151–165.

Kothari, S. P. and J. B. Warner, 1997, 'Measuring Long-Horizon Security Price Performance', *Journal of Financial Economics* 43, 301–341.

Krigman, L., W. H. Shaw, and K. L. Womack, 1999, 'The Persistence of IPO Mispricing and the Predictive Power of Flipping', *Journal of Finance* 54, 1015–1044.

—— —— —— 2001, 'Why Do Firms Switch Underwriters?', *Journal of Financial Economics* 60.

Kryzanowski, L. and I. Rakita, 1999, 'Assessment of the Short-Run Intraday Behaviour of Canadian IPOs using a Multi-Moment Market Model', mimeo, Concordia University.

Kunz, R. M. and R. Aggarwal, 1994, 'Why Initial Public Offerings are Underpriced: Evidence from Switzerland', *Journal of Banking and Finance* 18, 705–724.

La Chapelle, C. A. and B. M. Neuberger, 1983, 'Unseasoned New Issue Price Performance on Three Tiers: 1975–1980', *Financial Management* 12, 23–28.

Lee, I., 1997, 'Do Firms Knowingly Sell Overvalued Equity?', *Journal of Finance* 52, 1439–1466.

Lee, P. J., S. L. Taylor, and T. S. Walter, 1996, 'Australian IPO Pricing in the Short and Long Run', *Journal of Banking and Finance* 20, 1189–1210.

Leefeldt, E., 2000, 'Fixed Rates, Double Standards', *Bloomberg Magazine*, May: 36–40.

Leland, H. and D. Pyle, 1977, 'Informational Asymmetries, Financial Structure, and Financial Intermediation', *Journal of Finance* 32, 371–387.

Leleux, B. F., 1992, 'Information and Fads Components in IPO Pricing: A Survival Analysis', mimeo, INSEAD.

Lerner, J., 1994, 'Venture Capitalists and the Decision to Go Public', *Journal of Financial Economics* 35, 293–316.

Levis, M., 1990, 'The Winner's Curse Problem, Interest Costs, and the Underpricing of Initial Public Offerings', *Economic Journal* 100, 76–89.

—— 1993a, 'The Long-Run Performance of Initial Public Offerings: The UK Experience 1980–1988', *Financial Management* 22, 28–41.

Levis, M., 1993*b*, 'The First 1000 Days in the Life of an IPO', mimeo, City University Business School, London.

—— 1995, 'Second Equity Offerings and the Short and Long-Run Performance of IPOs in the UK', *European Financial Management*, 125–146.

Liaw, G., Y.-L. Liu, and K. C. J. Wei, 2000, 'On the Demand Elasticity of Initial Public Offerings: An Analysis of Discriminatory Auctions', mimeo, Hong Kong University of Science and Technology.

Lin, T. H. and R. L. Smith, 1998, 'Insider Reputation and Selling Decisions: The Unwinding of Venture Capital Investments during Equity IPOs', *Journal of Corporate Finance* 4, 241–263.

Ljungqvist, A. P., 1995*a*, 'The Timing, Pricing and Long-Term Performance of Initial Public Offerings', unpublished D.Phil. thesis, Nuffield College, Oxford University.

—— 1995*b*, 'When Do Firms Go Public? Poisson Evidence from Germany', mimeo, Said Business School, Oxford University.

—— 1996, 'Can Firms Outwit the Market? Timing Ability and the Long-Run Performance of IPOs', in M. Levis (ed.), *Empirical Issues in Raising Equity Capital*. Amsterdam: North-Holland.

—— 1997, 'Pricing Initial Public Offerings: Further Evidence from Germany', *European Economic Review* 41, 1309–1320.

—— and W. J. Wilhelm, 2001, 'IPO Allocations: Discriminatory or Discretionary?', paper presented at the NYSE conference on 'Global Equity Markets in Transition', Hawaii, February.

—— T. J. Jenkinson, and W. J. Wilhelm, 2000, 'Global Integration in Primary Equity Markets: The Role of US Banks and US Investors', mimeo, Stern School of Business, New York University.

Logue, D., 1973*a*, 'On the Pricing of Unseasoned Equity Issues, 1965–69', *Journal of Financial and Quantitative Analysis* 8, 91–103.

—— 1973*b*, 'Premia on Unseasoned Equity Issues, 1965–69', *Journal of Economics and Business* 25, 133–141.

Loughran, T., 1993, 'NYSE vs. NASDAQ Returns: Market Microstructure or the Poor Performance of Initial Public Offerings?', *Journal of Financial Economics* 33, 241–260.

—— and J. R. Ritter, 1995, 'The New Issues Puzzle', *Journal of Finance* 50, 23–51.

—— —— 1997, 'The Operating Performance of Firms Conducting Seasoned Equity Offerings', *Journal of Finance* 52, 1823–1850.

—— —— 2000, 'Uniformly Least Powerful Tests of Market Efficiency', *Journal of Financial Economics* 55, 361–389.

—— —— 2001, 'Why Don't Issuers Get Upset About Leaving Money on the Table in IPOs?', *Review of Financial Studies*, forthcoming.

—— —— and K. Rydqvist, 1994, 'Initial Public Offerings: International Insights', *Pacific Basin Finance Journal* 2, 165–199.

Lowry, M. and G. W. Schwert, 2000, 'IPO Market Cycles: An Exploratory Investigation', mimeo, University of Rochester.

—— and S. Shu, 2000, 'Litigation Risk and IPO Underpricing', mimeo, University of Southern California.

Macey, J. and H. Kanda, 1990, 'The Stock Exchange as a Firm: The Emergence of Close Substitutes for the New York and Tokyo Stock Exchanges', *Cornell Law Review* 75, 1007–1052.

Mandelker, G., 1974, 'Risk and Return: The Case of Merging Firms', *Journal of Financial Economics* 1, 303–335.

Manigart, S. and B. Rogiers, 1992, 'Empirical Examination of the Underpricing of Initial Public Offerings on the Brussels Stock Exchange', mimeo, Vlerick School for Management, University of Ghent.

Mauer, E. and L. Senbet, 1992, 'The Effect of the Secondary Market on the Pricing of Initial Public Offerings: Theory and Evidence', *Journal of Financial and Quantitative Analysis* 27, 55–79.

McConnell, J. and H. Servaes, 1990, 'Additional Evidence on Equity Ownership and Corporate Value', *Journal of Financial Economics* 27, 595–612.

McGuinness, P., 1992, 'An Examination of the Underpricing of Initial Public Offerings in Hong Kong: 1980–90', *Journal of Business Finance and Accounting* 19, 165–186.

—— 1993*a*, 'Investor- and Issuer-Related Perspectives of IPO Underpricing', *Omega International Journal of Management Sciences* 21, 377–392.

—— 1993*b*, 'The Post-Listing Return Performance of Unseasoned Issues of Common Stock in Hong Kong', *Journal of Business Finance and Accounting* 20, 167–194.

Megginson, W. and J. Netter, 2000, 'From State to Market: A Survey of Empirical Studies on Privatization', mimeo, University of Oklahoma.

—— and K. A. Weiss, 1991, 'Venture Capitalist Certification in Initial Public Offerings', *Journal of Finance* 46, 879–903.

Mello, A. S. and J. E. Parsons, 1998, 'Going Public and the Ownership Structure of the Firm', *Journal of Financial Economics* 49, 79–109.

Michaely, R. and W. H. Shaw, 1992, 'Asymmetric Information, Adverse Selection, and the Pricing of Initial Public Offerings', mimeo, Cornell University.

—— —— 1994, 'The Pricing of Initial Public Offerings: Tests of Adverse-Selection and Signaling Theories', *Review of Financial Studies* 7, 279–319.

—— and K. L. Womack, 1999, 'Conflict of Interest and the Credibility of Underwriter Analyst Recommendations', *Review of Financial Studies* 12, 653–686.

Mikkelson, W. H., M. M. Partch, and K. Shah, 1997, 'Ownership and Operating Performance of Firms that Go Public', *Journal of Financial Economics* 44, 281–307.

Miller, E. M., 1977, 'Risk, Uncertainty, and Divergence of Opinion', *Journal of Finance* 32, 1151–1168.

Miller, R. E. and F. K. Reilly, 1987, 'An Examination of Mispricing, Returns, and Uncertainty for Initial Public Offerings', *Financial Management* 16, 33–38.

Mitchell, M. and E. Stafford, 2000, 'Managerial Decisions and Long-term Stock Price Performance', *Journal of Business* 73, 287–329.

Modigliani, F. and M. H. Miller, 1958, 'The Cost of Capital, Corporation Finance and the Theory of Investment', *American Economic Review* 48, 261–297.

Mok, H. M. K. and Y. V. Hui, 1998, 'Underpricing and Aftermarket Performance of IPOs in Shanghai, China', *Pacific-Basin Finance Journal* 6, 453–474.

Mørck, R., A. Shleifer, and R. W. Vishny, 1988, 'Managerial Ownership and Market Valuation: An Empirical Analysis', *Journal of Financial Economics* 20, 293–315.

Muscarella, C. J. and M. R. Vetsuypens, 1989*a*, 'A Simple Test of Baron's Model of IPO Underpricing', *Journal of Financial Economics* 24, 125–135.

—— —— 1989*b*, 'The Underpricing of "Second" Initial Public Offerings', *Journal of Financial Research* 12, 183–192.

Myers, S. C. and N. S. Majluf, 1984, 'Corporate Financing and Investment Decisions when Firms Have Information that Investors Do Not Have', *Journal of Financial Economics* 13, 187–221.

Nanda, V. and Y. Yun, 1997, 'Reputation and Financial Intermediation: An Empirical Investigation of the Impact of IPO Mispricing on Underwriter Market Value', *Journal of Financial Intermediation* 6, 39–63.

—— J.-H. Yi, and Y. Yun, 1995, 'IPO Long-run Performance and Underwriter Reputation', mimeo, University of Michigan.

Ozer, B., 1997, 'Abnormal Returns of IPOs in the Istanbul Stock Exchange', mimeo, Bogazici University, Turkey.

Pagano, M., F. Panetta, and L. Zingales, 1998, 'Why Do Companies Go Public? An Empirical Analysis', *Journal of Finance* 53, 27–64.

Panagos, V. and G. Papachristou, 1993, 'A Note on the Effectiveness of the Price Guarantee Clause in the Greek Underwriting Contract: Evidence from the After-market Volatility of IPOs', mimeo, Aristotle University of Thessaloniki, Greece.

Paudyal, K., B. Saadouni, and R. J. Briston, 1998, 'Privatisation initial public offerings in Malaysia: Initial premium and long-run performance', *Pacific-Basin Finance Journal* 6, 427–451.

Prabhala, N. R. and M. Puri, 1998, 'How Does Underwriter Price Support Affect IPOs? Empirical Evidence', mimeo, Stanford University.

—— —— 1999, 'What Type of IPOs do Underwriters Support and Why? The Role of Price Support in the IPO Process', mimeo, Stanford University.

Rajan, R. and H. Servaes, 1994, 'The Effect of Market Conditions on Initial Public Offerings', mimeo, University of Chicago.

—— —— 1997, 'Analyst Following of Initial Public Offerings', *Journal of Finance* 52, 507–529.

Rangan, S., 1998, 'Earnings Management and the Performance of Seasoned Equity Offerings', *Journal of Financial Economics* 50, 101–122.

Reilly, F. K., 1977, 'New Issues Revisited', *Financial Management* 6, 28–42.

Ritter, J. R., 1984, 'The Hot Issue Market of 1980', *Journal of Business* 57, 215–240.

—— 1987, 'The Costs of Going Public', *Journal of Financial Economics* 19, 269–282.

—— 1991, 'The Long-Run Performance of Initial Public Offerings', *Journal of Finance* 46, 3–27.

Rock, K., 1986, 'Why New Issues Are Underpriced', *Journal of Financial Economics* 15, 187–212.

Roëll, A., 1996, 'The Decision to Go Public: An Overview', *European Economic Review* 40, 1071–1081.

Ruud, J. S., 1990, 'Underpricing of Initial Public Offerings: Goodwill, Price Shaving or Price Support', unpublished Ph.D. dissertation, Harvard University.

—— 1991, 'Another View of the Underpricing of Initial Public Offerings', *Federal Reserve Bank of New York Quarterly Review* 16, 83–85.

—— 1993, 'Underwriter Price Support and the IPO Underpricing Puzzle', *Journal of Financial Economics* 34, 135–151.

Rydqvist, K., 1993, 'Initial Public Offerings in Sweden', Working Paper no. 48, Stockholm School of Economics.

—— 1994, 'Compensation, Participation Restrictions and the Underpricing of Initial Public Offerings', mimeo, Stockholm School of Economics and Carnegie-Mellon University, Pittsburgh.

—— 1997, 'IPO Underpricing as Tax-Efficient Compensation', *Journal of Banking and Finance* 21, 295–313.

Safieddine, A. and W. J. Wilhelm, 1996, 'An Empirical Investigation of Short-Selling Activity Prior to Seasoned Equity Offerings', *Journal of Finance* 51, 729–749.

Schlag, C. and A. Wodrich, 2000, 'Has There Always Been Underpricing and Long-Run Underperformance? IPOs in Germany before World War I', mimeo, University of Frankfurt.

Schultz, P. H. and M. A. Zaman, 1994, 'After-market Support and Underpricing of Initial Public Offerings', *Journal of Financial Economics* 35, 199–219.

Securities and Exchange Commission (SEC), 1971, *Institutional Investor Study Report of the Securities and Exchange Commission*. Washington, DC: US Government Printing Office.

Shaw, D. C., 1971, 'The Performance of Primary Common Stock Offerings: A Canadian Comparison', *Journal of Finance* 26, 1101–1113.

Sherman, A., 2000, 'IPOs and Long-Term Relationships: An Advantage of Book Building', *Review of Financial Studies* 13, 697–714.

—— and S. Titman, 2000, 'Building the IPO Order Book: Underpricing and Participation Limits with Costly Information', National Bureau of Economic Research, Working Paper no. 7786.

Shleifer, A. and R. Vishny, 1986, 'Large Stakeholders and Corporate Control', *Journal of Political Economy* 94, 461–488.

Simon, C. J., 1989, 'The Effect of the 1933 Securities Act on Investor Information and the Performance of New Issues', *American Economic Review* 79, 295–318.

Slovin, M. B. and J. E. Young, 1990, 'Bank Lending and Initial Public Offerings', *Journal of Banking and Finance* 14, 729–740.

—— M. E. Sushka, and Y. M. Bendeck, 1994, 'Seasoned Common Stock Issuance Following an IPO', *Journal of Banking and Finance* 18, 207–226.

Smart, S. B. and C. J. Zutter, 2000, 'Control as a Motivation for Under-pricing: A Comparison of Dual- and Single-Class IPOs', mimeo, Indiana University.

Smith, C. W., 1986, 'Investment Banking and the Capital Acquisition Process', *Journal of Financial Economics* 15, 3–29.

Spence, A. M., 1974, *Market Signalling*. Cambridge, Mass.: Harvard University Press.

Spiess, D. K. and R. H. Pettway, 1997, 'The IPO and First Seasoned Equity Sale: Issue Proceeds, Owner/Managers' Wealth, and the Underpricing Signal', *Journal of Banking and Finance* 21, 967–988.

Sternberg, T. D., 1989, 'Bilateral Monopoly and the Dynamic Properties of Initial Public Offerings', mimeo, Vanderbilt University, Nashville.

Stigler, G. J., 1964a, 'Public Regulation of the Securities Markets', *Journal of Business* 37, 117–142.

—— 1964b, 'Comment', *Journal of Business* 37, 414–422.

Stoll, H. R. and A. J. Curley, 1970, 'Small Business and the New Issue Market for Equities', *Journal of Financial and Quantitative Analysis* 5, 309–322.

Stoughton, N. M. and J. Zechner, 1998, 'IPO Mechanisms, Monitoring and Ownership Structure', *Journal of Financial Economics* 49, 45–78.

—— K. P. Wong, and J. Zechner, 2001, 'IPOs and Product Quality', *Journal of Business* 74.

Stulz, R., 1988, 'Managerial Control of Voting Rights: Financing Policies and the Market for Corporate Control', *Journal of Financial Economics* 20, 25–54.

Sullivan, M. J. and A. A. Unite, 1998, 'Performance of Philippine Initial Public Offerings: Critique of Current Studies and Update', *Philippine Review of Economics and Business* 35, 187–207.

Teoh, S. H., T. J. Wong, and G. R. Rao, 1993, 'An Empirical Analysis of the Incentives for Earnings Management in Initial Public Offerings', mimeo, University of California, Los Angeles.

—— I. Welch, and T. J. Wong, 1998a, 'Earnings Management and the Underperformance of Seasoned Equity Offerings', *Journal of Financial Economics* 50, 63–99.

—— —— —— 1998b, 'Earnings Management and the Long-Term Performance of Initial Public Offerings', *Journal of Finance* 53, 1935–1974.

Tinic, S. M., 1988, 'Anatomy of Initial Public Offerings of Common Stock', *Journal of Finance* 43, 789–822.

Titman, S. and B. Trueman, 1986, 'Information Quality and the Valuation of New Issues', *Journal of Accounting and Economics* 8, 159–172.

Van Arsdell, P. M., 1958, *Corporate Finance*. New York: Ronald Press.

Vaughan, G. D., P. H. Grinyer, and S. J. Birley, 1977, *From Private to Public*. Cambridge: Woodhead-Faulkner.

Vos, E. A. and J. Cheung, 1992, 'New Zealand IPO Underpricing: The Reputation Factor', *Small Enterprise Research* 1, 13–22.

Wasserfallen, W. and C. Wittleder, 1994, 'Pricing Initial Public Offerings: Evidence from Germany', *European Economic Review* 38, 1505–1517.

Welch, I., 1989, 'Seasoned Offerings, Imitation Costs, and the Underpricing of Initial Public Offerings', *Journal of Finance* 44, 421–449.

—— 1991, 'An Empirical Examination of Models of Contract Choice in Initial Public Offerings', *Journal of Financial and Quantitative Analysis* 26, 497–518.

—— 1992, 'Sequential Sales, Learning and Cascades', *Journal of Finance* 47, 695–732.

—— 1996, 'Equity Offerings Following the IPO: Theory and Evidence', *Journal of Corporate Finance* 2, 227–259.

Wessels, R. E., 1989, 'The Market for Initial Public Offerings: An Analysis of the Amsterdam Stock Exchange (1982–87)', in R. M. C. Guimaraes, B. G. Kingsman, and S. J. Taylor (eds.), *A Reappraisal of the Efficiency of Financial Markets*. Berlin, Heidelberg: Springer-Verlag.

Wethyavivorn, K. and Y. Koo-smith, 1991, 'Initial Public Offerings in Thailand, 1988–89: Price and Return Patterns', in S. G. Rhee and R. P. Chang (eds.), *Pacific-Basin Capital Markets Research*, vol. 2. Amsterdam: North-Holland.

Wimmers, S., 1988, 'Aktien- und börsenrechtliche Deregulierung: Die Bewertung aktueller Reformvorschläge durch die Börsenneulinge der Jahre 1977–1986', in H. Albach (ed.), *Die private Aktiengesellschaft: Materialien zur Deregulierung des Aktienrechts*. Stuttgart: Poeschel.

Woo, L.-A., 2000, 'Primary Equity Formation in Australia', mimeo, University of New South Wales.

Zingales, L., 1995, 'Insider Ownership and the Decision to Go Public', *Review of Economic Studies* 62, 425–448.

Index

Note: **bold** page numbers denote references to tables and figures.